Conversations with Samuel R. Delany

Literary Conversations Series
Peggy Whitman Prenshaw
General Editor

Conversations with
Samuel R. Delany

Edited by
Carl Freedman

University Press of Mississippi
Jackson

www.upress.state.ms.us

The University Press of Mississippi is a member of the Association of American University Presses.

Copyright © 2009 by University Press of Mississippi
All rights reserved
Manufactured in the United States of America

First printing 2009
∞
Library of Congress Cataloging-in-Publication Data

Delany, Samuel R.
    Conversations with Samuel R. Delany / edited by Carl Freedman.
        p.   cm. — (Literary conversations series)
    Includes index.
    ISBN 978-1-60473-277-1 (alk. paper) — ISBN 978-1-60473-278-8 (pbk. : alk. paper)
1. Delany, Samuel R.—Interviews. 2. Authors, American—20th century—Interviews.
3. African American authors—Interviews. 4. Gay authors—United States—Interviews.
5. Critics—United States—Interviews. 6. Science fiction—Authorship. 7. Authorship.
I. Freedman, Carl Howard. II. Title.
    PS3554.E437Z46 2009
    813'.54—dc22

                                                                2009004197

British Library Cataloging-in-Publication Data available

Books by Samuel Delany

Fiction:

The Jewels of Aptor. New York: Ace Books, 1962.

The Fall of the Towers (trilogy):

Out of the Dead City [originally published as *Captives of the Flame*]. New York: Ace Books, 1963.

The Towers of Toron. New York: Ace Books, 1964.

City of a Thousand Suns. New York: Ace Books, 1965.

The Ballad of Beta-2. New York: Ace Books, 1965.

Babel-17. New York: Ace Books, 1966.

Empire Star. New York: Ace Books, 1966.

The Einstein Intersection. New York: Ace Books, 1967.

Nova. Garden City, NJ: Doubleday & Company, 1968.

Driftglass (stories). Garden City, NJ: Nelson Doubleday, 1971.

Equinox [originally published as *The Tides of Lust*]. New York: Lancer Books, 1973.

Dhalgren. New York: Bantam Books, 1975.

Trouble on Triton [originally published as *Triton*]. New York: Bantam Books, 1976.

Distant Stars (stories). New York: Bantam Books, 1981.

Stars in My Pocket Like Grains of Sand. New York: Bantam Books, 1984.

Return to Nevèrÿon (tetralogy):

Tales of Nevèrÿon. New York: Bantam Books, 1979.

Neveryóna. New York: Bantam Books, 1983.

Flight from Nevèrÿon. New York: Bantam Books, 1985.

Return to Nevèrÿon [originally published as *The Bridge of Lost Desire*]. New York: Arbor House, 1987.

They Fly at Çiron. Seattle: Incunabula, 1993.

The Mad Man. New York: Masquerade Books, 1994.

Atlantis: Three Tales. Seattle: Incunabula, 1995.

Hogg. Normal, IL: Black Ice Books, 1995.

Aye, and Gomorrah, and Other Stories (collected stories). New York: Vintage Books, 2003.

Phallos. Whitmore Lake, MI: Bamberger Books, 2004.

Dark Reflections. New York: Carroll & Graf, 2007.

Graphic Novels:

Empire (drawn by Howard Chaykin). New York: Berkley Books, 1978.

Bread & Wine: An Erotic Tale of New York (drawn by Mia Wolff). New York: Juno Books, 1999.

Nonfiction:

The Jewel-Hinged Jaw: Notes on the Language of Science Fiction. Elizabethtown, NJ: Dragon Press, 1977.

The American Shore: Meditations on a Tale of Science Fiction by Thomas M. Disch—
"Angouleme." Elizabethtown, NJ: Dragon Press, 1978.

Heavenly Breakfast: An Essay on the Winter of Love. New York: Bantam Books, 1979.

Starboard Wine: More Notes on the Language of Science Fiction. Elizabethtown, NJ: Dragon
Press, 1984.

The Motion of Light in Water: Sex and Science Fiction Writing in the East Village, 1957–1965.
New York: Arbor House, 1988.

Wagner/Artaud: A Play of 19th and 20th Century Critical Fictions. New York: Ansatz
Press, 1988.

The Straits of Messina. Seattle: Serconia Press, 1988.

Silent Interviews: On Language, Race, Sex, Science Fiction, and Some Comics. Hanover, NH:
Wesleyan University Press, 1994.

Longer Views: Extended Essays. Hanover, NH: Wesleyan University Press, 1996.

Times Square Red, Times Square Blue. New York: New York University Press, 1999.

Shorter Views: Queer Thoughts & the Politics of the Paraliterary. Hanover, NH: Wesleyan
University Press, 1999.

1984: Selected Letters. Rutherford, NJ: Voyant Publishing, 2000.

About Writing: Seven Essays, Four Letters, and Five Interviews. Middletown, CT: Wesleyan
University Press, 2005.

Contents

Introduction

One characteristic of the genuine intellectual—as distinguished from a mere member of the *intelligentsia*, that is, those who earn their living by primarily intellectual labor—is the refusal ever to take anything completely for granted. The true intellectual is engaged in a practice of endless dialectical revision—a practice of unceasing questioning and self-questioning—in which nothing is ever taken on pure faith. This practice must, of course, be sharply distinguished from that ungrounded eclecticism that the liberal and empiricist ideologies dominant in our society generally uphold as evidence of an "open mind." Authentic intellectual work cannot be undertaken except from a definite, engaged viewpoint. But the real intellectual never allows a viewpoint to ossify into a dogma, and always leaves open the possibility that even fundamental assumptions sometimes need to be rethought. One might say (at least as a counsel of perfection) that an intellectual is someone who is actually thinking—and not just recycling conventional wisdom—*all the time.*

It is in this way that Samuel Delany—"Chip Delany," to those who know him personally, "Samuel R. Delany" as he appears on the title pages of his books—counts as one of the most genuine intellectuals among current American authors. For there are few writers in the United States today—or anywhere else, for that matter—who can match Delany in the number of topics that engage his attention or the supple, self-reflexive intelligence with which he treats them; and the exuberant cognitive energy of his mind can be found on nearly every page of each of the numerous works he has produced.

For instance, even if he had never written a line of fiction, Delany's dozen or so books of critical prose (not to mention an almost countless number of shorter, uncollected critical pieces) would by themselves establish him as one of the important and genuinely intellectual authors of our time. His critical career began with science-fiction criticism, most notably with his first nonfiction volume, *The Jewel-Hinged Jaw: Notes on the Language of Science Fiction* (1977), which at the time of publication counted as by far the most intelligent and useful book about

science fiction yet produced—and which today, two generations later, remains indispensable in a field that during the intervening years has grown prodigiously
in both quantity and quality. During these years Delany's active critical interests
also mushroomed. He has written widely not only on science fiction but on a huge
number of other literary, cultural, and political matters, from pre-Socratic philosophy to the politics of the AIDS epidemic, from Wagnerian opera to everyday
life in Harlem, from the classic French novel to the significance of modern technological innovation; and he has consistently handled such diverse topics with
such searching intelligence and in such clear, lively, accessible prose that more
than one commentator (myself included) has paid him what some would regard
as the ultimate tribute: namely, suggesting him as a worthy successor to Edmund
Wilson. No critic at work today more dependably pursues the "adventures of
the dialectic," to invoke a phrase I once used to title a review-essay of Delany's
longest critical book, *Shorter Views: Queer Thoughts & the Politics of the Paraliterary* (1999).

But it is by no means only in his expository prose that Delany appears as an
intellectual of the highest order. To suppose so would be a radical misunderstanding of Delany's achievement as a whole. He has not only mastered a number
of different genres—science fiction, sword-and-sorcery, historical fiction, contemporary realism, pornography, and autobiography, in addition to criticism—
but has always remained alert to (as I think he would put it) how porous and permeable the boundaries between genres may be or (as I would myself put it) how
various may be the different generic tendencies at work in a single text. Which-
ever formulation one prefers, Delany self-consciously glories in generic impurity, pursuing his intellectual interests at a high level of conceptual sophistication
in novels and stories as well as in essays. One can observe this pursuit already in
his early science-fiction novels (the books that first won him fame), for instance
Babel-17 (1966), which amounts to, *inter alia*, a meditation on the function of language and the power of poetry, or *The Einstein Intersection* (1967), which, just
below the surface of its quest narrative, maintains a subtle but unswerving po-
lemic in protest against the essentially conservative nature of myth. In such later
works as *Trouble on Triton* (1976) and, even more, the four volumes of the sword-
and-sorcery Nevèrÿon sequence (1979–1987)—which probably counts as his supreme masterpiece—the basic generic border between fiction and nonfiction,
between narrative and theory, breaks down almost completely. We read, for instance, provocative and original critical essays composed by entirely imaginary
figures, while the narrative action is often interrupted, complicated, and enriched
by dialectical meditations in linguistic, psychoanalytic, and Marxist theory.

Rarely since the Tolstoy of *War and Peace* has a great novelist so unashamedly used fiction for avowedly intellectual purposes; and, as the Tolstoyan precedent may suggest, it is often when Delany is at his most unabashedly intellectual that his characters are most engaging and his narratives most exciting.

This same sort of generic impurity, and this same irresistibly intellectual impulse, are also at work in Delany's extensive work as an autobiographer—so that, for instance, his formal autobiography *The Motion of Light in Water* (1988) offers a wide-ranging cultural history of New York City during the 1950s and 1960s; while *Times Square Red, Times Square Blue* (1999), an essay in Marxist urban sociology, tells its story partly through detailed and extremely graphic accounts of the author's sexual exploits. Like the French poststructuralists that have influenced him so profoundly—most notably Michel Foucault, Jacques Derrida, and Roland Barthes—Delany is an author for whom the act of writing itself is more compelling and more actual than any generic delimitation; and that act, for Delany, should always aim at making us think.

It is in this context of Delany as the most rigorously and, as it were, *insistently* intellectual of writers that we can begin to grasp the importance which the interview—the literary conversation—possesses for him: an importance rather different than that which it has for most other authors. Despite a few well-known exceptions (J. D. Salinger, Thomas Pynchon), most writers whose output has attracted wide attention do give interviews from time to time; and readers interested in the writings by which an author has made a reputation usually find such interviews (or at least the better ones) to be also of interest, both as enjoyable reading in themselves and for the light they may throw on the novels or poems or other literary works for which the authors are primarily known. Such is the founding premise, for example, of the extremely popular series of (by now) over three hundred "writers at work" interviews launched by *The Paris Review* in 1953. Such is also the premise, of course, of the University Press of Mississippi's Literary Conversations series, in which the current volume appears, which aims to collect in individual volumes the best interviews with a large variety of authors. In the main, however, even the best literary interviews typically have an interest, both for the authors who give them and for the readers who read them, that is distinctly *secondary* to the interest taken in the author's "own" work. Excellent interviews are available with, say, William Faulkner or Ursula Le Guin, but one probably reads them as auxiliary to the reading of Faulkner's novels and stories, or the reading of Le Guin's novels, stories, poems, criticism, and children's fiction. "Interviewee" is not, in general, one of the major literary identities even of writers who have participated in a large number of literary conversations.

But Delany is an exception. Precisely because the literary dialogue is an especially fruitful form for the generation of ideas, for the dialectical process of conceptual give and take, Delany has made it not a detour from his own work but an
integral part of it. He insists that all interviews with him be "silent," i.e., written, partly because experience has taught him that the interviewee cannot count
on being represented with precise accuracy by the interviewer's notes or even tape
recorder: but also because the written interview possesses greater conceptual resources, more intellectual elbow-room, as it were, than an interview conducted
viva voce. A Delany interview is as *literary,* in the strictest and strongest sense, as
an essay or novel. Delany does not turn aside from the writing he regards as his
actual work in order to indulge an interviewer's request; and, unlike many famous writers, he has never disparaged the literary interview as a form. Instead, he
actively welcomes the opportunity that an interview provides, an opportunity *not*
for a casual chat but for a serious piece of critical writing done in dialectical collaboration with the interviewer (though challenging some of the premises that lie
behind the interviewer's questions is sometimes, for Delany, a necessary intellectual move in this kind of writing). The seriousness with which Delany takes his
interviews is indicated by the fact that he has incorporated many of them into his
own critical books. Indeed, one of these books—*Silent Interviews: On Language,
Race, Sex, Science Fiction, and Some Comics* (1994)—is composed of nothing other
than a selection of his literary conversations.

One might say that Delany's interviews are akin to dialogues in the most robust philosophic sense. But to put the matter thus is inevitably to suggest the Platonic precedent: and so it ought to be made clear that it is the *contrast* between
Plato and Delany that really helps us to understand the latter. As a Marxist and a
materialist, Delany upholds an ontology and an epistemology that are resolutely
anti-Platonic: he insists upon the priority of temporal flux and of contradiction
against all idealism, all thought that is based on identity, stasis, and eternality.
Like Walter Pater (one of the really distinctive influences on Delany's later work,
whose 1893 volume *Plato and Platonism* has had a particular importance for him),
Delany sees not Plato but Heraclitus, the founder of the dialectic, as the true beginning of philosophy and the first eminent model in Western culture of how to
think. Though passionately interested in the significance of form, Delany always
sees form as irreducibly material and historical in a way radically opposed to the
timeless Forms of Plato.

Furthermore—and relatedly—it is also in his approach to the form of the interview itself that Delany is resolutely anti-Platonic. If Delany's robust sexual
practices mark him as, in this respect, the antithesis of the notoriously abstemi-

ous Platonic Socrates, the same can be said for the way that he approaches intellectual exchange. As careful readers of Plato have long noticed, the famed "Socratic method," so frequently and naively commended as a pedagogic model, is
actually constructed on an extensive tissue of irony that (thinly) veils the single-
minded authoritarianism with which Plato's Socrates expounds the Platonic
idealism. Though Socrates often pretends, with elaborate *faux*-courtesy, to take
the views of his interlocutors seriously, he in fact uses the latter only as rhetorical
foils in the presentation of a philosophy fully worked out before the conversation
has begun. The Platonic dialogues contain little real dialectic, little intellectual
give and take. Indeed, though technically dialogic—an effect, it has been said, of
Plato's aborted youthful ambitions to become a playwright—they are in substantive philosophic terms relentlessly *monologic.*

Plato's monologic idealism finds its opposite in the genuinely dialogic and dialectical materialism of Delany. Avoiding all traces of the condescending Socratic
false modesty, Delany treats the interlocutors who are his collaborators with real
respect. He takes their ideas seriously, which means sometimes rejecting them
as decisively wrong but never sneering at them from a quasi-Socratic position
of smug superiority. What is at issue here is not just human courtesy—though I
may add, in a personal aside, that I have known Delany well for about a decade
and that he has always seemed to me, in his acute awareness of and responsive-
ness to the feelings of others, one of the most deeply courteous and generous individuals I have ever met—but, again, the priority that Delany gives to thought
at its most insistent, genuine, and self-reflexive. For Delany as for any real dialectician, valid ideas emerge from (and are tested in) intellectual clash and contradiction; and the philosophic process is necessarily collaborative in fundamental rather than (as in Plato) merely formal ways. To be sure, to value collaboration
as a sign (and frequent condition) of authentic intellectual work is not necessarily to posit any simple mathematical equality among the collaborators. As the
reader of this volume will discover, Delany as an interviewee often "talks" (or actually, of course, writes) for many pages at a time; and, as might be expected from
one of the first American intellectuals to take a serious interest in Derrida's theory
of writing, a Delany interview makes no attempt to camouflage itself as the tran-
script of a "live" conversation spoken in real time. But this absence of false modesty co-exists with the true modesty expressed by the way that Delany's own discourse in a literary conversation—however extensive his share of the conversation
may be—always remains in alert dialogue with that of the interviewer.

Indeed, a Delany interview is collaborative and dialogic to a degree that is
particularly evident if one has taken the role of interviewer; and I will add a few

details rooted in my own experience as one of Delany's many interviewers, an experience whose most recent product is the final selection in this volume. My Delany interviews have been conducted by e-mail—a wonderful technological innovation that makes the silent interview far more practically feasible than it had ever been before—and, in the first instance, Delany and I each composed passages that, by the technical artifice of the dialogue form, are feigned to be spoken by the respective participants. But, as in any real literary endeavor, initial composition provides only the raw materials that are then worked upon in an elaborate revisionary process—revision being, of course, an indispensable feature of dialectical thought. Not only did each of us revise and rework aspects of our "own" contributions, but we sometimes suggested changes in the passages attributed to the other as well; and, prior to our agreement on the final shape of the whole interview, we also sometimes discussed—"off-stage," as it were—issues that the interview might handle and how they might be dealt with. If one reads an interview as the unmediated record of an actual oral exchange, such a procedure may seem odd and even faintly dishonest. But Delany and I have both taken the pressure of the crucial Derridean insight that written language is never, in fact, the mere second-order representation or counterfeit of spoken language. The binary opposition between speech and writing is as incomplete and misleading as any other binary opposition: and writing is a practice that from ancient times has enjoyed its own autonomy and internal complexity.

Writing is also the practice to which Delany has primarily devoted his life (as he explicitly says in his recent nonfiction work, *About Writing: Seven Essays, Four Letters, and Five Interviews* [2005]), and this book joins his many others as splendid evidence of this devotion. As with any series of literary conversations, many of the exchanges in this book concern Delany's own published work. But Delany is the least self-absorbed of interviewees, and, as the reader will soon discover, he engages a range of issues here as wide as in his fiction and nonfiction as a whole. Open this book at random and you may find Delany reflecting on one of his own novels, but you are just as likely (or more likely) to find him expounding on the historical development of the novel form, or on sexual practices today, or on the politics of philosophy, or on any number of a thousand other issues.

I will conclude with a few words about the selection of the pieces that follow and their place in the Delany *oeuvre* as a whole—though I will not offer a comprehensive overview of that *oeuvre*, partly because I have already done so in other places, which the interested reader may consult.[1] Space limitations meant that— even after eliminating all Delany interviews that he had incorporated into his own books—there were still far more excellent pieces available than could be included in this volume. Allowing for some difficult judgment calls, and for some

interviews that I would like to have included but could not, there were two major
principles that guided my choices. First, longer interviews were usually preferred
to shorter ones. A mind as acute and as amply stocked as Delany's tends to need
a pretty high word count to show what it can really do. Indeed, this principle applies not only to Delany's interviews but to his work as a whole. Though he has
written some excellent free-standing short stories, probably no other American
science-fiction writer of remotely comparable stature has done so little work in
the short-story form. He has always preferred novels to tales, and it is no accident
that his longest single work—the Nevèrÿon sequence, a vast and imaginatively
quite roomy cycle of novels, novellas, stories, and essays—is, at least arguably,
his best. Even his best free-standing tales—such as "The Star Pit" (1967), "We, in
Some Strange Power's Employ, Move on a Rigorous Line" (1968), and "Time Considered as a Helix of Semi-precious Stones" (1968)—are often significantly longer
than the average short story.

I have also tended to choose more recent as against older interviews. The earlier interviews are naturally allied to Delany's earlier fiction and essays. Though
this work—almost entirely science fiction and science-fiction criticism—certainly
remains of the highest interest, its much deserved fame means that it is likely to
be already fairly well known to most of those reading this book. Delany's newer
work, by contrast, has of course had less time to establish itself and so tends to
be less familiar to readers. Delany remains most widely known in science-fiction
circles, and most Delany critics would, I think, agree that his work in the field as
both practitioner and critic remains the core of his achievement. But we need to
remember that he has not published a work that is clearly and inarguably science-
fictional since *Stars in My Pocket Like Grains of Sand* in 1984, or a work that is by
any plausible construction science-fictional since the conclusion in 1987 of the
Nevèrÿon sequence (which I, for one, have argued to be, ultimately, a kind of science fiction). As monumental as his stature as a science-fiction writer and critic
is—and several of his novels, such as *Dhalgren* (1975), *Trouble on Triton*, and *Stars
in My Pocket Like Grains of Sand*, are among the supreme achievements of the
genre—his more recent work by no means suffers in comparison with the earlier work: I am thinking, for instance, of brilliant novels in various genres like
The Mad Man (1994), *Phallos* (2004), and *Dark Reflections* (2007); the superb stories brought together in *Atlantis: Three Tales* (1995); and nonfiction like the often
highly personal urban sociology of *Times Square Red, Times Square Blue* (1999),
the remarkable personal letters collected in *1984* (2000), and the acute (and practically very useful) meditations on Delany's own craft found in *About Writing*
(2005). The interviews that follow contain a good deal of discussion of the later
works and, no less, of the issues that the later works themselves raise: not, to be

sure, to the exclusion of Delany's science fiction, but in addition to it, so as to give a more balanced picture of the whole range of Delany's interests and accomplishments. Though Delany's established readership naturally forms the main presumptive audience of this volume, I have hopes that even the reader who happens to come upon it without having read anything else by Delany will find it well worth reading—both in itself and as a spur to read more by one of the most challenging and rewarding authors of our time.

It remains only to express my appreciation for several individuals without whom this volume would never have come into being. The most obvious debt, of course, is to Chip Delany himself. In compiling a collection like this one with a living author, the author's cooperation is, to put it mildly, useful. But Chip's participation has gone far beyond mere cooperation. In working on the interview that concludes this volume and in numerous other ways as well, he has devoted substantial amounts of time from an always very busy schedule to helping to make this book the excellent work I believe it to be. The generosity, energy, and helpfulness he displayed were extraordinary, though quite typical—as I and many others can testify—of the man himself. Since, however, I have made no effort, in this introduction or elsewhere, to conceal the personal respect, admiration, and affection I feel for Delany, the reader may well wonder how such feelings comport with the impersonal disinterestedness that scholarship is generally reckoned to involve. It is a fair question, and one that a dialectician ought not to avoid.

In the nature of the case, it is, of course, always a tricky matter to gauge and account for one's own biases. I will only suggest a few considerations that incline me to think that my integrity as a Delany scholar has not been fatally compromised by personal friendship. In the first place, though Chip has indeed become one of my most valued friends over the past decade, my admiration for his writings has not been any greater during this period than it was during the preceding quarter century, when I not only had no personal relationship whatever with him but also never supposed that I was likely to have one. I remember well, for instance, the excitement I felt upon reading *Stars in My Pocket Like Grains of Sand* (consistently my personal favorite among Delany's novels) when it first came out in 1984; every word of praise I offered in the critical foreword that I wrote to the 2004 reprint was already implicit in my initial reaction twenty years earlier. It therefore seems to me reasonable to believe that, insofar as there is a meaningful relation between my admiration for the work and my friendship for the man, the former has been one of the motives for the latter—not the other way around. Furthermore, as anyone who knows Chip will, I think, agree, he would surely regard any disingenuous or uncritical profession of admiration to be a very poor token of friendship. As an intellectual of rigor and integrity, he values the honest, vigorous play of ideas above all.

I suspect that any book published by the University Press of Mississippi owes a considerable debt to Seetha Srinivasan, for many years the press's director and chief guiding spirit. That is certainly the case with the present volume, the third that I have worked on with Seetha; and none of them would have come close to seeing print without her support, advice, and encouragement. Since, as of this writing, she has recently announced her impending retirement, I should like this book to stand as a particular tribute to her long and devoted service to authors and editors—and, of course, to readers. That the press is likely to remain in good hands even after her departure is suggested by the productive working relationship I have already formed with my editor Walter Biggins, whose attention and assistance have been exemplary.

Nobody has worked harder on this book than Rich Cooper, my research assistant, my student during his undergraduate and now during his graduate education, and my friend. This is the second book I have produced in collaboration with him, and I earlier praised him as "virtually the Platonic ideal of what a research assistant ought to be." Though quite sincerely meant, this phrase now seems to me to provide a pertinent example of the essential fallaciousness of Platonic (and all other) idealism—and hence of any language that borrows, even tactically, from the terminology of the ideal. For, if one took the phrase literally, it would be logically impossible for me to state what is, in fact, the truth: that Rich's research skills have become even sharper and more wide-ranging over the past year, and that it was with an even easier mind than before that I depended on him for a thousand things large and small in the preparation of the manuscript. The share of the credit that Rich deserves for the strengths of the book is large indeed, though all responsibility for the book's shortcomings is of course mine alone. I feel fortunate to be working with Rich at the beginning of what I am confident will be a very fine intellectual career.

Finally, I should mention my beloved wife Annette. I will not particularize the debts I owe her, except to note that they include making the earth turn, the sun shine, and life worth living.

CF

Note

1. I have offered a basic survey of Delany's career in "Samuel Delany: A Biographical and Critical Overview," in *A Companion to Science Fiction*, ed. David Seed (Oxford: Blackwell, 2005), pp. 398–407. A less thoroughgoing synoptic account, but one done in greater

conceptual detail (and which I delivered orally as a keynote address at an academic conference devoted to Delany's work), is "About Delany Writing: An Anatomical Meditation," *Extrapolation*, Summer 2006, pp. 16–29. The following pieces of mine (listed here in reverse chronological order) represent more specialized work in Delany studies: "Foreword" to reissue of Samuel Delany, *Stars in My Pocket Like Grains of Sand* (Middletown: Wesleyan University Press, 2004), pp. xi–xiv; "Racing Delany" [review of Jeffrey Allen Tucker, *A Sense of Wonder: Samuel R. Delany, Race, Identity, and Difference*], *Science-Fiction Studies*, November 2004, pp. 476–79; "A Note on Marxism and Fantasy," *Historical Materialism*, vol. 10:4 (2002), pp. 261–71; "Adventures of the Dialectic: or, On Delany as Critic" [review of Samuel Delany, *Shorter Views: Queer Thoughts and the Politics of the Paraliterary*], *Science-Fiction Studies*, March 2001, pp. 107–18; "An Anatomy of Hope" [review of Samuel Delany, *1984: Selected Letters*], *Science-Fiction Studies*, November 2000, pp. 523–26; "Of Cities and Bodies" [review of Samuel Delany, *Times Square Red, Times Square Blue* and *Bread & Wine: An Erotic Tale of New York*], *Science-Fiction Studies*, July 2000, pp. 356–57; "*Stars in My Pocket Like Grains of Sand*: Samuel Delany and the Dialectics of Difference," in Carl Freedman, *Critical Theory and Science Fiction* (Hanover and London: Wesleyan University Press and University Press of New England, 2000), pp. 146–64.

Chronology

1942	Born as Samuel Ray Delany, Jr., on April 1 in New York City, to Samuel Ray Delany, Sr., a Harlem funeral director, and Margaret Delany, a court stenographer.
1945–56	Attends New York private schools on scholarship.
1952	Around this time discovers his primary sexual orientation to be homosexual; gives himself the nickname "Chip," which endures to this day.
1956–60	Attends the Bronx High School of Science; writes his first (unpublished) novels, and also writes stories and essays and composes music.
1960	Father dies of lung cancer.
1960–61	Attends City College of New York.
1961	Marries his Bronx Science classmate (later the renowned poet) Marilyn Hacker.
1962	Publishes his first novel, *The Jewels of Aptor*.
1967	Wins his first Nebula Award for *Babel-17*.
1967–68	Is a member of the rock group and urban commune Heavenly Breakfast, which is chronicled in his autobiographical work *Heavenly Breakfast: An Essay on the Winter of Love*.
1968	Wins his second and third Nebula Awards for *The Einstein Intersection* and the short story "Aye, and Gomorrah."
1969	Wins his fourth Nebula Award for the long story "Time Considered as a Helix of Semi-precious Stones."
1970	Wins his first Hugo Award for "Time Considered as a Helix of Semi-precious Stones."
1970–71	With Marilyn Hacker, publishes the journal *Quark*.
1972	Visiting writer at Wesleyan University's Center for the Humanities.
1974	Daughter Iva Hacker-Delany born.
1975	At the invitation of the famed literary critic Leslie Fiedler, takes his first (visiting) academic position as Butler Professor of English, SUNY-Buffalo.

1977   Senior fellow at the Center for Twentieth-Century Studies at the University of Wisconsin; publishes his first critical book, *The Jewel-Hinged Jaw: Notes on the Language of Science Fiction.*

1978   Writer in residence at SUNY-Albany.

1980   Is divorced from Marilyn Hacker after being separated since 1975.

1985   Honored with the Pilgrim Award from the Science Fiction Research Association for lifetime achievement in science-fiction scholarship.

1987   Senior fellow at Cornell University's Society for the Humanities.

1988   Takes his first tenured academic position as professor of comparative literature at the University of Massachusetts at Amherst.

1989   Wins his second Hugo Award for his autobiography *The Motion of Light in Water*; is included by *Lambda Book Report* among its "Fifty Men and Women Who Have Done Most to Change Our Attitudes Toward Gayness in the Last Hundred Years"; wins the lifetime achievement award from the Dark Room, the black students' collective at Harvard University.

1991   Begins living with the previously homeless street vendor Dennis Rickett; their relationship (which endures to this day) is the subject of the autobiographical graphic novel *Bread and Wine: An Erotic Tale of New York* (drawings by Mia Wolff).

1993   Receives the William Whitehead Memorial Award for lifetime achievement in gay and lesbian writing.

1993–2007 Takes visiting academic positions at the University of Michigan's Humanities Center, the University of Kansas, the University of Idaho, the University of Minnesota, the Honors College of Michigan State University, the Atlantic Center for the Arts, and the Naropa Institute.

1995   Is guest of honor at the World Science Fiction Convention in Glasgow, Scotland.

1997   Honored with the Kessler Award from the Center for Lesbian and Gay Studies at the City University of New York.

1998   Leaves the University of Massachusetts for a tenured professorship in the Poetics Program of the English Department at SUNY-Buffalo.

2000   Leaves Buffalo to take his current academic position as professor of English and creative writing at Temple University in Philadelphia.

2002   Inducted into the Science Fiction Hall of Fame.

Conversations with Samuel R. Delany

Samuel R. Delany:
The Possibility of Possibilities
Joseph Beam/1986

Beam: I'm certain that there are many black gay male writers who write only "heterosexually." You and James Baldwin, in recent times, are the only two major writers who have dared write about black gay men and from a black gay male perspective. What has allowed and enabled you to write as a black, openly gay man? What events precipitated that courageous choice?

Delany: Courage doesn't have much to do with it. Rather, I think, it's a kind of education. I don't mean school. I mean the social education you get in the world—what the nineteenth century called an education of the sentiments.

Also, remember, my first five science fiction novels were written as "heterosexually" as any homophobe could wish.

It must have been sometime in the late fifties, when I was still in my teens, that it hit me: if everybody knew that *all* of us were queer—that's the word I used, thinking about it to myself then—nobody could blackmail us any more.

Today, with the Annual Gay Pride Day March, and a widely distributed gay press (and not so well-distributed books such as this one), and the Phil Donahue Show, we forget the biggest fear we used to have as gay men, in the forties and fifties, black or white, was of someone's finding out: anyone who knew you were gay, especially if they were straight, had life-and-death power over you. That person could lose you your job, get you evicted, or have you generally hounded out of town. The House Un-American Activities Committee was hunting up gays right along with Communists back in the early fifties—because we were more susceptible to blackmail, and therefore bigger security risks! Well, it went through a lot of people's minds that if it *was* all out, this awful power any straight person immediately assumed over every gay person would vanish. I don't know when or where, a few years later in the sixties, I first read this detailed clearly—it was well before Stonewall.

But the reason I can't recall the particular article is that by the time I'd read it, it was such a frequently rehearsed idea. The specific piece merely confirmed something I—and many other gay people—had thought many times.

In terms of any long-range, large-scale program, as many of us making ourselves known to as many people as possible was the only sane political alternative to end our greatest fear and oppression. And the more people who did it, the safer it would be for the rest of us. It's still not easy, but it's easier now than it was in 1960.

As a black man, I tended to straddle worlds: white and black. As a gay man, I straddled them too: straight and gay. I'd been leading a pretty active gay sexual life from the time I was seventeen. But on my second or third heterosexual experiment, I found myself on my way to being a father. So, at nineteen I got married. Although my wife was wholly aware of my sexual orientation (and we'd discussed the possibility of a then-illegal abortion), we decided to marry anyway and have the baby. And I found myself with all the privileges and pressures of a heterosexual coupling. My wife miscarried a few months later. But we stayed married for the next thirteen years—till after, indeed, we had another child.

Anyway.

My father, who died about ten months before I dropped out of City College to run off to Detroit and get myself hitched with this brilliant, eighteen-year-old Jewish poet, had owned a funeral home in Harlem. The organist who played for the services when I was a kid was a brown, round, roly-poly, irrepressibly effeminate man named Herman. It was an open secret Herman was gay. The adults in my family joked about it all the time. Herman certainly never tried to hide it—I don't know whether he could have.

Herman was very fond of me and my younger sister. From somewhere, he'd gotten the idea that I liked shad roe. (I didn't. What seven- or eight-year-old does? But then, perhaps he was teasing. He was so flamboyant in his every phrase and gesture, there was no way to be sure.) From various trips to see one sister in Baltimore, or another in Washington, D.C., Herman would bring back large, oval tins of shad roe as a present for me. And Sundays my mother would serve it for breakfast, exhorting me to eat just a taste, and, later, on some visit, while I waited, silent and awed at her untruth, would tell Herman how much I'd *loved* it!

In August, bent nearly double, his shirt sleeves rolled up over wet, teak-colored arms, some black delivery man would push a bronze and mahogany casket on the collapsible rubber-tired catafalque, slowly and step by step, into the chapel, where

Herman, in his navy suit and scarlet tie, was practicing. (At the actual service a black tie would replace it. But, during practice, as he put it, "Mother needs *some* color about her or things will be just *too* dreary—don't you think?") Herman would glance over, see the man, break into an organ fanfare, rise from the bench, clasp both hands to his heart, flutter them and his eyelids, roll his pupils toward heaven, and exclaim: "Oh, my smellin' salts! Get me my smellin' salts! Boy, you come in here and do that to a woman like me, lookin' like that? My heart can't take it! I may just faint right here, you pretty thing!"

If the delivery man had been through this before, he might stop, stand up over the coffin with sweat drops under his rough hair, and say: "What's a'matter with you, Herman? You one of them faggots that likes men?"

But Herman's eyes would widen in astonishment, and, drawing back, one hand to his tie, he'd declare: "Me? Oh, chile, chile, you must be ill or something!" Then he would march up, take the young man's chin in his hand, and examine his face with peering eyes. "Me? One of *them?* Why, you must have a fever, boy! I swear, you must have been workin' out in the heat too long today. I do believe you must be sick!" Here he would feel the man's forehead, then, removing his hand, look at the sweat that had come off on his own palm, touch his forefinger to his tongue, and declare: "Oh, my lord, you *are* tasty! Here," he would go on before the man could say anything, putting both his hands flat on the delivery man's chest, between the open shirt buttons, and push the shirt back off the dark arms, "let me just massage them fine, strong muscles of yours and relax you and get you all comfortable so them awful and hideous ideas about me can fly out of your head forever and ever and ever, Amen! Don't that feel good? Don't you want a nice, lovely massage to relax all them big, beautiful muscles you got? *Umm?* Boy, how did you get so strong? Now don't tell me you don't like that! That's lovely, just lovely the way it feels, isn't it? Imagine, honey! Thinkin' such nastiness like that about a woman like me! I mean, I just might faint right here, and you gonna have to carry me to a chair and fan me and bring my smellin' salts!" Meanwhile, he would be rubbing the man's chest and arms. "Ooooh, that feels so good, I can hardly stand it myself!" His voice would go up real high and he'd grin. "Honey, you feelin' a little better now?"

In the chapel corner the floor fan purred, its blades a metallic haze behind circular wires. In seersucker shorts and sandals, on the first row of wooden folding chairs painted gold with maroon plush seats, I sat, watching all this.

Different men would put up with Herman's antics for different lengths of time; and the casket delivery man (or the coal man or the plumber's assistant) would finally shrug away, laughing and pulling his shirt back up: "Aw, Herman,

cut it out, now . . . !" and my father, in his vest and shirt sleeves, would come from
the embalming room at the chapel back, chuckling at the whole thing, followed
by a smiling Freddy, Dad's chief embalmer.

I'd smile, too. Although I wasn't sure what exactly I was smiling at.

One thing I realized was that this kind of fooling around (the word "camping"
I didn't hear for another half dozen years or more) was strictly masculine. It was
1948 or '49. And if my mother or another woman were present, Herman's horse-
play stopped just as assuredly as would my father's occasional "goddamn," "shit,"
or "nigger, this" or "nigger, that." Yet the change of rhetoric did not seem, with
Herman, at all the general male politeness/shyness before women as was the case
with my father and his other, rougher friends. Herman was, if anything, more
attentive to my mother than any of the others. And she was clearly fond of him.
With her, he was always full of questions about us children and advice on paint
and slipcovers, and consolation, sympathy, and humor about any of her domestic
complaints (not to mention cans of shad roe, packages of flowered stationery, and
bags of salt-water taffy from Atlantic City), all delivered with his balding, brown
head far closer to my mother's, it seemed, when they talked over coffee upstairs in
the kitchen, than my father's or anyone else's ever got.

A few years later, when I was fourteen or fifteen, I remember Herman, bent
over, sweating, fat, stopping in to visit Freddy or my father at the funeral parlor,
walking slowly, carrying some bulging shopping bag. (He no longer played the
organ for us.) I would ask him how he was, and he would shake his head and declare: "I ain't well, honey. I ain't a well woman at *all!* Pray to the Lord you never
get as sick as I been most of the last year! But you lookin' just wonderful, boy!
Wonderful! Mmmm!" And when I was seventeen or eighteen, I remember going
to look at him, grown from fat to obese, squeezed into his own coffin in the back
chapel—the one time he got to wear his red tie at a service, which only added
to that uneasy feeling always haunting funerals of friends that this was not real
death, only practice. I also realized I had no notion what actual sexual outlets
there'd been in Herman's life. Had he gone to bars? Had he gone to baths? Had
he picked up people in the afternoon in Forty-second Street movie houses or in
the evenings along the benches beside Central Park West? Once a month, did he
spend a night cruising the halls in the YMCA, over on 135th Street, where, on Sat-
urday afternoons I used to go so innocently swimming? Had there been a long-
term lover, waiting for him at home, un-met by, and un-mentioned to, people like
my father he worked for? Or had his encounters been confined to the touch teased
from some workman; or had it even been his arm around my shoulder, his thigh
against my own, when, years before, beside me on the organ bench, he'd taught

me the proper fingering for the scale on the chapel console, before running to my parents to exclaim: "You *must* get that boy some piano lessons! You must! There's so much talent in his little hands, I tell you, it just breaks my heart!"—an exhortation my parents took no more seriously than they did any of his other outrageousness. (I was already studying the violin.) I had no way to know. Herman was fat and forty when, as a child, I met him. By his fifties he was dead of diabetic complications.

Herman's funeral was among the many my father was never paid for, which changed him, in Mom's mind, from a dear and amusing friend to one of the "characters" she claimed were always latching on to my father, to live off him, to drain him of money and affection, and finally to die on him.

Today, I like shad roe a lot. And, somehow, by the time I was nineteen and married, I had decided—from Herman and several other gay black men I'd seen or met—that *some* blacks were more open about being gay than many whites. My own explanation was, I suppose, that because we had less to begin with, in the end we had less to lose. Still, the openness Herman showed, as did a number of other gay men, black and white, never seemed an option for me. But I always treasured the image of Herman's outrageous and defiant freedom to say absolutely anything . . .

Anything except, of course, I *am* queer, and I like men sexually better than women.

At the time I would have analyzed my own "lack of options" this way: I wasn't personally attracted to effeminate men. Therefore, I couldn't imagine the men I would *be* attracted to attracted in turn to someone who *was* effeminate. *Ergo*, I'd better *not* swish—not if I wanted the kind of sexual partners I thought I did, Q.E.D.

Today, of course, my *"ergo"* looks pretty shaky. What was really going on was closer to this: I wasn't particularly attracted to effeminate men—okay, we'll take that as a given. But the second assumption was: since I was terrified someone might find out I *was* gay, I just assumed any male I was attracted to would be equally terrified of discovery. Therefore, no swishing for *either* of us! If nothing else, his would get me in trouble; mine would get him in trouble. And when I look back on it now, it's pretty hard to separate that terror of discovery from the initial sexualization of "straight looking" (whatever that is) men in the first place.

It's kind of sad, isn't it?

But, for better or worse, that's the kind of sentimental education on which what was to come was based.

The next big step came when I was about twenty-two. I'd been married for three years. I'd already published four novels, with a fifth due out soon. Then, I had a kind of breakdown and was in a city mental hospital, where I was in a ward-wide therapy group. Each of the group's eighteen patients had individual therapy once a week with Dr. Grossman. But daily, all together, we had a group session. My group had blacks, Hispanics, and whites in about equal numbers. In my individual hour, the first thing I brought up with Dr. Grossman was my homosexuality. After all, homosexuality was a "mental problem," if not a "mental illness"—at least in 1964. But in group sessions, I didn't mention it. Not talking about something like that in a therapy session seemed to me then a contradiction in terms. I discussed it with Dr. Grossman, who said, bless his soul, that if talking to the group about my homosexuality made me uncomfortable, he didn't feel there was any pressing need for it. But that felt wrong to me; I decided to bring it up anyway.

Was I scared? Yes!

But I was also scared not to. My breakdown had frightened me. I had no idea, at twenty-two, if group therapy in a city mental hospital would help. But since I was there, it seemed idiotic to waste the therapy time if it was available. Therapy to me meant talking precisely about such things.

Therefore, talk, I decided, is what I'd better do.

Most of the group didn't threaten me. One Hispanic woman was there because she'd killed her baby and had somehow ended up in the hospital, rather than in jail. One poor, pear-shaped, working class white man was obsessed with his stomach—should he walk around with it held out (rich and successful men always seemed to do this), or should he hold it in (because sometimes that's what it seemed they did)? While he was there, he never did quite get that his problem *was* his problem—rather than his inability to resolve it. His earliest memory, he told us, was of his father bloodying his mother's nose with a punch, while she clutched him, as an infant, in her arms and the blood gushed down over him. And there was an elderly Jewish woman who had flipped out, apparently, when her eighty-six-year-old and terminally ill mother had committed suicide in the Park Avenue apartment downstairs from hers. She'd been placed in the hospital by her husband, to be "cured" by the time his vacation came around. And, indeed, the day the vacation began, he summarily removed her from the hospital, over the protests of the doctors. I remember she left us, on her husband's arm, babbling on about how of course she was better, she had to be better, it was time to go on va-cation, and, yes, she was really much better now, she felt perfectly fine, oh, she'd be just wonderful, she'd be really fine once they got started on the drive to Colo-rado, everything would be wonderful, they'd have a wonderful time, he'd see how much better she was—then she'd bite viciously at the lace-rimmed handkerchief pulled tight around her foreknuckle, and try to squeeze back tears, grinding her teeth loud enough for us to hear across the lobby, while her white-haired, pin-striped husband tugged her, stumbling, toward the glass doors and the waiting car outside. Also in the group was an older, white-haired man, named Joe, who, from his demeanor, manicure, and sweaters, I just assumed was gay, though he'd mentioned it in group session no more than I had. There was also a black twenty-year-old named Beverly. Endless arguments and fights between her mother and a succession of her mother's lovers had finally driven her to live on her apartment house roof—which is where she'd been found before she had been brought into Mt. Sinai. In all the nontherapy programs, Beverly presented herself as a ballsy black dyke. But, with the same people, during the group session she withdrew into paralyzed silence, though she claimed to have no problems talking to Dr. Grossman in her weekly individual hour; and his presence, along with the slightly more formal seating arrangement, was the only difference in the gathering she'd seemed so comfortable with minutes before the official therapy hour, or indeed, minutes afterwards.

Next to these guys, I guess, I felt pretty sane.

My fear of talking about my own homosexuality, however, centered on one patient. Call him Hank.

Hank was white, about my age, and a pretty aggressive fellow. Once a young woman patient had become hysterical because she didn't want to take some medication. Nurses, orderlies, and a resident had had to restrain her physically to give her an injection—when Hank had rushed up at her screams and started punching, putting a very surprised psychiatric resident on the floor. "Hey! She don't want it. Don't *give* it to her!" And because she immediately calmed down—doubtless astonished at her common-sense rescuer—they didn't. Hank's own problem, as I recall, was something wrong with his feet. They were perpetually sore, and it was painful for him to walk. Nothing physical had been found wrong with him, and he'd been transferred to the mental ward for observation on the chance that his ailment was psychosomatic. Aside from occasional moments of belligerence, he was a pretty affable guy. I rather liked him and, I guess, wanted him to like me. But his affability also included the odd "faggot" joke, which left me dubious over talking with him about being gay, even in "group."

Nevertheless, I'd made up my mind.

So, Monday morning, when the eighteen of us were seated around the room on our aluminum folding chairs, I launched in: as I recall, it was the most abject of confessions. I explained the whole thing, looking fixedly at the white and black floor tile. I had this problem—I was homosexual, but I was really "working on it." I was sure that, with help, I could "get better." I went on and on like this for about five minutes, and finally glanced up at Hank—whom I'd been afraid to look at since I'd started, and for whom, in a kind of negative way, the whole performance was geared.

And I saw something:

First, he wasn't paying much attention. He was squirming around in his chair. And you could tell: his feet hurt him a *whole* lot. Now I explained that I'd really been most worried about *his* reaction—to which, as I recall, he was kind of surprised. He looked up at me, a little bemused, and said that homosexuality was just something that, Gee, he didn't know too much about.

Joe, I remember, made a measured comment during one of the silences in the discussion that followed:

"I've had sexual experiences with men before," he began. "Maybe this is just something you're going through, Chip. I mean you're married—comparatively happily, I gather—and you say you don't have any sexual problems there. Perhaps it's just something you're trying out. Soon it'll be behind you. And it won't worry you any more."

"No," I said. "No, I don't think so. First off, I've been going through it ever since I was a kid. And, second, I don't want it to stop. I like it too much. But . . ."

Which returned us to that unanswerable silence that seemed, if anything, more and more the heart of my "therapeutic" confession.

Hank's only real comment came about an hour later, when most of us from group were now in another room, making our potholders or picture frames. Hank suddenly turned to Joe (in his lavender angora sweater) and baldly announced, "Now, you see I figured *you* were that way—"while Joe raised a silvery eyebrow in a refined Caucasian version of Herman's grandly black and preposterous protest so many years before.

It was lost on Hank. "But you?" He turned to me. "Now that really surprised me. I never would have figured that for somebody like you. That's real strange."

I don't know about Joe; but that was when I made the connection with that all-but-forgotten article; I began to suspect that perhaps the "therapeutic" value of my confession, after all, may not have been psychological so much as sociological. Certainly Hank wasn't any *less* friendly to me after that, as we continued through lunch and the various occupational sessions for the rest of the day. But he didn't tell any more "faggot" jokes—not when Joe or I was around.

The most important part of the lesson resolved for me that night however, while I was lying in bed, thinking over the day:

Thanks to my unfounded fear of Hank's anger (the guy—like most of the world—had too many problems of his own), I'd talked like someone miserable, troubled, and sick over being gay; and that wasn't who I was. On the contrary, my actual feeling was that, despite my marriage, the gay aspects of my life, from the social to the sexual, were the most educational, the most supportive, the most creative, and the most opening parts of my life. Being gay had meant everything to me from the fact that I knew I could survive on my own fairly comfortably in just about any medium-sized or large American city, to an exposure to aspects of art, theater, and literature I simply never would have gotten had I been straight. Where had all the things I'd said that morning come from?

I began to understand where they'd come from that night. They'd come from a book by the infamous Dr. Burgler I had read as a teenager that had explained how homosexuals were psychically retarded. They came from an appendix to another psychology book that told how homosexuals were all alcoholics who committed suicide. They had come from the section on "Inversion" by Kraft Von Ebbing in *Psychopathia Sexualis* that I'd also read; some of it had come from Vidal's *The City and the Pillar* (before he revised the ending) and some from Andre Tellier's *The Twilight Men*. Some of it had come from the pathos of Theodore Sturgeon's science fiction story "The World Well Lost" and his Western story, "Scars." And some had come from Cocteau's *The White Paper* and some came from Gide's *Corydon*. Some, even, had come from Baldwin's *Giovanni's Room*.

It had come from tragic-comic portraits by Proust of Baron Charlus, by Balzac of M. Vautrin, by Petronius of Enculpias.

When you talk about something openly for the first time—and that, certainly, was the first time I'd talked to a public *group* about being gay—for better or worse you use the public language you've been given. It's only later, alone in the night, that maybe, if you're a writer, you ask yourself how closely that language reflects your experience. And that night I realized my experience had been betrayed.

For all their "faggot" jokes, the Hanks of this world just weren't *interested* in my abjection and my apologies, one way or the other. They'd been a waste of time. They only wounded my soul—and had misinformed anyone who'd actually bothered to listen.

I thought about Herman. I thought about any number of other gay men, black and white, some friends, some casual sex partners among the many hundred I'd had over the last six years since I was seventeen. I also thought about Petronius, Baldwin, Vidal, Gide, Cocteau, and Tellier again. They, at least, had talked about it. And however full of death and darkness their accounts had been, they'd at least essayed a certain personal honesty. And the thing about honesty is that all of ours is different. Maybe I just had to try my own.

The next day, at the hospital, it happened that I was to be interviewed by a bunch of medical students and interns interested in going into psychiatry. While the white-smocked students listened and took notes, the chief psychiatrist, an iron-haired, balding man in his late forties, asked the questions.

The whole effect was very different from the one of the day before.

I explained to them that I was a writer, I was black, I was homosexual, I was married, I was twenty-two, and I had published five novels (a fifth had come out)—but whatever problems I had, they didn't *seem* to lie in the sexual area. While I was talking, I felt pretty self-assured, and probably sounded it—I remember wondering, vaguely, if that made me sound to them even *more* disturbed; but since it was the truth, it was their problem, not mine. And I talked, of course, about what I thought to be the actual pressures that had contributed to my breakdown. The questioning psychiatrist's tongue kept slipping and he would accidentally call me "Dr. Delany . . ." The students would laugh, and, embarrassed, he would correct himself and call me "Mr." for a while, till his tongue slipped again. Once more I became, "Doctor . . . I mean *Mister* Delany." And again they'd laugh.

Later, to my therapy group, I even explained what I felt had happened with my "confession"—how I'd needlessly and inaccurately presented myself so much as a victim, in order not to offend them and to assuage their (i.e., Hank's) imagined anger.

Straight, white Hank wasn't much more interested in *that* than he'd been in the original confession.

A few days later the suicide of another patient (she was not in our group; still, some of us had known her: it was the woman Hank had tried to defend from the doctors who'd been trying to force medication on her) shifted us all into another mode. Deirdre had been eighteen; she was pregnant by another patient, and suffered from grueling headaches. She had not been able to get the doctors to authorize a therapeutic abortion for her: she was too "unstable," they claimed, for such a "psychologically difficult" operation—though she had wanted an abortion desperately. Refused one once again, she had hung herself in the third-floor bathroom with a towel from the shower-curtain pole.

Her death broke up a number of people in our group, especially Hank and Beverly.

A few weeks later, I was released from the program.

Maybe six weeks after that, I was crossing Cooper Square at Astor Place, when I heard someone call: "Hey! Hello!"

I looked back, to recognize Hank, waving at me with a great grin and hobbling forward.

"Guess what!" was the first thing he said to me. "It's physical, Chip! They finally found some goddamned pinched nerve, which is why my feet hurt me all the time! So I'm not crazy after all! Isn't that great? Can you imagine, after all that, it turns out to be *physical*?"

"That's great!" I said.

He was a very happy young man, very happy to be telling me about it; and I was happy for him.

Well, it was my next novel that I decided I wanted to base at least some sections of it on some of my real experiences. In this case, I was in the middle of a very satisfying triple relationship with my wife and another man, where we all lived quite pleasantly together and slept—quite actively—in the same bed. It's not in the foreground of the book. It's just used as a kind of decoration. But I wonder if it's an accident that *that's* the first of my SF novels (*Babel-17*) anyone paid any real attention to, when it appeared, a year or so later.

Beam: Poet Sonia Sanchez writes from midnight to 3 a.m., after her twin sons have gone to sleep; and novelist Maya Angelou rents a hotel room where she writes from 7 a.m. until 2 p.m. How do you fit writing into your life?

Delany: Back there in my twenties, I used to keep to Lord Byron's romantic schedule. You know: rise at one in the afternoon, socialize till five, dine till nine, then start to work and continue writing all through the night, till dawn pales in eastern panes—then I'd crash . . . starting all over next afternoon.

It didn't do Byron much good either—he was dead at thirty-six.

About a dozen years back, however, I became a parent: it pretty much foxed *that* sybaritic routine. For maybe half the time since, I've been a one-parent family. So for the past dozen years, it's been up at four or five in the morning and work till one or two in the afternoon—with an hour out to get my kid to school. Then, once she comes home, it's on to correspondence, essays, interviews, and the like (generally things that can be interrupted by homework and the real world). Somewhere in the middle of it, I cook dinner.

And I'm in bed by 9:30.

It sounds more organized than it is. But it's the only way to get anything done if you have a kid, unless you have a wife (of whatever sex) and/or servants. And I don't have or want either.

Beam: Poet Judy Grahn, in her recent book, *Another Mother Tongue: Gay Worlds, Gay Words*, speaks of gay and lesbian people as society's visionaries and seers. She

maintains that gay people have been present in most cultures and have often fulfilled respected, honorable functions such as village magicians, tribal shamans,
and medicine women. As a creator of futuristic cultures and worlds, a visionary
by literal definition, what is your personal vision?

Delany: I don't have *a* personal vision. I have any number of visions, many of
them quite contradictory. I distrust people with only one—especially if it's too
complete, and they want to thrust everyone into it.

Some of my very fragmentary and incomplete visions are quite bleak and
scary. There's room for those too, you know.

Others are optimistic as hell.

When, in a science fiction story, one or another vision is doing its job best,
then it's engaging in heated dialogue with *your* visions, which I assume are just as
plural, fragmentary, and alive as mine. The way to start that dialogue is, of course,
by reading some of my SF stories or SF novels and letting them engage you.

Now if you just mean how would I like to see life improved—well, that doesn't
require anything so grandiose as a "vision."

There're lots of small, local problems I'd like to see remedied by the applica-
tion of some local institutional and collective energy.

I think it's a societal flaw when social forces nudge gay people toward a single
(or limited group of) social function(s). And it doesn't matter whether that social function is that of the medicine woman in one society, or that of the hair-
dresser in another, or that of the prostitute in a third. No matter how great an
individual's contribution is in any of these fields, if the choice for gay people is
conceived of as singularly limited by the general populace, then none of the three
societies provide real freedom.

And that's what we should be talking about, no?

In a recent sword and sorcery novel of mine, *The Tale of Plagues and Carnivals* (1985), a gay male character works, for a while, as a leather tanner, in the particular society he lives in. Halfway through the story, you learn that, in his culture, the tanning industry is almost wholly gay: everyone knows that leather
tanners are "that way," and, indeed, in that society, many are. I hope my readers—
gay and straight—will, first, recognize the syndrome involved. At the same time I
hope that, because of the distance the fantasy setting provides, they get at least an
inkling of how wasteful, oppressive, and arbitrary it is to have all gays herded toward any one (or any one kind of) profession.

The dialogue of multiple, partial, plural visions is great political training—
training for that most difficult of political tasks: dealing with new problems in
practical terms when they come along. But the training comes from considering

one vision, *then* another. It comes from going back and forth *between* visions, from ferreting out the parts that are coherent, from recognizing the parts that are contradictory, and locating the parts that are incomplete as one vision highlights another. That's what's really valuable—far more so than the content of any single one.

Writing about the uses of criticism, T. S. Eliot says somewhere: "About someone so great as Shakespeare, it is probable that we can never be right; and if we can never be right, it is better that we should from time to time change our way of being wrong." Well, the world is even more great and complicated than Shakespeare. Individual personal visions of the best way to organize the future— whether Marx's, Jefferson's, Sade's, Fourier's, John Stuart Mill's, Rosa Luxemberg's, or Spengler's—just aren't going to *be* entirely right. Therefore the needed talent is to be able to move from vision to vision, to get the benefits that fall from each.

There's a simple fact we science fiction writers know a bit better than anyone else: You really can't predict what the world will be like in five or fifty-five years. If any individual science fiction story happens to coincide, in part, with something that comes to pass, it's a scatter-shot effect: with *all* the various SF visions of the future, one or another *will* turn out correct—at least if you look at it with the proper squint. But nobody's going to know which one till after the fact. The visionaries' job is, I think, to provide mental practice in dealing with a whole *range* of different situations (at least the SF visionaries')—situations different from what we have now *and* different from one another.

But in the same way that courage is a small part of writing about your own life situations honestly (when compared to the obvious social disasters that accrue to writing about them dishonestly or not writing about them at all), single, prophetic visions are a very small part of writing about the future—compared to the social gain in mental flexibility that comes from contemplating a range of possible futures in a real world where the future is as unpredictable as ours.

Beam: You've known Harlem Renaissance artist-writer Bruce Nugent since you were about seventeen. Will you talk about your friendship with him?
Delany: Well, Bruce was born in 1906, the same year as my father, and I wasn't born till 1942. When I met him in '58 or '59, he was already a man in his fifties. We met at the West End Avenue apartment of some friends of mine, Bernard and Iva Kay. Bernie and Bruce had been friends since they were, respectively, nineteen and twenty-three. Bernie had prepared me for the meeting by showing me some of Bruce's privately printed and beautifully illustrated pamphlets. That spring

or summer afternoon, while I was sitting around in the living room, and Bruce dropped over, I remember him as a tall, coffee-complected black man, with an extraordinarily delicate voice, which moved from gentle humor to an equally gentle intensity, over just about everything he talked of. Bruce had spent some time in Italy, living in Florence and Rome. He spoke Italian, and was enamoured of (almost) all things Italianate. Bernie had spent some time living in Puerto Rico, near Ponce, and was equally enamored of things Hispanic. Years later, when Bernie was running a translation bureau, Bruce worked there doing the Italian translations. When I would drop into the Forty-second Street offices on the nineteenth floor of the Candler Building to say hello, they would be at their respective desks, working away at those appalling international business letters—usually about machine parts, invoices, or die castings.

About four years ago, Bruce was honored with a symposium at the extraordinary Hatch-Billops Collection, here in New York, down in the industrial part of the city. After the reception, Bruce was interviewed, in the long, narrow, semi-loft apartment, one wall lined with books, while a lot of his old and new friends sat around and, when the interview opened up to questions, also asked questions, and gave their own comments and reminiscences.

Bernie, who was then seventy-five and was very ill with lung cancer, still insisted on going. So I and my lover drove him down; it was a wonderful afternoon, and for the first time I saw actual copies of *Fire!!* and other Harlem Renaissance publications. But at one point early in the interview, Bruce told the man with the recording microphone: "You really should be interviewing Bernie, there. We've been friends since we were *children!* He knows much more about me than *I* do!" Bernie had a spectacular memory for anecdotes. (I have about twenty hours of his reminiscences on tape. Bruce may have been right.) At one point in the symposium Bernie told us about a winter night in the twenties when Bruce gave away his shoes to a cold and barefoot black man, then walked barefoot himself in the snow to get another pair from Bernie—and I realized this was the incredible kind and heroically sensitive black artist whom I had known, however slightly, for the past twenty-five years. (White Americans writers seldom *have* to give their shoes away to their fellows.) Bernie also used to say that for every piece of writing or work of art by Bruce that survived, five or ten had been lost or given to people who would probably do little or nothing to preserve them.

Bruce of course was sixty-three back in 1969. And it was very easy to see the gay activism of the last of the 'sixties and the early 'seventies leaving men like Bruce (and Bernie) behind. A number of times I heard Bruce say, in passing, "I just don't see why everyone has to be labeled. I just don't think words like homosexual—or gay—do anything for anybody." And I would hold my counsel and rack it up to age. But later, when young historians, like David Lewis, Robert Hemingway, Eric Garber, and half a dozen others, discovered what a treasure of information and insight Bruce was (you run into his name today as a research source in practically every work on the Harlem Renaissance that gets published), it was astonishing—and warming—to watch him catch up; and, indeed, to be able to provide first-hand historical insight into what *is* going on today thanks to his astute observations on what was going on thirty, fifty, and sixty years back.

I last saw Bruce at Bernie's memorial service, three years ago. We arrived early and had coffee together at the Olympia Coffee Shop around on Broadway. After the service, when actor Earl Hymen's beautiful eulogy was over (though Bernie was a white New Englander with impeccable religious connections in New Hampshire, two of his three eulogists were black, and over half the mourners at the memorial service were black or Hispanic), I walked with Bruce from the church, while he cried openly and unabashedly for his dead friend. Since then, I've spoken to him a few times on the phone.

But, sadly, I haven't made the trip over to Hoboken to see him.

Beam: In your interview with Christopher Caspar, which appeared in Donald Keller's *Inscape* (Seattle, 1983), you speak of "the possibility of possibilities." Often, as black men, the only dreams we are permitted to pursue are those of the athletic star, entertainer, or lotto winner. Will you elaborate on this notion? **Delany:** In that interview I said that the possibility of possibilities is what we had to teach our people. The fact that, in large part, we don't is something I remember my father complaining about at least as far back as when I was ten years old.

But for all my father's complaints, for all mine, the black kid on the street today just doesn't know about black scientists and inventors like Benjamin Banneker, Ernest E. Just—or, today, even George Washington Carver, with his peanuts and nectarines. They don't know about black Captain Hugh Mulzac; maybe one out of twenty knows the first man killed in the American Revolution was a black man, Crispus Attucks; but do one out of a hundred know the first man to reach the North Pole was a black explorer, Matthew Henson—part of Admiral Perry's discovery expedition? I mean, it was only two weeks ago I first learned that black opera singer Leontyne Price's brother was *General* Price—and I'm supposed to be more or less informed! I suppose you have to put things like that in some perspective: What is it? Six out of ten Americans don't know for sure the name of the President of the United States? But the fact is, white people can afford to be that stupid. *We* can't. When we are, we pay far more heavily.

A point I made in the interview you cited, and that I'd like to make again: a simple *list* of black achievements and black achievers won't do it. What's necessary is some understanding of how they relate to each other. (When I was eight my parents, as did the parents of how many other Harlem children, took me to *meet* Mr. Henson, the great North Pole explorer. A small, frail, brown old man, not unlike my mother's gentle father, Mr. Henson lived with his daughter in the Dunbar Houses. Standing before his armchair, with my hands folded in front of me, while the sunlight from the venetian blinds made bars over the taupe wall, I asked, very tentatively, what the North Pole had been like. He smiled at me over his pipe and said, "Well, it was *very* cold." But my parents wanted me to know that the man who had first set foot on the North Pole was black, was real, and lived in Harlem like I did . . . and they hoped, as did a lot of other black parents who took their children to meet him, that I just might make the mental leap: Therefore, *I* can do something memorable in the world, too. That goes double for, say, a list of black gay male achievers. Lists alone are ephemeral. Over the years names drop off them with appalling frequency. Only a clear understanding of relationships and real historical processes, events, and influences can hold them in their right constellations with any permanency.

That's why it's such a joy to see the burgeoning of interest, research, and scholarship in that wonderful period of black writing, the Harlem Renaissance— a good number of whose writers were gay as well.

Beam: If you had one minute in which to address (via satellite, phone lines, computer terminals, etc.) the entire world, what would you say?

Delany: Understand, you're talking to a guy who deeply distrusts that sort of totalizing gesture. To me, the question falls in with, "What are the ten greatest novels in the world?" or "What's the greatest minute of symphonic music ever written?" To do anything but laugh at such questions is simply to betray one's vast naïveté about the range and complexity of excellences available in the field one is presuming to judge.

The fact is, even if all practical translation problems were solved, I don't think there *is* anything to say in one minute that everyone in the world would understand—if only because of the huge societal differences that make up our world—differences that are, themselves, constitutive of the world's societies; there's certainly not much you could say in a minute that would *change* things. *Your* question betrays, I suspect, a somewhat naïve vision of the world as much smaller (and much more homogenized) than it could possibly be—a vision that *one* of my "personal visions," as you'll find it in some of my recent science fiction, is specifically and heartedly in contest with. I think it's important to have both images—so the argument can occur.

Still, that doesn't stop me from believing one side's right and one side's wrong.

Look, I don't even know what I'd want to say to all the gay black males in the very small United States of America. Let me see. How about, "There're maybe a goodly handful of millions of us, and we have a tough row to hoe, brothers. But don't let the bastards get you down"? Somehow, I don't think that's saying anything most of us don't know already. And as far as everybody in the whole, very wide *world*...?

I'd rather trade my "minute with the world" for, say, half an hour with the people currently heading the Times Square redevelopment and rehabilitation program.

For some time now that historic strip of sleazy entertainments has been slated for demolition. Office towers will replace most of the movie houses and sex shops. Much of what's left will be squeezed into a mall at one end—and a *very* few of the theaters are supposed to be renovated! This week's *Village Voice* has a cover story explaining that there's as much corruption, tax favoring, and general mismanagement in this urban project as there usually is in any such—maybe a little more.

The victims the article cites are the usual: the elderly, the black, the Hispanic, and the young. Delaying suits have been filed. But nowhere does the article even mention that this area has traditionally been a center for *much*, to put it mildly, of New York City's homosexual activity. And much of that activity is among black and brown working-class gay men. Indeed, in the area slated for demolition and replacement by offices stands one of the city's most established black gay bars: Blue's. If I *were* given that half an hour, I'd need to do about two or three weeks' research before I got what I wanted to say together. But you can be sure there's something to *be* said there. And I think it might have a better chance of doing some good than a minute-long worldwide homily.

But I really believe the answer to a better world is lots of local groups putting out lots of local energy into solving the immediate local problems by which oppression manifests itself. (A political program that doesn't start by dealing with your problems and my problems in the particular part of the world we live in, here and now, is no political program for you and me!) Only then will the solutions link up, support, and stabilize larger patterns of liberation. That we inhabit a country in which, for all its murderously real problems, this is a feasible vision is a great privilege . . . especially when you envision it in world terms.

Samuel R. Delany

Lance Olsen/1989

From *Rebel Yell: A Short Guide to Fiction Writing.* Cambrian Publications, 1989, 17–22. Reprinted by permission of Lance Olsen.

Q: Why do you write, and, more interestingly, why do you choose to write alternative fiction?

A: Of all explanations for why artists create, Harold Bloom's feels to me the most accurate: Bloom sees creativity as a radical rebellion against the pervasive failure to create—a failure which, in some infantile part of the artist's mind, is equated with death itself. Creativity grows out of the fear, the terror of death.

Alternative fiction might be seen as fiction in which the pressure of observation and the complexity of organization are simply at a different level from where they're set in normative endeavors. But (or, better, therefore), save on the most contingent, provisional level, I don't see the fundamental enterprise of, say, Dickens, Joyce, and Kathy Acker to be particularly, meaningfully different.

The variable in all three cases are variables in observation and organization. In the work of each writer, observation is aimed in one direction or another, then adjusted up or down as one moves along through the text. Organization of the textual material in each case is either complex, or formal, or simple, or informal.

In much alternative fiction the observation and the organization are simpler than they are in normative fiction—the simplicity highlights and makes us aware of the observation and the organization *per se.* Because normative fiction still makes up most of what people read, for many of us it still seems somehow "natural." One thing that alternative fiction does is "denature" normative fiction and make us more aware of how it functions as artifice.

When I conscientiously choose to write something that might be more easily called alternative fiction than not, usually it's because somehow I want to highlight some aspect of process—either of its organization or its observation.

Q: How has the marketplace changed since you arrived on it and why?

A: Marketplace questions are rarely, if ever, questions about alternative fiction. A novel of mine that many people consider to have some aspects of alternative fiction about it—*Dhalgren*—was published by Bantam books in 1975. Over a period of a dozen years, it sold quite well—somewhat over a million copies. What your question may be addressing is the situation that a publishing executive at Bantam Books was addressing when he said to me in 1987, a few years before he left the company to work somewhere less constraining: "If *Dhalgren* came in today, Chip, we probably couldn't publish it."

Notice he was not an editor but a publishing executive. Nor did he say: "We couldn't accept it editorially." He said, specifically, "We . . . couldn't publish it." Publishing a book is a complex process in which an editor's acceptance is only the first step.

Publishing includes marketing, distribution, and promotion. And that's what the publisher would not be set up to do today. That has to do with the prevalence of what are called publishing "slots."

In the late sixties there were a hundred-plus sizable publishers in New York City. By 1980, there were only seventy-nine. By 1995, there were fifteen. And with the recent merger of HarperCollins and Bantam-Doubleday-Dell, that number has gone down to five.

In the five major companies, the first thing that must happen to be a book today is that it must be fitted into a "slot." It must be put in an official category. And that category will determine everything from the kind of packaging it gets to the amount of money that will be spent on its advertising to the target number of copies the publisher hopes to sell, and is therefore willing to print.

Some slots have the possibility of best-sellerdom built into them. But most do not—which is to say, the assumption is that, with most categories of book, the book can only be but so successful, and thus there is no possibility that the book put in such and such a slot will break out and run away. The advantage to this system—and there *are* some advantages—is that books do not compete with one another. They only compete with books in the same slot—books that are already judged to be of the same type. A book only needs to do well in terms of its own category: a book of short stories by a new writer, say, only has to do well vis-à-vis other books of short stories by new writers. It will be spoken about within the company as a success if it does well in that context. It doesn't have to outsell the newest best sellers by Belva Plane to be considered a success. The disadvantages are, however, self-evident from the remainder of my story.

Here's how my editor, Fred Pohl, told me he was able to publish the book at Bantam:

Bantam had invited me to edit a line of books for them, to appear as "Frederick Pohl Selections," and they wanted to see what I could do. For starters, they were more or less letting me have my way. When I accepted *Dhalgren*, I told everybody in the company: "I'm doing this big, solid novel by Delany. It's highly sexual, too. Real best seller material." To some people I would say, "You know, I'm doing this strange, mysterious, wacky kind of novel, very experimental, that personally I think is just wonderful . . ." But I went out of my way not to mention that the two books were the same—until finally, at the sales conference, it came out. Then, when everyone was a little confused and wondering what was supposed to happen next, I stood up and said, very forcefully, to the sales representatives: "Look, if you get out there and place that book, it will sell. It will make money! People will buy it up like hotcakes." Now while I was saying it, I was scared to death. They could have gone out there, pushed the book—and we could have had 90 percent returns! But because it was SF—because it was my line of books and I was being given my head—the sales force went out and did just what I told them. And the book sold. Within weeks we were back for a second printing. Then there was a third—even before the official publication date. Four months later, we'd gone through two more printings.

Without ever becoming a bona fide best seller, *Dhalgren* sold half a million copies in its first year and another half million or so over the next dozen. When the publishing executive told me, a decade later, that the book could not be published if it had come in today, what he meant specifically is that there was now no "publishing slot" that the book could fit into.

Since (arbitrarily) 1976, with the Simplified Copyright Law, the Thor Power Tool Decision, and the host of economic changes that have restructured American mainstream publishing over the last twenty years, the first thing that happens to a book today once it's accepted (which was not true in 1973 when Pohl accepted *Dhalgren* at Bantam Books), is that the editor sends a memo around to the rest of the company telling what "slot" his newly accepted book goes into, which immediately triggers a set of marketing procedures, a certain sort of advertising, a certain type of sales approach, that is coordinated throughout the company for all books that go in that particular slot.

If there is no slot for the book, it is—by definition, today—unmarketable and therefore unpublishable.

And there is simply no "slot" today in any major publisher that is set out for eight-hundred-page-plus novels that are strange, mysterious, highly sexual, and experimental—which is what *Dhalgren* was. And that, in a nutshell, is how the market has changed.

Q: In what sense, if any, do you think writing can be taught?
A: I honestly don't know if writing on the level we are speaking about can be taught.

The mechanics of grammar and various rules of organization and style can be taught. Frankly, I would like to see them taught more thoroughly than they are.

On the level we're discussing, however, when we speak of creative writing, writing presupposes a certain kind of reading. Now reading *can* be taught. When I teach reading, and point out various patterns in the text, be it at the level of the phrase, the sentence, the scene, or some larger structure, I feel I'm much closer to teaching writing than I am when I actually run a workshop and people hand in their attempts at stories, essays, or poems.

In one important respect, all there is to learn about writing is a number of patterns, on all those levels (phrase, sentence, scene . . .) that writing can conform to. New levels of observation and organization make us violate (or, indeed, conform to) some of these patterns. The existence of these previous patterns alone is what makes the new patterns (of alternative fiction, say) signify.

Well. You now know all I know *about* writing.

Anything else would be what I know *of* writing itself.

And the only way to learn that is by reading . . .

No, I wonder seriously if writing can be taught, in the usual sense: of explanation, practice, and repetition, leading to mastery.

To me, as I've written before, good writing (especially the more experimental) feels much more like submission than mastery. And that's why I think all rhetoric that points to, that leads towards the notion of "mastery" in matters aesthetic is deeply misguided.

Q: Is there a difference between teaching how to write mainstream fiction and alternative fiction? If so, can you articulate the difference?
A: If we hold onto the provisionality and contingency of the differences between the two types of fiction, of course there are differences in teaching them.

Any exercise that urges us to observe in a different way becomes a route to new fictive material that will likely register as alternative; any exercise that suggests new ways of organizing the materials of writing—from words, to sentences, to scenes, to whole works—will also likely generate alternative fiction.

Spend a single day during which you write three descriptive sentences about every object you encounter (which you stop and look at closely for a minimum three minutes) that begins with the letter "b"—and *only* those that begin with the letter "b." (You might call it "Being and Time.") Fulfilling such a writerly task may well produce an interesting fiction.

Or—depending on the quality of your descriptive sentences—it may produce a very dull one. But until you try it, until you actually spend some time inhabiting such an Oulipo-esque schema, there's no way to know or to judge the results beforehand.

Q: You wrote a number of sentences in *Dhalgren*, the novel many (including myself) consider your magnum opus, on individual cards before inserting them into the text. Why craft so carefully when so few will notice?
A: Emily Dickinson once wrote: "Nothing survives except fine execution." I encountered that statement as a kid—and bought it. Yes, I'd like my work to survive, if only a little longer than it might had I not worked on it as hard as I did.

In *Dhalgren*, by the by, more sentences were written at the head of notebook pages than on index cards—because I needed to rework each sentence to bring it in line with iron and crystal. I gave up on index cards fairly quickly (yes, an idea initially borrowed from Nabokov); there wasn't enough room.

And people do notice. I can tell the difference between writing that is carefully worked over and writing that is not. You only have to read a paragraph or page of Ethan Canin or Joanna Russ or Guy Davenport—three very different writers—to know that all three put real thought into which word is going to follow which; which also means not only does each make all sorts of wonderful verbal choices, but that each has forbidden him- or herself all sorts of commonplace choices. There are dozens of ways that ordinary writers allow themselves to negotiate sentences that Canin and Russ and Davenport are just not interested in using. The modes of mental organization they represent are too facile. The commonplace observations and received dogma they allow the writer to slip in are just not ones these writers want to promote. With a Gass or Nabokov, recognizing the difference between their prose and the ordinary is like recognizing the difference between someone who gets up and walks across the room and someone who leaps up, to grab a trapeze hanging from the ceiling, vaults into the air and spins, balances, and flips. Most of the time, though, it's more like telling the difference between walking and dancing.

People recognize the difference, and they take pleasure in the dancing—even if they themselves can't execute such steps.

Q: Many of your characters—Hogg, for instance—are less than likable, even frightening and repulsive. Why choose to write about such social pariahs, and how do you ease the reader into coming along for the narratological ride? In other words, what can we learn about the nature of characterization from your choices?

A: I don't like to talk about "easing the reader." I'm not terribly interested in character the way it's usually conceived—that is, as a ground bodying forth certain psychological truths—or as a playing field to display the usual emotional pyrotechnics we associate with "good characters": sympathy, antipathy, identification. I'm interested in characters only as each is a locus for allowing certain sorts of sentences to be uttered—by the character or about the character.

But, as I've written elsewhere, I begin a sentence lover. It's at the level of the sentence you're more likely to *find* me, as a writer. Now I'm interested in the larger structures sentences can fit and generate. Still, for me, writing *begins* as an excuse to put together certain sorts of particularly satisfying sentences.

Q: Is there a question along writing lines you always wanted to ask?
A: Again, only of the practical and provisional sort. Goethe once remarked, in terms of his own writing, "Why, once a man accomplishes something admirable, does the entire universe conspire to see he never does it again?"

I want to write more books that I, personally, can be proud of.

So, yes, I spend a lot of time wondering why the very institutions that seem to be most appreciative of what I've done (the academy, the SF readership that enjoyed my earlier work, the publishers for whom my work has had its limited measure of success) are the very institutions that make it hardest for me to go on writing.

An Interview with Samuel Delany

Charles H. Rowell/1998

From *Callaloo*, 23.1 (2000) 247–67. Copyright © Charles H. Rowell. Reprinted by permission of the Johns Hopkins University Press. This interview took place between Charlottesville, Virginia, and New York, New York, in May 1998.

Rowell: You are the first African American whose career is science fiction writing. Of course, a few—and that means very few—have followed, but you and Octavia Butler are certainly the most visible figures. What did it mean for you to enter an area of creative writing which was for a long time a white male preserve and make a career of it? Was your entering the area considered a transgression—by whites or blacks or by your own family?

Delany: Octavia's story, of course, I can't tell you. After—briefly—being my student at the Clarion Science Fiction Writers' Workshop, she entered the field with her first story "Crossover" in 1971 and her first novel *Patternmaster* in 1976— fourteen years after my own first novel appeared in the winter of 1962. But she recounts her story with brio and insight. Everyone was very glad to see her!

For myself, however, let me answer you with a tale.

With five days to go in my twenty-fifth year, on March 25, 1967, my sixth science fiction novel *Babel-17* won a Nebula Award (a tie, actually) from the Science Fiction Writers of America. That same day the first copies of my eighth, *The Einstein Intersection*, became available at my publishers' office. (Because of publishing schedules, my seventh, *Empire Star*, had preceded the sixth into print the previous Spring.) At home on my desk at the back of an apartment I shared with my then-lover on St. Mark's place, my ninth, *Nova*, was a little more than three months from completion.

On February 10, a month and a half before the March awards, in its partially completed state *Nova* had been purchased by Doubleday & Co.

Well . . .

Three months *after* the awards banquet, in June, when it was done, with that first Nebula under my belt, I submitted *Nova* for serialization to the famous SF editor of *Analog Magazine*, John W. Campbell, Jr.

Campbell rejected it, with a note and phone call to my agent explaining that he didn't feel his readership would be able to relate to a black main character.

That was one of my first direct encounters, as a professional writer, with the slippery and always commercialized form of liberal American prejudice: Campbell had nothing against *my* being black, you understand. (There still exists a letter from him to horror writer Dean Koontz, from only a year or two later, in which Campbell argues in all seriousness that a technologically advanced black civilization is a social and biological impossibility . . .) No, perish the thought! Surely there was not a prejudiced bone in his body! It's just that I had, by pure happenstance, chosen to write about someone whose mother was from Senegal (and whose father was from Norway), and it was the poor benighted readers, out there in America, who would be too upset . . .

It was all handled as though I'd just *happened* to have dressed my main character in a purple brocade dinner jacket. (In the phone call Campbell made it fairly clear that this was his only reason for rejecting the book. Otherwise, he rather liked it . . .) Purple brocade just wasn't big with the buyers that season. Sorry . . .

Today if something like that happened, I would probably give the information to those people who feel it their job to make such things as widely known as possible. At the time, however, I swallowed it—a mark of how both the times and I have changed. I told myself I was too busy writing.

The most profitable trajectory for a successful science-fiction novel in those days was for the book to start life as a magazine serial, move on to hardcover publication, and finally be reprinted as a mass market paperback. If you were writing a novel a year (or, say, three novels every two years, which was then almost what I was averaging), that was the only way to push your annual income up, at the time, from four to five figures—and the low five figures at that. But now I knew I was not going to make the kind of money (little enough!) that, only months before, at the Awards, I'd let myself imagine. Things I wrote in the future were going to be more, not less, controversial. The percentage of purple brocade was only going to go up.

The next installment of my story concerns the first time the word "Negro" was said to me, in direct reference to my racial origins, by someone in the science fiction community. Understand that, since the late 1930s, that community, that world, had been largely Jewish, highly liberal, and with notable exceptions leaned to the left. Even its right-wing mavens, Heinlein or Poul Anderson (or Campbell himself), would have far preferred to go to a leftist party and have a friendly argument with some smart socialists than actually to hang out with the right-wing and libertarian organizations which they may well have supported in principle and, in Heinlein's case, with donations.

April 24, 1968, a year and—perhaps—a shy month later, was the night of the next Nebula Awards Banquet. A bit over three weeks before, I'd turned twenty-six. That year my eighth novel, *The Einstein Intersection* (which had materialized as an object on the day of the previous year's), and my short story "Aye, and Gomorrah . . ." were, the both of them, up.

The banquet was black tie with upwards of 150 guests at a midtown hotel-restaurant. Quite incidentally, it was a time of upheaval and uncertainty in my personal life (which, I suspect, is tantamount to saying I *was* a twenty-six year old writer). But that evening my mother and sister and a friend, as well as my wife, were at my table.

My novel won—and the presentation of the glittering Lucite trophy was followed by a discomforting speech from an eminent member of the SFWA. Perhaps you've heard such disgruntled talks: They begin, as did this one, "What I have to say tonight, many of you are not going to like . . ." and went on to castigate the organization for letting itself be taken in by (the phrase was, or was something very like) "pretentious literary nonsense," unto granting it awards, and abandoning the old values of good, solid, craftsman-like story-telling. My name was not mentioned, but it was evident I was (along with Roger Zelazny, not present) the brunt of this fusillade. It's an odd experience, I must tell you, to accept an award from a hall full of people in tuxedos and evening gowns and then, from the same podium at which you accepted it, hear a half-hour jeremiad from an *eminence grise* declaring that award to be worthless and the people who voted it to you duped fools. It's not paranoia: By count I caught more than a dozen sets of eyes sweeping between me and the speaker going on about the triviality of work such as mine and the foolishness of the hundred plus writers who had voted for it.

As you might imagine, the applause was slight, uncomfortable, and scattered. There was more coughing and chair scraping than clapping. By the end of the speech, I was drenched with the tricklings of mortification and wondering what I'd done to deserve them.

The master of ceremonies, Robert Silverberg, took the podium and said, "Well, I guess we've all been put in our place." There was a bitter chuckle. And the next award was announced.

It again went to me—for my short story, "Aye, and Gomorrah . . ."

I had, by that time, forgotten it was in the running.

For the second time that evening I got up and went to the podium to accept my trophy (it sits on a shelf above my desk about two feet away from me as I write), but, in dazzled embarrassment, it occurred to me as I was walking to the front of the hall that I *must* say something in my defense, though mistily I perceived it had best be as indirect as the attack. With my sweat-soaked undershirt beneath my formal turtle-neck, peeling and unpeeling from my back at each step, I took the podium and my second trophy of the evening. Into the microphone I said, as calmly as I could manage: "I write the novels and stories that I do and work on them as hard as I can to make them the best I can. That you've chosen to honor them—and twice in one night—is warming. Thank you."

This time I received a standing ovation—though I was aware it was as much in reaction to the upbraiding of the nay-sayer as it was in support of anything *I* had done.

I walked back down toward my seat, but as I passed one of the tables, a woman agent (not my own) who had several times written me and been supportive of my work, took my arm as I went by and pulled me down to say, "*That* was elegant, Chip . . . !" while the applause continued.

At the same time, I felt a hand on my other sleeve—in the arm that held the Lucite block of the Nebula itself—and I turned to Isaac Asimov (whom I'd met for the first time at the banquet the year before), sitting on the other side and now pulling me toward him. With a large smile, wholly saturated with evident self-irony, he leaned toward me to say: "You know, Chip, we *only* voted you those awards because you're Negro . . . !"

(This was 1968; the term "black" was not yet common parlance.)

I smiled back (there was no possibility he had *intended* the remark in any way seriously—as anything other than an attempt to cut through the evening's many tensions . . . Still, part of me rolled my eyes silently to heaven and said: Do I really need to hear this right at *this* moment?) and returned to my table.

The way I read his statement then (and the way I read it today; indeed, anything else would be a historical misreading) is that he was trying to use a self-evidently tasteless absurdity to defuse some of the considerable anxiety in the hall that night; it is a standard male trope, needless to say; I think he was *trying* to say that race probably took little or no part in his or any other of the voters' minds who had voted for me.

But such ironies cut in several directions. I don't know whether Asimov realized he was saying this as well, but as an old historical materialist, if only as an afterthought, he must have realized that he was saying also: No one here will ever look at you, read a word you write, or consider you in any situation, no matter whether the roof is falling in or the money is pouring in, without saying to him- or herself (whether in an attempt to count it or to discount it), "Negro . . ." The racial situation, permeable as it might sometimes seem (and it is, yes, highly permeable), is nevertheless your total surround. Don't you ever forget it . . .

And I never have.

The fact that this particular "joke" emerged just then, at that most anxiety-torn moment, when the only-three-year-old, volatile organization of feisty science fiction writers saw itself under a virulent battering from internal conflicts over shifting esthetic values, meant that, though the word had not yet been said to me or written about me till then (and, from then on, it was, interestingly, written regularly, though I did not in any way change my own self presentation), it had clearly inhered in every step and stage of my then just-six years as a professional writer.

Here the story takes a sanguine turn.

The man who'd made the speech had apparently not yet actually *read* my nominated novel when he wrote his talk. He had merely had it described to him by a friend, a notoriously eccentric reader, who had fulminated that the work was clearly and obviously beneath consideration as a serious science fiction novel: Each chapter began with a set of quotes from literary texts that had nothing to do with science at all! Our nay-sayer had gone along with this evaluation, at least as far as putting together his rebarbative speech.

When, a week or two later, he decided to *read* the book for himself (in case he was challenged on specifics), he found, to his surprise, he liked it—and, from what embarrassment I can only guess, became one of my staunchest and most articulate supporters, as an editor and as a critic. (A lesson about reading here: Do your share, and you can save yourself and others a *lot* of embarrassment.) And *Nova*, after its Doubleday appearance in 1968 and some pretty stunning reviews ("Samuel R. Delany, right now, as of this book, *Nova*, not as of some future book or some accumulated body of work, is the best science fiction writer in the world, at a time when competition for that status is intense. I don't see how a science fiction writer can do more than wring your heart while telling you how it works. No writer can . . ." wrote Algis Budrys, in his January 1969 review in *Galaxy*, who also had been there that evening), garnered what was then a record advance for an SF novel paid to date by Bantam Books (a record broken briefly), ushering in the twenty years when I could actually support myself (almost) by writing alone.

But what Asimov's quip also tells us is that, for any black artist (and you'll forgive me if I stick to the nomenclature of my young manhood, that my friends and contemporaries, appropriating it from Dr. Du Bois, fought to set in place, breaking into libraries through the summer of 1968 and taking down the signs saying Negro Literature and replacing them with signs saying "black literature"—

the small "b" on "black" is a *very* significant letter, an attempt to ironize and de-transcendentalize the whole concept of race, to render it provisional and contingent, a significance that many young people today, white and black, who lackadaisically capitalize it, have lost track of), the concept of race informed everything about me, so that it could surface—and did surface—precisely at those moments of highest anxiety, a manifesting brought about precisely by the white gaze, if you will, whenever it turned, discommoded for *whatever* reason, in my direction.

You ask if I perceived my entrance into science fiction as a transgression.

Certainly not *at* the entrance point, in any way. But it's clear from my story, I hope (and I have told many others about that fraught evening), transgression inheres, however unarticulated, in every aspect of the black writer's career in America. That it emerged in such a charged moment is, if anything, only to be expected in such a society as ours. How could it be otherwise?

Rowell: Do you know what led you to the writing of science fiction, genre fiction, as opposed to literary fiction? You have written that you "began writing science fiction because a handful of writers I read in my adolescence (Sturgeon, Bester, Heinlein, and MacLean) wrote a few stories and novels that I found more moving and stimulating than anything I'd ever read." I might add that at the time, you tell us, you were also reading James Baldwin, Albert Camus, Samuel Beckett, and Jean Genet.

Delany: As I've explained in other interviews, my turning to SF was all but an accident. I read it, enjoyed it—enjoyed it exorbitantly. But my adolescent ambition was simply to write novels—of whatever sort. Shortly after I married—at nineteen—I decided to write a science fiction novel as a kind of jape for my then wife, working—at eighteen—as an editorial assistant at a paperback science fiction publisher. Once she read it, she suggested I submit it—and we did, under a pseudonym. The book sold: Three science fiction novels later (I was now twenty-one and in the middle of another), it occurred to me I'd become a science fiction writer.

Since then, I've put a great deal of thought into how to become a *better* science fiction writer.

But as to becoming a science fiction writer in the first place: No decision was made. It simply happened.

Rowell: How important was reading to you when you were beginning your writing career? How important is reading to the beginning writer? How important is reading to you as a writer? Your work reveals a critical working knowledge of numerous and various kinds of texts; you and Jay Wright appear to be the most widely read of our writers, that is, your creative and critical voices suggest as much.

Delany: As I've said—and written repeatedly—in the process I used to call "literary creation" and, since 1978, have called "fictive creation," reading is the most important practice there is.

It's important on the level we can call the vocabulary of incident—so that when creation, at its most oppositional, erupts, the writer will know what *not* to write about. How many young radical writers have we seen, fired up with the most salutary energy and outrage, with so little command of the tradition that they waste their effort reinventing rhetorical wheels whose semantic tires blew out and went flat decades ago?

It's important on the level we can call the discourse of genres/the genre of discourses—where we absorb the forms of the forces that produce the objects and subjects that comprise our universe. Talk of forms and objects sounds a lot like Plato. And I wouldn't be surprised if Plato's notion of the forms wasn't a theocritized apprehension of the mechanics of discourse itself—precisely how discourse might have been inferred by someone for whom reading had not yet become *the* metaphor for materialist abstraction, held free of idealism by the complexities and resonances provided by images of mechanical reproduction.

You ask, how important was reading to me personally—as a person. Like anyone who has been immersed—reader or writer—as I have been, life long, in the reading and writing processes (for there are many of each), I too am tempted to rush forward to say that reading more than anything else has *made* me a person.

It is a center of my subjecthood.

But as someone who has also spent lots of time around people who *don't* read—as a teacher with my students, as a New Yorker around my neighbors, as a writer in several social circles which were picked, most self-protectively, from among people who at least don't read *my* work (it requires a fair amount of honesty, *savoir faire*, and, yes, reticence, to be both my reader and my friend)—I can and must observe how reading also rigidifies (as it preserves), how it excludes (as it selects), how it lulls into acceptance (as it excites to understanding).

This is why there will always be people who have never read a book in their lives who, nevertheless, have something important to say. (Shouldn't we African Americans, with what the readers among us try so ineffectually to tame with the phrase "oral tradition," be particularly aware of this?) It behooves us as readers to be able to hear as well as read. The only thing a lack of reading disempowers us to pronounce on is books—and what comes from them. No matter how much shelf space they take up in our apartments, they are—sadly—not that large a part of the world.

My life partner of nine years, Dennis, who, by his own admission has read only a single book cover to cover (Clavell's *Shogun*, which he picked entirely on the criterion of size: When, after he met me, he decided he better read at *least* one, he figured he'd best make it a big one), walked through the living room just this morning, as I was talking on the phone with a long-time journalist friend, enthusing over some structurally serendipitous discovery I'd made in a recent reading of the incomplete draft of my current novel. Dennis gave a wonderfully generous laugh and declared: "You guys are *crazy . . . !*" before, with a grin, he left to meet a friend of *his* and go walking in the Sunday morning street fair out on Broadway.

Rowell: As an African American writing science fiction, you were a pioneer. Who were your models when you began writing?

Delany: I've always taken for models people about whom my knowledge was scanty: two or three dramatic "biographemes," possibly some dates, and the rest a wax tablet rubbed bare by my own ignorances, onto which I could inscribe what I wanted a model—what I desperately *needed* a model—to be.

When I was a young writer, say between fourteen and twenty (I was twenty when that first novel was published), my models tended to be other young writers: Keats, Rimbaud, Radiguet, Chatterton, Büchner, Carson McCullers, Shena McKay, Truman Capote, Minut Druët, Harlan Ellison, Francoise Sagan . . .

James Baldwin became a model for me on the publication of *Another Country.* Yes, I'd been reading his essays steadily up until then; and—steadily—I'd been impressed by his thinking since my middle teens. But I hadn't been mooning over him, walking for blocks in the street wondering about him, pondering what he might have done were he in my position (as I did with these others) until, as I said, *Another Country* came out and, in my Lower Eastside apartment on the dead end of Fifth Street, I read it.

I hated the book.

I thought it a bad, sloppy, unstructured novel. (I am much less vehement about its flaws today.) It was about everything in my life (sex, death, race, art . . .). But instead of proffering the reassuring message that it is the novel's mandate to offer the young (however chaotic it looks, this life-material is negotiable and though the contradictions it engenders may wreak death and havoc among these or those major or minor characters caught up in a subplot, the true hero, through knowledge, strength, and grace, can still prevail . . .), *this* novel shrieked and gibbered and babbled banalities and sobbed and rambled and screamed, and screamed, and *screamed* in all modes of awe and terror before life's mystery, wonder, and horror. In short, it dramatized in its form, in however distorted a manner, a truth. It just wasn't the particular truth I needed, right then, to hear.

But because it seemed to me that *my* life was the book's betrayed substance, it never occurred to me (at least when I was twenty or twenty-one) to grant Baldwin the prize simply for turning to face this material in a way that neither, say, Djuna Barnes nor Nelson Algren had been able to in, respectively, the 1930s or the 1940s.

Around the same time, I encountered two quips, one about Baldwin and one by him. The first came in a passing conversation about Baldwin's new novel with poet Marie Ponsot, whom I used to visit at her house in Queens, where she lived with her bear-like painter husband and their half-a-dozen-plus children. One day when I was lamenting the structural failures of Baldwin's book, and decrying Mailer's misunderstanding of him in *The White Negro*, Marie said: "If Baldwin thought he was anywhere near as good a writer as *I* think he is, he'd be a much better writer."

It brought me up short.

What *could* this twenty-seven year-old white woman, who spoke Latin and French and argued Catholic theology *intelligently* and who kept a terminally messy house, and was a wonderful mother to seven kids, and who talked about not only the excellences but the *flaws* as well in the style of Rimbaud and Perse and Michaux and Senghor—and who, a few years before, had given me my first (hardcover, it didn't yet exist in paperback) copy of *Nightwood* to read—and owned a well-thumbed copy of *Finnegans Wake* and who said it certainly felt to *her* as if there were two *intensities* of orgasms for women, even if there weren't exactly two kinds, no matter what *my* wife said, and that Auden's "Canzone" was one of the greatest poems of the twentieth century and that Keats' "Then glut thy sorrows on a morning rose, or on a wealth of globed peonies" was the sexiest line of poetry in the English language, and who had actually published a book of poems, *True Minds* (today we would call it a chapbook, though it had come out in Lawrence Ferlinghetti's Pocket Poet Series, the volume just after Ginsberg's *Howl and Other Poems*), *what could she know* about writing that gave her a concept of it that could solve *my* problem with *this* writer . . . ?

The second quip was a line by Baldwin himself that I stumbled over in an essay of his a bit later. "The writer must tell all the truth he can bear, and then some."

My astonishment here was just as great as it had been with Marie's comment. I realized Baldwin was wrong. He was as wrong in his statement here as he had been wrong about how to deal with the material of *Another Country*. No: The writer must tell the truth. The question of whether he or she can *bear* it or not, or bear more of it or less of it, is not to hand in *this* part of the argument. That he'd been afraid he might not have been able to bear it had ruined his attempt at a major novel—ruined it, at any rate, for me. The way to deal with the truth Baldwin was wrestling with in *Another Country* was not to slough off form, but to invent/reformulate a new one (e.g., Sterne's *Tristram Shandy*, Toomer's *Cane*, Ellison's *Invisible Man*, Guyotat's *Eden, Eden, Eden*, Russ's *The Female Man*, Silliman's *Ketjak*, Barnes's *Flaubert's Parrot* . . .).

Between the two, it dawned on me that the writer's—the artist's—job in this society is not set by the writer himself. (Neither is the form of the novel; the form of the poem . . .) It begins as a concept of art accessible to any poet or student or reader or person able to envision—in our world—a better one: to anyone who will read.

You submit to that vision. Or you don't. But once you do, your job is to report *on* that vision. You have to tell the truth—or in some way dramatize the truth— about what you've seen. If, in the course of it, you have to adjust the form of the novel, the form of the poem, you'd better be prepared to work like Flaubert, like Wagner, like Joyce, like Proust. But you cannot just shrug it off or give up on it.

One may fail—and fail miserably. (The statistics on the enterprise are overwhelming that one will fail.) But excuses, in any way, shape, or form, are beside the point—irrevocably, uncompromisingly, totally. But that's when I began to re-read Baldwin of the nonfiction prose, the Baldwin who knew the price of the ticket (the discursive forms of the persuasive argument) in his bones, and who, in those writings, had (as had Thoreau in his *Journals*) won—and who had won wonderfully, with logic, lucidity, and passion.

From then on, Baldwin *was* my model writer—difficult, complex, and a very different and more immediate model than any of those romantic others.

Rowell: In 1972, you wrote a piece called "Letter to a Critic: Popular Culture, High Art; and the S-F Landscape," which was originally published in *The Little Magazine* (Vol. 6, No. 4) in 1973. There you said, "I write the books I have an overwhelming desire to read but cannot find on library shelf or bookstore rack." Will you comment on that statement? Did this position motivate you in the writing, for example, of two of your most recent books, *The Mad Man* and *Shoat Rumblin*? I should add *Equinox* and *Hogg* to the list.

Delany: Discourse is the objectifying element in any subjective undertaking. (It's Fanon's insight that begins Chapter One of *Peau Noire, Masques Blancs*: "I ascribe a basic importance to the phenomenon of language . . . [I]t is implicit that to speak is to exist absolutely for the other.") That's what I'd learned from Marie—though I could have just as easily learned it from Fanon, once his works of 1952 and 1961 were translated.

That "overwhelming desire" that I spoke of in your question above is simply one metaphor for what the early German Romantics called up with another, "*Begeisterung*": inspiriting / inspiration / enthusiasm. What desire must overwhelm is the discursive inertia that actively whispers, in all our ears, just below perception's limen, "You are not an artist. You are not a hero. You have no right to change anything at all. Be silent. Be still. Obey the King . . ."

Those bookstore shelves and library shelves are, coordinately, a metonym for the discourse that structures the range of fictions into which, if we are lucky, we are released once those discursive barriers of silence and stasis are breached.

Is desire the motivation for my recent books as much as for my earlier ones? Yes. Probably more so.

Rowell: Why did you find it necessary to write a disclaimer for *The Mad Man*? How do you want us to read these novels? Are we to read them as departures from the fiction of yours that precedes them? Where do you place them in your evolution as a writer? Are you aware that some of your readers have called *The Mad Man* pornographic?

Delany: How do I want you to read them? I'm just happy when anyone reads them at all.

The books themselves try to erect, in their small ways, internal road signs to guide the reader once within. But the reader who wants to ignore those signs and read against the grain is just as welcome—if, in any way, you can call such texts welcoming—as the reader who wants to let extant rhetorical expectations take her or him from sentence to sentence, page to page, chapter to chapter.

As to the Disclaimer: Does it *really* yield any particularly interesting information for me to say that two of the exemplars I had in mind, as I wrote it (in both cases, as with Baldwin, they were complex models, with intricately interconnected negative and positive aspects), were Balzac's *Avant propos* and Hugo's prefatory paragraph to *Les Misérables* written at Hauteville House in 1862? I am, alas, the sort of reader who can hardly write *anything* without thinking of *some* other text.

The rhetorical ease with which certain readers sling about our "Balzac," "Fanon," and "Hugo" often signals (to certain others) that such name-slinging is finally one with name-dropping. They take it, possibly rightly, as an elitist attempt to intimidate. Such models can often be more silencing than they are inspirational.

Does the fiction depart? Well, certainly these more recent novels are a different genre. They're not science fiction.

And, finally, am I aware that some readers have called *The Mad Man* pornographic?

But I am among them.

Rowell: Did you set out to add another dimension to science fiction as a genre? What did you want to do for/to the form? Do you think you succeed in doing so? Ultimately, this question implies that your presence in the field has had an impact. What do you view as or hope that impact is?

Delany: Talking about your "impact," or even your influence, is the way to sound like a pompous poseur—in a genre (the writer's interview) that courts pomposity at every turn.

What impact do I hope to have?

My hopes are far less clamorous than that.

I hope only for time and a life situation that will let me finish a few more novels, a few more essays, to write and receive a few more letters to and from a few more of my friends.

Rowell: In my opinion, your presence on the U.S. American literary scene is transgressive. *The Mad Man* (1994, revised 1996) is a transgressive act in the same sense that the nonfiction texts in *Longer Views: Extended Essays* (1996) are transgressive in form. I relate these acts of transgression to your 1972 statement about your desire to write books you want to read but cannot find in libraries or in bookstores. Please talk about the deliberate intervention your prose fiction and nonfiction prose have made in terms of forms and ideologies.

Delany: Deliberation tends, in my case, to fall elsewhere.

In a time when identity politics is sustaining a necessary and clarifying attack/analysis that will doubtless leave it forever changed into something more flexible and useful, more provisional and provisioned, I am interested in the "identities" (I use the term in its most informal manner) of those who have fallen through the categorical cracks without having slipped wholly free of the nets of desire.

I can easily imagine a black, gay man, of, say, fifty-six, who sustained a nervous breakdown in his early twenties toward the beginning of thirteen years of marriage, and who is today largely in agreement with the most radical arm of the women's movement, the gay rights movement and its offspring, queer politics, the

movement for African-American rights, and who—for his writerly work—a decade ago won a professorship in a New England state university, where he now
teaches and pursues his literary work.

As such a man might be imagined by hundreds of thousands of well-meaning
liberals, radicals, or conservatives—as such a man might even represent, for a
handful of people, some sort of model—the fact is, I cannot imagine someone
more boring, more ideologically irrelevant, less creative, unable to think a thought
outside the constraints of the wholly platitudinous, if not the thoroughly bubble-
headed. And though, as I'm sure you recognize, I have only described my "self,"
the only way I am at all interested in that self is precisely where it is in excess of
what can be categorized so easily even as that, precisely where it is non-identical
to the categories that try to contain him: that is, to say, where, to me, I am a
question.

All identities—even that one—only become interesting when they start to
"leak." And the leaking process causes them to slide against and seal with others,
from which they can never get free:

Black with white, white with black . . .

Gay with straight, straight with gay . . .

Male with female, female with male . . .

Mad with sane, sane with mad . . .

—just for the easiest (and, still, the most unsettling) of openers; and progress-
ing at least as far as artist and non-artist.

Briefly, there's nothing that you can say *about* me (must we add, "categori-
cally"? All identifying aspects are) that guarantees in any way that, on the level
where it counts, I have a brain in my head. Similarly, there's little that you can
say about a book, in the same ways, that *guarantees* the experience of reading it
will be in any way pleasurable and/or worthwhile. To the extent they are reading an interview by a writer whose books—even if only some of them—they have
not read, people, all of us, yearn for the guarantees of authorship/authority (con-
sistency of quality, values, ideas, styles, and topics). But there's no way to give it.
Thus, it's a topic I'd rather remain silent about.

The truth is, Charles, I have the old, modernist discomfort with telling people
what they should make of my books or how to use those texts. (Though it doesn't
seem to be a failure that has carried over into postmodernism, Lord-love-a-duck!)
Such considerations seem to me unseemly. As a teacher, I am concerned that my
students engineer for themselves the richest encounter possible with the texts
that we read together. I see myself pressing them toward such encounters by any
pedagogical means I can dredge up. Certainty I would be pleased if, somewhere,

someone was engineering—for herself or himself—such an encounter with one of *my* texts. That is to say, if, somewhere, I were being read by an intelligent reader.

But whether it is an unsettled apprehension of conflict of interest or just some odd class snobbery, I can only function, these days, with a more or less absolute division between teacher-critic on the one side and writer-critic on the other.

I do believe the works—with the help, if I am hugely lucky, of a few other critics—might themselves teach people how to read them.

(Is this finally just a retreat to my New Critical roots? In no way do I see the text as autonomous. Is it just a convention, possibly outmoded, in the sociality of art . . . ?)

Perhaps others of my texts can.

But *I* can't.

It's not a matter (of lack of or privileges) of powers. It's a matter of rights.

Perhaps that means respect for the powers of others.

Anything else would be disrespectful.

Rowell: Your revision or reinvention or remaking of forms is part of your intervention. Will you talk about the form of such pieces of nonfiction prose as "Reading at Work," "Shadows," and *The American Shore*? In these texts the essay as a form becomes something other than that traditional thing we read or teach as the essay. What does your invention do that the traditional essay cannot?

Delany: "Reading at Work," "Shadows" less so, and *The American Shore* more so are all works that rely heavily on one or several modes of critical rhapsody.

The structuralists and poststructuralists represent a stylistic explosion that recalls Carlyle, Ruskin, Pater in the nineteenth century: the alignment of discursive insight with rhetorical ecstasy is a powerful one, and the fact that the academy is still reeling is a sign of that power.

Of course rhapsody resided in lots of pre-structuralist criticism as well. *Are* there any more rhapsodic works than John Livingston Lowes's *Road to Xanadu*, Fiedler's *Love and Death in the American Novel*, or Kenneth Burke's *Language as Symbolic Action*, or—to step only a little afield—Eric Auerbach's *Mimesis*? And, in cultural criticism we have Du Bois's equally ecstatic *Souls of Black Folk*.

The works of mine you ask about are just a case of a critic venting the delirium of his momentary intensities. I'm rather fond of all of them—especially the *Shore*.

Rowell: You cannot deny that you are a disturber of bourgeois peace, that you smash borders which the middle class perpetually erects, and that you interrogate and mock the ideologies and values the middle class deems sacred. I surmise that your project is similar to that of Michel Foucault: You seem to want to expose that which keeps us from seeing (you show us the mask and what the mask hides) and, in doing so, you show us other ways of reading the world. What are you trying to do to your reader? What do you view as the relationship of the author to his/her readers?

Is that relationship the same in your nonfiction prose as it is in prose fiction? How do you respond to David Samuelson's contention that your "ultimate goal as a writer seems to be to bring about a recognition of the power of language to de-center the role of convention in life as much as in fiction"?

Delany: You pay me the compliment of looking at my minuscule critical violences through the magnifying glass of your own generous insight.

I thank you for it. I'm afraid, though, it might be more accurate to say that, rather than smashing borders, I wander where I wish to—because no one really pays that much attention to me. If borders are breached in the process, well ...

I look at statements like Professor Samuelson's, however, with some bemusement. I'm too much of a marxian (as Professor Samuelson knows well) to believe that language on its own can decenter (or center, for that matter) much of anything, except temporarily in our attention for the length of a text—and perhaps a few breaths more. It's superstructural: Thus the best it can do, by itself, is to stabilize (or destabilize). At worst it distracts—and, of course, lies. The recognition Professor Samuelson claims I want to bring about is not a recognition I, as yet, recognize.

The reason I'm a marxian with a small "m" is because, I suppose, I'm still too much of a capitalist. The way you decenter conventions in life (as in fiction) is to organize things at the infrastructural level so that other conventions, ones you approve of, perhaps, will be more profitable to pursue. When that process brings profit or pleasure to the people, I jump up and down and sing and write and celebrate and generally stabilize my ass off. When that process pulls both, along with power, from peoples' hands, I do as much destabilizing as I can (by showing the process up for what it is); then I go look for something else to write about.

A focus of my critical enterprise, that I do share with Foucault, is an attempt to make clear to those of my students, my readers, who can hear it, who can read it, the primacy of discourse. When Braudel remarked, "Without theory, there is no history," I believe the modular basis for that particular *obiter dictum* was some apprehension of the irrevocable necessity of discourse, if we are to have any notion of historical change as other than mere projection of a mystifacatory notion of some "eternal present," some "unchanging human nature."

True, I enjoy shocking my wonderfully liberal and "unshockable" graduate students by sending them to Chapter Five of Philippe Aries's *Centuries of Child-hood* (1961) for his account of the sexual practices (aristocratic, wholly sanctioned by the church and the best society of the times) of pre-revolutionary France: It makes much of what goes on in *Hogg*, or, indeed, my current novel, *Shoat Rumblin*, look very tame: Days were regularly set aside in which dozens of men and women came to feel and fondle publicly the genitals of the eight- or nine-year-old royal heirs, just to make sure they functioned, while, enjoying it all, the children sat on the laps of their parents, who led and directed the touching and stimulation . . . for starters. Nights were spent in bed [in the case of the eleven-year-old prince] with their mother and a pair of lusty young peasants, male and female, who demonstrated sexual positions and engaged the child in sexual play, while the Queen, in the same bed, approved and caressed through the night . . . In a world where working-class children started to labor at age six and many middle-class children at age eight, our attempts to protect our children from all active sexuality could easily have been considered criminally naive by those aris-tocrats; and our response when those attempts sometimes fail considered terror-istic and inhumanly cruel . . . to the child. Needless to say, I offer no absolute ap-proval to the sexual practices of *either* time. I point up the differences only to suggest that all such moral approval is a social construction, not a God-given law. In that sense, I only go where people have already gone and—sometimes—return with my very paltry accounts of what I've seen people doing.

Paradoxically, the only things *really* (read: politically) transgressive about my report is that I never let myself pretend, in my various ecstasies, that I have somehow transgressed the social—so that I will not think I have freed myself of the responsibility of telling the entailed social truths I see.

Rowell: What would you say to your detractors (academic critics are especially among them) who would ask you why you chose science fiction as your genre (or, indeed, pornography), considering how the academy treats it? In fact, there are those critics who treat it as a "lesser form" than fiction by, let's say, Robert Stone, John Cheever, and Toni Morrison, for example. How do you answer those detractors?
Delany: Isn't there something rather high-handed in the *form* of the basic ques-tion that supports your careful qualifications? What would you say (O young, starving, literary artist!) to those who ask you why you choose to associate with the poor, considering how everyone else in society looks down on them, rather than associate with the Astors, the Vanderbilts, the Mellons . . . ?

I mean, what if I happen to be poor myself?

I could answer, certainly, in the mode you ask: One reason I *remain* a science fiction writer is because science fiction acknowledged my talent, welcomed me as a writer, published my books, gave me a living (as best it could), heaped its awards on me, and sedimented the basis for whatever reputation I have. I believe loyalty is a virtue.

But, of course, I also think you're asking: What do you say to people who don't like science fiction?

I've analyzed the nature of that dislike at some length in various essays. It's fascinating, actually—nor is it by any means an innocent dislike, a temperamental disposition akin to a preference for Keats over Shelley. It's highly moral, hugely indignant, rigidly class bound, and drenched in social exclusions.

To those dozens and dozens and *dozens* of people who, say, at parties over the years, when they hear there is a science fiction writer present, feel morally obliged, once I am pointed out to them, to make their way through the crowd and, without an introduction, plant themselves in front of me and announce, "I hear you write science fiction. You know, I don't really *like* science fiction . . . ," what I would *like* to say to them is, "First, I didn't ask you. Second, I don't care. But the fact is—third—you are insufferably rude," then walk away.

Far more people, if they are honest, "don't like" poetry than "don't like" science fiction. But I can't imagine, in this society, anyone coming up out of the blue to confront a poet in that manner—as I am confronted regularly (at least once!), at almost every social occasion I attend . . .

What I do say, of course, is: "Well, many people don't." Then I smile and, sooner or later, depending on my conversational energies, excuse myself.

But the fact is, most of my detractors are cut from much the same cloth. In both cases, the discourse that impels and controls their actions is a vague feeling that, as science fiction is concerned with both unreal events and technology, it must be morally dangerous—and low class. By acting as they do they are making some gesture toward a kind of cultural prophylaxis or social cleansing. Indeed, it is precisely the people who, caught up in the notion of the esthetic, use that notion of the esthetic to justify their behavior to themselves, who are most mired in a process that, in its structure if not its intensity, is all but indistinguishable from a sort of racism. (Historically, indeed, the whole process is closely allied with anti-Semitism. Though that's *another* book of essays, as yet unwritten.)

To the extent you are really asking about a choice, the fact is: I was very young and wrote what I liked to read. Certainly it's more complicated than that; I've teased out some of those complications in other places. But, in brief, that's the basis of any further answer.

Now as far as answering critics: That's a risky business. When it's a matter of competing discourses and you simply feel that one of them is not addressing you, depending on your inner resources, sometimes I think it's best to remain silent.

Rowell: Apparently you were anticipating such detractors when you wrote "Letter to a Critic: Popular Culture, High Art, and the S-F Landscape," a defense of science fiction, which you reprinted as the opening piece for your book of essays, *The Jewel-Hinged Jaw* (1977). Will you discuss the autobiography of that essay/letter? Do you still stand by what you said then? Is there any more to the subject you would add as words to detractors of science fiction?

What did you mean when you said that "the science fiction enterprise is richer than the enterprise of mundane fiction"? What are you referring to in the term "mundane fiction"? Why do you place it against science fiction? What are we talking about when we use the term "science fiction" anyway?

Delany: That letter is a version of one written to critic Leslie Fiedler, after he gave a talk on science fiction at a Science Fiction Writers of America function. After several more letters continuing in the same vein, his generous response was to propose me for a visiting professorship that year, 1975, at SUNY Buffalo—my first academic appointment.

Only last month, when I was passing through Buffalo to talk at the University there, I called him up—he's now eighty-one—and asked Sally and him to join me for dinner. "I thought you might like to see the monster you created," I told him. He laughed.

And a very pleasant dinner it was.

When I made the statement you quote about the comparative richness of the genres, I was appealing to a limited mathematical model for the sentence. In the context in which I said it, you recall, I was simply saying that the number of possible word combinations was greater for science fiction texts than for mundane fiction texts. (Call it naturalistic fiction, if you prefer.) In naturalistic fiction you can say, "The door opened," or "The door swung back," or "The door eased in . . ." and that pretty much suggests, if it does not exhaust, the limits on what predicates ordinary doors, in ordinary fiction, can ordinarily combine with when opening. In science fiction, you can write all those, of course; but you can write as well, "The door dilated . . . ," "The door deliquesced . . . ," "The door appeared from nowhere . . ." Thus, and by extension, there are a greater number of possible sentences for science fiction than for mundane.

But allow me, twenty-five years later, to critique my own modular presumptions: Looked at in another light, what I was saying there is not too far from: "There are more integers altogether than there are odd numbers." Well, mathematically speaking, paradoxical as it seems, that's false. Using the codes of mathematics, there's an order of infinity of both. The statement in the form I made it only makes sense when you set some sort of provisional cut-off on the *size* of the number. There are twice as many natural numbers as there are odd numbers between zero and eighty-seven non-inclusive. There are one more than twice as many natural numbers as odd numbers between zero and two-hundred-fifty-billion-trillion-and-six. It's only the fact that sentences tend not to run over a few hundred words in length that makes that in any way a meaningful statement. If sentences could be infinitely long, my statement *wouldn't* hold.

Well, precisely to the extent that the upper cut-off for the length of sentences in fiction is imprecise and muzzy, a trend or tendency rather than a fixed and immovable point, my statement is equally imprecise and muzzy; and, when all is said and done, not very useful, unless science fiction writers use it specifically as a goad to search out the full richness, *at* the sentence level, at the level of word choice and combination, of what they can write. In short, it functions only as a writerly exhortation, not any sort of analytical tool.

As to what we mean by "science fiction" and "mundane fiction": Well, both are informal terms. They refer to practices of writing that, by and large, most readers can recognize, though there are always going to be moot examples. The terms are definable no more than are the terms poetry, drama, tragedy, comedy, the novel, the short story, or criticism—other practices of writing equally recognizable, equally undefinable, all with their moot texts. All such genre distinctions (and genre collections, such as literature—which includes: epics, lyrics, histories, essays, novels, comedies, and tragedies . . . Or paraliterature—which includes: science fiction, mysteries, pornography, comic books, and academic criticism . . .) have their provisional use; but none of them is in any way absolute. Mundane fiction is a particularly amusing designation. In its very carefully controlled etymology, it derives from the Latin *mundus*, meaning "the world," and by extension the here and now. Thus, it just suggests fiction that takes place in some provisionally real world, at some provisional here and now.

But in English "mundane" already exists as a pejorative connoting the ordinary, the earth-bound, that which doesn't soar . . .

Well, the etymological meaning is there for any educated person to figure out. The connotations are there as a kind of dig to all those "Hey, I hear you write science fiction . . ." folk at all the parties. The bright science fiction fans in the 1930s or 1940s who coined the term, they figured, "Turnabout is fair play."

Rowell: In "Letter to a Critic," you state up front the purpose of the piece: "I'd like to talk specifically about science fiction—not about what motivates a given writer to create a given story, or even how a particular story may be constructed, but rather about the attitudes and values of the people who contract and pay for it, and publish it once it is written, as well as those who read it and make it profitable to publish—the landscape in which I work." I am especially interested in what you said "Letter to a Critic" was *not* about. Actually, the essays that follow in *The Jewel-Hinged Jaw* are about some of the architectonics of fiction writing. In the section focusing on character, for example, you comment on story: "a story is ultimately not what happens in an author's mind that makes her write down a series of words . . . ; it is what a given series of words cause to happen in the reader's [mind]."

Delany: Well, we're talking about the overlap of subject and object here. What I'm saying between the two passages you pull out is no more complicated than that what goes on in the mind has a lot to do with what goes on in the world. And vice versa.

A general literary abuse is to assume that what goes on in the mind is a self-contained and inviolate process that has at best, only to do with itself and, just possibly, *other* minds. But, as an uncritical assumption, this tends to arise only in groups of folk who don't have to *worry* about what goes on in the world. Traditionally and fortunately, this has not been most novelists in English—nor novelists in most other European languages, for that matter.

Rowell: Is your sense of action the same as the three kinds you have commented on in fiction, "purposeful, habitual, and gratuitous"?

Delany: Again, I am something of a philosophical conservative. I don't usually designate what goes on within the brain, as I don't designate what goes on within an electronic circuit, with the word action: a mental event, if you will—though clearly in both cases brain events or circuit events (what goes on in each) can *lead* to physical/mechanical actions.

The sort of actions I was speaking of there are actions performed by subjects, actions that can be perceived by people, in the world, as having a purpose, or as having fallen into habit, or as appearing more or less gratuitous. But these categories are basically suggestive, provisional, and contingent. They do not produce a hard-edged grid allowing some sort of easy analysis. Some writers simply find them suggesting a useful set of questions to ask about their own characters in terms of their own tales.

Others don't.

Rowell: In *The Jewels of Aptor* (1962), Iimmi tells Geo, "Each action is a reconciliation of the duality of motivation." What is the meaning and significance of Iimmi's words to Geo?

Delany: I'll be honest: When I think of the age at which I *wrote* my first published novel, it's a wonder anything any of the characters in it said meant anything!

But, as I recall its adolescent allegory, at nearing forty years' distance, the book is set up so that Iimmi (pronounced "Jimmy," by the way) is the voice of criticism and action. Geo, to whom he speaks, is the wounded poet, the creator of art.

Well, poets (and male poets in particular), as I perceived them at nineteen, tended to live in pretty fundamentally conservative universes. The sun really rose and set. (No planetary orbits for these guys.) Things were of the head or of the heart for them. (Negative capability was the best they could come up with.) The book has been, up till that point, about the multiplicity of motivations behind any human action. And Geo has been asking in effect (and has been physically wounded by his failure to find an answer) when all this multiplicity finally resolves.

Iimmi has just reminded him that anything that is actually *done* in the physical word in which we live is precisely such a resolution: a resolution of its several (or, in this particular case, an exemplary two) motivations.

Rowell: Your concern for language in writing and speech acts is broad. You open "Thickening the Plot" with a statement that supports my long held position about the linguistic limitations of our current literary discourse. You say that "a vocabulary that has grown from a discussion of effects is only of limited use in a discussion of causes." I am not convinced that we have developed a form of English, for example, which is adequate for discussing literary productions or for discussing the creative process, the act of creating a literary text. Isn't *Dhalgren* about what you call "the grammar of the language of human signs"? "It tries to focus," you write, "on the grammar of that language by a science fictional reorganization to those signs' textual production/reproduction."

Will you use the following statement you made in "Thickening the Plot" to discuss the creative process as you experienced it, for example, in the creation of *Dhalgren*, or as Kid might have experienced it in the creation of *Brass Orchids*? What is the function of *Brass Orchids* in *Dhalgren*?

> When I am writing I am trying to allow/construct an image of what I want to write about in my mind's sensory theater. Then I describe it as accurately as I can. The most interesting point I've noticed is that the writing down of words (or at least the choosing/arranging of words to write down) causes the vision itself to change.

Delany: The first thing I feel obliged to say is that "Thickening the Plot" and the various essays I've written atomizing aspects of the writing or reading process purely through introspection ("Thickening the Plot," "Characters," "Of Doubts and Dreams," "About 5,750 Words," or, more recently, "Some Notes for the Intermediate and Advanced Creative Writing Student") have been among my essays over which people have been most generous with their attentions. One of the legacies of Behaviorism is that "Introspection," from the 1950s onward, was just not looked upon with much faith, in a psychology menaced (the only word for it) on all sides by a very sophisticated notion of the unconscious. Nevertheless, there are some processes we have no other access to besides introspection: Creativity is foremost among them. So even the little bit of introspection that I've allowed myself, people are often hungry for.

It tastes very good to them.

But this doesn't mean that, as critical models, these descriptions of mine are any less reductive than any others. The process I describe, while a number of writers have felt it has the ring of truth, will nevertheless, no matter how slavishly you follow it, in no way *necessarily* produce—or account for—the production of *high quality* narrative. It will not produce well structured—or interestingly structured—stories. All it will produce is a narrative procession or narrative progression, as likely to be slovenly and unfocussed as not. As soon as we want to raise one level above the production of merely more or less coherent narrative verbiage, other forces must come into play—forces of, indeed, the sort I speak of in "Some Notes."

For that reason, I can't see how talking about it in relation to a specific passage—much less a near-900-page novel—can be possible, much less interesting. Its most intriguing aspect is that it's a self-destruct process, obliterating the earlier preparatory stages by replacing them with richer, more fully realized ones.

I don't know if poetry is necessarily written by the same process. I speak of the process by which I think sentences in general are written in my essay on Hart Crane, "Atlantis Rose . . ." (*Longer Views*, pages 193f; tangential to this discussion is the discussion of the part intention plays in language production in my account of Artaud's *Correspondence with Jacques Riviére*, in *Longer Views*, "Wagner/Artaud," pages 23–31). The passages in *Dhalgren* which show Kid writing and rewriting the sentences that move, though their several revisions, toward the versions (which ultimately we never see) that take their places in his poems in *Brass Orchids* are a somewhat misty attempt to dramatize my vision of the process *avant la lettre* of the later theoretical elaboration—with all that elaboration's necessary/inescapable theoretical reductions.

Within the larger architectonics of *Dhalgren*, of course, I don't think I'm telling any secrets by saying *Brass Orchids* plays the part of any more or less postmodern art object in the general allegory in terms of the social microcosm that Bellona represents.

Rowell: You wrote your essay "Characters" back in the 1960s. Here in 1998 would you like to add more to what you say about characters—i.e., about psychological veracity and what the character does, the character's actions?
Delany: Those essays, of which, yes, "Characters" is one, tend to be somewhat hard-edged, even executive in their approach, which is probably part of what little appeal they still have, in a time when most writing about the topic is rather soft-edged and wishy-washy. Still, most of what I have to say about them today is in the form of rather (wishy-washy, soft-edged) caveats and qualifications.

First, the basic ability to come up with believable characters—to know what details to assemble that will, among the interstices, generate a believable, interesting character—is, when all is said and done, a talent, not a skill. At the core of that talent, as much as selection, is a willingness, even a delight, in distorting and exaggerating, combined with a feel for psychological veracity—that is, what not to distort by any means, a sense of what one must fight to remain true to so that veracity does not go out the same window that has been opened to let in novelty, interest, and delight. Chaucer, Shakespeare, and Dickens are, among them, still the great exemplars in English. Add Balzac's and Dante's respective *Comedies*, Human and Divine, and while there is a lot other writers can teach you about writing *per se*, there is very little else to be learned about character—save Wilde's brilliant observation: The more you analyze your characters, the more they all come to sound alike.

Listening to me take refuge in Great Literature like this, I sound to myself a bit of a fuddy-duddy. Certainly the first lesson that anyone reading those Harvard Five-Foot Bookshelf Greats will take away is: Look first very carefully at the people around you. They will supply both major templates and all specific detail.

What does literature supply, then?

A way of looking at both. It will suggest distances at which to put the material so that various traits can be highlighted. And *some* of that, yes, you *can* reinvent on your own. Though, without question, you have a leg up if you've watched— and paid attention to—the way the Masters do it.

Rowell: In your essay "Quarks" (1970), you used the term "aesthetic discipline." What were your referring to?
Delany: The structures that must be absorbed, internalized, and submitted to if one is to write anything from a sentence to a scene to a multi-volume Encyclopedia of Everything or a *roman fleuve*.

Rowell: You ended your essay "Letter to a Critic" with a note which tells as much about your writing project and, whether you intended it or not, critiques, however indirectly, much early African-American fiction. You wrote that "all socially beneficial functions of art are minimal before this esthetic one: It allows the present meaning; it allows the future to exist."

Delany: That is one of those terminal apothegms that strains to say more than a sentence can say. If it still speaks to anyone after all these years, I can only be pleased I was lucky enough to have once been in a position to write it down.

Rowell: I think *The Jewel-Hinged Jaw: Notes on the Language of Science Fiction* (1977) is a very important book. Will you talk about its place in your writing career?

Delany: Well, it's a first collection of occasional essays by a young writer who, in many ways, was an even younger critic. Dragon Press, who urged me to gather those pieces, was run by David Hartwell. The first edition of the book was a labor of love and riddled with more typographical errors than almost any other book I know of. Three years later, a corrected edition appeared in trade paperback from Berkeley Windhover Books. But even that contains some whoppers.

One that still sets my teeth on edge occurs in the essay "Prisoner's Sleep," a reading of a dream scene in Thomas M. Disch's superb novel *Camp Concentration*. About a third of the way down page 211, the line occurs: "What is this dream about?" A provisional paragraph follows. Then, in the page's center, comes the line: "Our question, however, is: What is this dream about?" It should have been, of course, "What is about this dream?" but it was "corrected" by an overzealous proofreader going *much* too quickly.

Alas, there are many more.

It appeared when I was thirty-five, after I had published eleven novels—the most recent of which had been something of a success. The sales of *Dhalgren* and *Trouble on Triton* doubtless made it feasible to bring out a collection of essays by the author. But the earliest ones among those essays were written in 1968 and 1969. By and large they reflect my thinking before I'd had any significant encounter with what today we call critical theory.

When I tell people this today, sometimes they (quite wrongly) assume I mean I wrote them before I read any literary criticism at all. That's nonsense. I've been a lover of good critical writing since my teens. Fiedler's *Love and Death in the American Novel* and Wilson's *Axel's Castle* were both books I read, and read carefully, before I was twenty-one. Auerbach's *Mimesis* and Arthur Symons's *The Symbolist Movement in Literature* were both major critical revelations for me—all of which I read *well* before I began my five years' work on *Dhalgren* in 1969. But I had already sloshed about in the *Well Wrought Urn* and poured over *Form and Value in Modem Poetry.*

And, as I said, Baldwin's essays were among my early readerly enthusiasms.

Eventually I would find support for the kind of microscopic retardation of the ordinary reading and writing processes that I undertook in essays like "About 5,750 Words" and "Thickening the Plot" in the equally patient readings of Barthes and, later, Derrida. But this was my critical bent before I had their examples or their vocabulary among my tools.

One is always pleased when someone else takes pleasure in what you've written. But largely, except for things like the theoretical sections in "To Read *The Dispossessed*," most of the ideas retain interest for me only as take-off points for later theorizations—and often ones more critical than not of the parent ideas expressed there.

Rowell: Why do you write literary criticism at all? Certainly not to explain or justify what you do in your prose fiction. How did you come to writing it?
Delany: Reading is as much an experience for a certain sort of intellectual as climbing a mountain is for a certain sort of adventurer. Eventually the adventurer wants to tell people about what he's learned both *from* climbing and about the best way (and the most interesting and effective ways) to climb, with concrete examples taken from different mountains. As a reader, I had a very similar desire to tell people the same sorts of things about some of my reading experiences. (The fact that I'm highly dyslexic may give a little more weight, in my case, to the comparison of texts with mountains than it has with the luckily more lexic.)

In my early years, I confined my essays pretty much to what I'd learned about reading science fiction *per se*. But, after I became a professor, the restriction came to seem somewhat artificial.

In 1986, when I was taking a break from a term as Senior Fellow at the Society for the Humanities at Cornell to teach a three-week creative writing workshop at Lawrence, Kansas, an interviewer asked me: "How do you teach literature?"

I answered, "I don't. I teach science fiction," meaning nothing more than that, in the eleven years since my first visiting professorship at SUNY Buffalo, I had never been *asked* to teach anything other than courses in science fiction. Science fiction classes comprised the only ones I'd ever taught. A little later, a couple of professors, now writing articles on my work, came upon the published interview and, unable to conceive of how someone who had, by that time, been a Senior Fellow at three major research institutions at Universities around the country, could have meant something so prosaic—so political—sent me early drafts of articles in which they declared: "Samuel Delany teaches all literature as though it were science fiction . . ." and went on to ask how I accomplished this generic distortion—and why? One (who'd never sat in on a single class I'd ever taught), when I wrote back explaining what I'd meant, even went so far as to argue with me. He swore up and down that that was *not* what I'd written (though I have quoted you the question and my answer verbatim [cf. "Toto, We're Back! The *Cottonwood Review* Interview," page 78, *Silent Interviews*, Wesleyan, 1994]). But we have to remember that there are always readers who will avoid the obvious reading in favor of the intriguingly lunatic. There is no way for a writer to protect himself or herself from that.

As you point out, I'd read a great deal more than science fiction—as much as I enjoyed reading it, as much as I enjoyed writing it. The major criticism I received for my early nonfiction efforts centered on my tendency toward what some wag once dubbed "promiscuous autobiographizing."

I was fortunate to have early come across Cocteau's advice to young artists: "What your friends find to criticize about you, cultivate. It is you." The result was, a few years on, my autobiographical memoir, *The Motion of Light in Water* (1988), certainly among the books of mine that readers have been kindest to in the last twenty years—another genre crosser, in this case, between criticism and memoir.

Rowell: I am convinced your critical texts are irrevocably tied up with your prose fiction: they reinforce each other. Whom do you imagine as the audience for these two forms? Are they—do you assume—one and the same?

Delany: I certainly think those audiences are closer—or presume a different relationship—than, say, the initial audiences for D. H. Lawrence's fiction and *his* criticism. On the other hand, the only audience one can really speak of for criticism in this country is finally academic and/or professional. Possibly the audience for my fiction overspills those boundaries.

When I tell people I'm just not concerned about my audience, they often look at me surprised. "But you're supposed to be a professional writer," they say. "Don't professional writers spend sleepless nights worried over what the audience will say or think, fearful that you might drive them away? . . . But you're a critic with a burning vision," they go on. "Aren't you concerned that people actually *get* it?" Well, I don't and I'm not. For what little it's worth, the responses I've been most pleased with have been most numerous precisely over the works I wrote as rigorously as I could the way *I* wanted to. (I'm a formalist; I like to write both my

fiction and my nonfiction in a variety of formal ways.) At this point, I go into a
new work thinking pretty much only of myself: It has to be clear so *I* can understand it. That's the only critical talisman I carry with me at this point. I have to
be true to what I know, what I've seen, what I've learned—even when it invali-
dates something I wrote a day or a decade ago. I have to be true to the concept of
the form in which I'm working; that alone allows me to vary, emend, or develop
that form. I don't know whether it's superstition, luck, or self delusion. But that's
the way I do it. As for sales, other than at Tax time and then only in passing, I just
don't pay attention to them.

I've always written for readers who can read and are willing to re-read. (Publishers and writers who try to write and sell books to people who don't read I
think are . . . well, weird.) I've been fortunate: Since my very first novels, these are
often the readers I've gotten.

A woman in San Mateo, California, has read *Dhalgren* once a year since it came
out in the last days of 1974. Needless to say, she's become quite an expert on the
text and has several times helped me prepare correction sheets. I've never met her,
but we've corresponded desultorily. Eventually I dedicated one of my nonfiction
books to her: *The Straits of Messina.*

Rowell: How important is it for you to tell us—your readers—the following?

I am black, I have spent time in a mental hospital, and much of my adult life
has been passed on society's margins. My attraction to . . . [the preceding con-
texts] . . . is not so much the desire to write autobiography, but the far more
parochial desire to set matters straight.

Delany: I made that statement in response to some questions about *Dhalgren*—in
effect, why did I choose to write about the "depressing" things and not particularly "up-lifting" people I focused on in that novel.

Was it necessary? In that case answering was merely politeness.

At least one academic, otherwise quite supportive of me, had finally confessed
(or, more accurately, erupted): "I'm just not *interested* in the people you write
about, Chip! I just don't see how they're at all important in the greater scheme
of things." Behind such a statement are resonances going back to Aristotle's defense of tragedy: It's only good as long as it's written about kings and noblemen;
and his collateral contention that similar stories about ordinary men and women
would not be tragic, merely pathetic.

Like many writers, I've felt that the form of esthetic attention can itself en-
noble a topic.

It requires a lot of verbal tap dancing, however, to body forth that interest through the rhetoric itself.

But if you've noticed that the world works differently from the way most people have been told it does, and you can explain what you see of that working (are Proust or Musil or even Auden *anything* else, page after page, volume after volume? The answer is, of course, "Yes") clearly and convincingly—i.e., with the ring of truth—I think you have a leg up.

A Silent Interview with Samuel R. Delany

Eric Lorberer and Rudi Dornemann/2000

From *Rain Taxi Review of Books*, Winter 2000/2001. Online Edition. Reprinted by permission of Eric Lorberer.

Samuel R. Delany's many books offer not only the beauty of well-turned phrases and the spark of provocative ideas, but an illumination won from the exacting exploration of self and society. In science fiction, literary criticism, comic books, memoir, or pornography, to read Delany is to discover. Showing us what we as readers didn't already know, he freshens our eyes for what we had always accepted as familiar.

Delany's writing career began in the precincts of science fiction in the early sixties—earning him the highest awards in the genre before he was thirty—and has continued through further SF landmarks (e.g., *Dhalgren* and *Stars in My Pocket Like Grains of Sand*), the four volumes of philosophical fantasy in his Return to Nevèrÿon series, transgressive novels (*Hogg* and *The Mad Man*), works of memoir and family history (*The Motion of Light in Water* and *Atlantis: Three Tales*), and numerous collections of essays and criticism. This year, he has added two books to his nonfiction column: *Shorter Views: Queer Thoughts & the Politics of the Paraliterary* and *1984*.

While the former of these new books speaks for itself, the latter may demand some explanation. In ironic homage to one of the classics of "literary" science-fiction, *1984* shows us the year of Orwell's nightmare prophecy from the vantage of the present, offering a well-chosen selection of Delany's letters written during that year. There are intriguing parallels to Orwell's vision; "Big Brother" here appears in the guise of the IRS, who lay their claim on every last cent Delany earns, while "sexcrime" is explored through Delany's musings on the changing pornographic underworld during the advent of AIDS and gentrification (a subject given his full critical scrutiny in last year's *Times Square Red, Times Square Blue*). With all the grace of an epistolary novel, *1984* is a riveting look at a year in the life of a struggling writer.

As is Delany's practice, the following is a "silent interview" in which the author responded to our questions in writing. A shorter version of this interview appears in Volume 5, Number 4 of *Rain Taxi Review of Books.*

Rain Taxi: References to poetry are sprinkled liberally throughout your writing—*1984*, to cite only the latest example, begins with a double-barreled meditation on the onset of AIDS and the death of poet Ted Berrigan. Clearly poetry is important to you, despite the fact that it's one of the few genres you haven't written. Can you talk about the role of poetry for non-poets?

Samuel R. Delany: Because I like to read poetry—and like to read *about* poetry—I'm tempted to start with the most pragmatic answer: As a prose writer, I work with language; and those who work with language turn to poetry for renewal. But that's a metaphor—and sometimes it's difficult to turn up the focus on the experience itself to analyze just what the reading of poetry gives.

Among my recent enthusiasms is the critical work of the late poet Gerald Burns. In a slim pamphlet called *Toward a Phenomenology of Written Art,* in "The Slate Notebook," the first of the two essays that comprise his book, Burns writes:

> Some writers know a great deal about how words should come at a reader; others study the ways words come to a writer. The second is likely to please passionate readers more, if only because the first is more likely to be vulnerable to literature as rule book, a catalogue of other men's effects. What saves him sometimes is reading very little. The second, whether reading or writing, is likely to pay less attention to the book of rules than to grass and how the ball looks coming at you, and the oddity of lines painted on a field. What he explores is the act of writing, as his readers explore the act of reading. There is nothing contemptible about traditionalist writing, but its readers are more likely to ignore the act of reading as part of the experience of what is read. In the first-quarto *Hamlet* Corambis asks, What doe you reade my Lord? and Hamlet says, Wordes, wordes. In the Folio he says, Words, words, words. It's not only funnier, it's truer, to his and our experience. The scribe may hate his pen as the painter his paint, but in another mood he will imitate Van Gogh and drink ink.

Around his baseball exemplary (borrowed, surely, from Jack Spicer), this kind of insight locates our attraction to poets from Pound of the *Cantos,* through Laura (Riding) Jackson, Charles Olson, Robert Duncan, and Jorie Graham—and is one you're only likely to hear *from* a poet. The writers of prose fiction whom I can easily think of who fall in with those writers more interested in how words come to the writer than to the reader are D. H. Lawrence and the greatly under-rated Paul Goodman. Today, language-aware prose is, indeed, more likely to be concerned with the reader. William Gass or Guy Davenport, Richard Powers or Edmund White are all writers primarily interested in the reader. As, I confess (my Nevèrÿon tales excepted), am I.

Still, from time to time it's interesting—as Burns suggests, obsessively so—to read writers who are interested first in how language comes to them.

In his long poem *The Alphabet* (the *Prelude* of our times), in the S-section, "Skies" (in the book *fl*, which includes three sections, "Quindecagon," "fl," and "Skies," Drogue Press: New York: 1999) Ron Silliman gives us the detritus of many days' looking at the sky—of going out and writing at least a sentence a day about it. The result? A sensuous, sumptuous, and remarkably analytical cascade of perceptions, focused on one great natural field. Another thing we turn to today's task-orientated poetry for is the performance of those language undertakings that we prose writers are just too lazy, or, yes, too insensitive, to try.

Hart Crane—to cite a poet I love and have written about, both in critical essays and as a character in fiction (*Atlantis: Three Tales*, Wesleyan, Middletown: 1996)—is a poet who lets me into a hyperarticulate universe, where I'm privileged to hear the entire inanimate world given voice. Considering gay history, it's fascinating that, in an incomplete poem ("A Traveler Born") written in 1930 about his various sailor conquests, a gay poet should mention the "Institute Pasteur" where the AIDS virus would eventually be isolated fifty-three years later. In Crane's poems, ships, waves, cables, rain, sea-kelp, and derricks all sigh, scream, choir, and return words, song, letters, and laughter for speech. Eliot meditated on the significance of what the thunder said through the medium of the second Brahmana of the fifth lesson of the *Bhradâranyaka Upanishad*. In his poem "Eternity," Crane crawled out from under the bed the next morning, sat down, and, amidst the wreckage, pretty much transcribed what he saw of its effects directly.

In some situations—though I'd be hard-pressed to give them a coherent characterization—this is not just invigorating. It's downright useful.

Gertrude Stein knew she was a genius, and she wanted to show that the way language comes to geniuses is insistently simple; it arrives in the mind of those who can really think with a clarity, a lucidity, and a strident and self-reaffirming simplicity that is all but one with the language of the child. When someone like Blanche McCrary Boyd advises writers today, "Write as simply as you can for the most intelligent person in the room," she is encapsulating—she's aphorizing—the dramatized wisdom of Stein's *Lectures in America* and *How to Write*.

I don't think I can leave your question without noting that those writers concerned with (that is to say, who fetishize) how language comes to them rather than how it goes out from them tend to be on the conservative side.

They're the writers who don't question why the words for the gallery of writing techniques come to them as "men's efforts."

Because that's the way it comes, that's reason enough for someone like Burns to preserve it.

In 1966 and '67, after I finished a novel called *Babel-17*, in the various articles I was writing here and there I began to use "she" and "her" as the general exemplary pronoun. In the sixties and seventies, copy editors regularly used to correct me, changing my "the writer she" back to "the writer he"—and, if I could, I'd put it back, though I didn't always get a chance. I'd never seen anyone else do it before. The decision was purely intellectual. But after having written a whole novel about the trials and tribulations of a woman poet, I just couldn't go on accepting the notion that everything from children to animals to writers to parents were composed of nothing but males. I know a few writers—specifically in the science fiction field—took the idea over from me and began to do it too.

Today, thirty-odd years later, it's a commonplace in the style of everyone from Gayatri Chakravorty Spivak to Richard Rorty. I'm quite prepared to believe other people—women and men—got the idea independently of me, or of any of the people who (like Joanna Russ) borrowed it from me. Possibly someone did it even before me. But this brings up the whole notion of voluntarism in language—a tricky and difficult topic. Conscientiously changing the language is only likely to be done by a writer who fetishizes how the words strike the *reader*. But the experience of the modern "man" from the fifteenth century on has been that of the language which society gives her or him not describing the world she or he knows to be the case. Whether it's the suggestion (that comes directly from the classical languages) that the child (that is, the important child in the family, the one who will be a citizen, the one who will inherit) as soon as it stops being an "it," becomes a "he," or that the sun rises and sets (instead of stays in one place while the earth turns above it), or that, by seeing and hearing things, the subject does something *to* them, rather than being neurologically excited *by* them in some way, or that electricity runs from positive to negative (shortly after the poles were assigned, of course, it was discovered that the electrons actually moved the other way), language constantly remains inadequate to describe accurately what we know of the world—unless we're willing to take it by its neck and, well . . . after wringing it and slapping it around a *little*, voluntarily changing it.

Most of the time, we negotiate this inadequacy by developing twin rhetorical traditions. We still say that the sun rises in the east—even as we talk, in terms of time differences, of the earth turning "beneath" (itself a ridiculous concept, since, during its night, Australia is in the same orientation toward the solar center as is daytime Canada: only the earth's globe lies between) the sun. The logical way to speak of it, however, would be to say that the whole earth moves in an orbit ninety-three million miles *above* the sun, as the moon orbits *above* the earth—and, indeed, as the sun revolves thirty thousand light years above and about the massive black hole probably at our galaxy's center. "Above," in this situation, is new diction. It hasn't been used before. The anti-volunteerists say that you *can't* change language voluntarily. I say, if it makes sense to you, use it; now; from now on—and we *will* have changed the language, just as those of us who started using "she" as an exemplary pronoun comparable with "he" changed it in the late sixties and seventies.

RT: *1984* is titled after one of the best known works of literature (or some would say science fiction). What is it you want to remind us of Orwell's relevance as his apocalyptic date recedes into the past?
SRD: I was going for irony: A science fiction writer writing a nonfiction book about a time in the actual past that was, for so long (and still is, by so many) considered to *be* science fiction. In that sense, I used the title in a poetic (if comic) way, rather than as a hard-edged reference to some synopsizable Orwellian politics. Some of those poetic relationships between what Orwell was doing and what I was up to are beautifully and intelligently unpacked and teased apart by Kenneth James in his "Introduction" to the letters that largely make up the book.

RT: You've constructed fictions which implicitly and/or explicitly reference large intellectual frameworks such as semiotics or deconstruction. Do you see any relation between ways in which your work is informed by literary/critical thinking and ways in which the works of other SF writers have been informed by other bodies of thought—for example, theories of history and Isaac Asimov's Foundation series, or eco-political ideas and Kim Stanley Robinson's Mars and California trilogies?
SRD: You've hit the nail on its head with your question. In stories trying to put over some notion from cultural or theoretical studies, really the writers aren't doing anything very different from what Asimov was trying for in his Foundation tales. The first handful of stories in *Foundation*—the first volume—attempt to get across some of the fundamentals of historical materialism. You know: A society that has a scarcity of metals is likely to develop differently from one in which

metals are in excess. A society that is all water and wood is likely to develop differently from one with a plethora of ceramics.

People are pretty comfortable with the notion of SF as the literature of ideas. Well, personally I've been trying to pull that firmly tucked-in blanket up over the shoulder of Sword & Sorcery awhile now. In the midst of my more grandiose day dreamings, I've suggested that the Nevèrÿon stories are in the same line as Isak Dinesen's "gothic" tales. But the mumbled truth is that they're even closer to all those lunatic volumes Frank Herbert kept turning out before he wrote his Dune books—novels which nobody ever looks at any more.

SF writers have always liked to play with ideas of history. The idea that ecology is a major historical force—as it is in Stan Robinson's vision of the terraforming of Mars—resonates clearly with some of the work of Braudel and the *Annales* historians and other historians of the long *durée*.

RT: In other interviews, you've talked about the process of using memories in which you perceive a certain "beauty and formal order" as a starting point for writing—even when your subject matter is outside what is usually treated artistically. And you've written about the idea that "human beings have an aesthetic register," which "manifests itself as a desire to recognize patterns." Have your ideas/perception of what constitutes "beauty and formal order" changed over time? Do you discover different aesthetic patterns in your experience of the world now than you did when you were first writing?
SRD: They've changed surprisingly little. I still believe pattern fascinates on its own. And three-sevenths of a pattern, or even a smaller fragment, can fascinate still more—get us really hunkering down, trying to tease out the whole of the figure in the carpet. Pattern is repetition of symmetry. And, as Freud told us in *Beyond the Pleasure Principle*, "Repetition is desire." Classical antiquarians used to call it *ex pede Herculem*—from only the statue's marble foot, they would try to reconstruct the entire form of the luminous, lowering demi-god.

Certainly there's new content to write about.

As certainly we are all drawn to some content—emotional, political, sexual—more than others.

But over time we can all watch what once seemed inescapably pressing *because* of the strident relevance of its content lose more and more of its interest till it's nothing but a formal arrangement.

From *The Red and the Black* (1830) through *Huckleberry Finn* (1884–85) and *The Way of All Flesh* (1904), a whole stream comprising some of the most revered works in Western fiction turns on the oedipal notion that the older generation feels it's due respect and deference from the younger because it's lived more, seen more, and done more—while the young rebel, claiming they must be allowed to discover the machinery of the world for themselves if for no other reason than the workings of that machinery is always in flux. There have always been many people for whom you only had to state the idea to raise in them a *frisson* of recognition, a thrill of identification.

Well, a few years ago, I had a surprising revelation. A significant proportion of my undergraduate literature students simply didn't relate in any major way to that "universal" notion, through no more complex a situation than having grown up with moderately reasonable parents, who simply weren't concerned with those orders and strictures of formal deference. That whole concept of intergenerational respect leans with ponderous weight on the notion of huge amounts of land, labor, and wealth passed from generation to generation.

Well, save some pots and pans, a ring, and some linen, I received no direct inheritance from either of my parents. Once an aunt of mine left me a legacy amounting to slightly under three months rent. Alas, whatever I leave my daughter is likely to be equally minimal.

The nineteenth-century concept of independent incomes passed from parents to children—incomes without which civilized life would be inconceivable—is simply not a part of the current standard order of all civilized life for most of us—though it was *the* topic of the eighteenth- *and* the nineteenth-century novel. With all that economic responsibility unto eternity lifted from the shoulders of parents and children, life has probably been—locally—happier for lots of us. That means there's a growing generation for which any image of the good and forgiving father doesn't immediately bring tears to the eyes with the deep and tragic realization that, in their childhoods, they have never had one. (He was too busy building up something to leave you to be bothered to love you. Oedipus himself was, after all, a displaced prince, who won back his kingdom through murder most foul.) The tyrannical father doesn't immediately enlist them in a pact of identificatory anger that can now be turned against all unfair authority. These students' appreciation for the works that appealed to these patterns was primarily intellectual, and their esthetic response was limited to what greater and more intricate patterns the writers had embedded this oedipal material within.

Despite the creeping (and rather Spenglarian) Manicheanism of Slavoj Zizek, I don't think this is necessarily a bad thing—even as it moves some of the works I think of as personally and wonderfully powerful over or out a notch in the generally stabilizing canon structure.

RT: Are there artistic movements or particular artists you find particularly interesting, new ways of seeing the world in fiction or science fiction, comics or poetry, drama or visual arts? Conversely, do you feel there are parts of social reality for which there isn't currently an adequate artistic language in which to convey/reflect/express/discuss them?

SRD: I have been teaching for the last few years. The tragedy of that situation is the restrictions it imposes of how much of the world—especially the world of art—I get to explore. The Poetics Program at the State University of Buffalo where I teach has brought me in contact with an exciting stream of poets. But to say that Nick Piombino has some extraordinary ideas about poetry, which, in conjunction with his work as a psychoanalyst, have produced some fascinating essays and poems; or to say that Nicole Brossard has penned some scrupulously elegant fictions that attack the edges of poetry and appropriate them for themselves; or to say that Christian Bök's constructivist energy and historical intelligence is jaw dropping—well, I'm not sure what that says about anything other than my own enforced provincialism over the last few years.

What we now have to realize more and more, as high art becomes more and more democratically accessible, however, is that we only become more and more provincial.

I've been delighted and entranced with all of Alan Moore's ABC comics—*Top Ten, Promethea, Tom Strong,* and that wonderful camp extravaganza of paraliterary ironies, *The League of Extraordinary Gentlemen,* with its intrepid leader Mina Harkner (née Murray), escaped from (but not unscarred by) Dracula's clutches. And I was wonderfully glad to see the single-volume edition of the Moore/Campbell *From Hell.* (Are you as curious about the movie, due for next summer's release, as I am?) *Hellblazer* seems to have gotten a new shot of ingenuity from wherever. (Did you ever read Maggie [*The Book of the Penis*] Paley's wonderful novel from 1986, *Bad Manners?* It wrings more esthetic use out of the telephone than any work since Cocteau's *Le Voix humain.* And I was intrigued by, if I didn't exactly enjoy, Coetzee's *Disgrace.*) *White Out* and *White Out Melt* were—as the kids used to say—awesome. The *Sin City* volumes and *300* were extraordinary offerings from Frank Miller. And since *The Preacher* recently concluded, yes, I've missed it.

The point, of course, is that there is a great deal of artistic energy in flux and a-swarm out and around in the making world. Turning to authorities to validate this or that section of it may be a necessary evil. What makes it an evil is, however (and keeps it from becoming a contribution to the aesthetic landscape's general health), the lack of an adequate language in which the general public for art can express its own enthusiasms, its own interpretations, its agile and motile movements of attention.

But then, I suspect most of life takes place in the interstices of what's already been articulated. We call it discourse. Finally I think a question like yours has always got to be posed as part of a two-way process. After I give my answer, I am obliged to ask immediately, as if, indeed, the asking were only an extension of my response: And what new works and artists are currently exciting *you*?

Without that reciprocity (again I want to put the ball back in the *reader's* court), the question—and any given answer from any given person—must be, as some of us have lately been known to murmur, radically incomplete.

RT: In the last book of your Return to Nevèrÿon series (*Return to Nevèrÿon* [1987]), you claim you "write yearning for a world in which all these stories might be merely 'beautiful,'" and go on to write that such a world might be possible in ten or twenty years, and that "That world would be, in many ways, the world I conceived of as Utopia." Is that world any closer now?
SRD: Paradoxically, I'm the last person to answer that. Whatever determines my worldview, *really* determines it. I have to remain blind to it. For me, no, those stories can never be "merely" beautiful.

That's something for our children to decide—or our children's children. We fashion meticulously and with as much strength as we can a wrung for the ladder we only hope, once those children, grown now, climb it, they can finally throw away. Politics is the *most* quixotic element of art . . . Still, I think those critics who believe it doesn't belong there at all are deluded. Was there ever a more political writer than Shakespeare? Those histories were all colored by, as they commented on, contemporary politics. The wheat riots in *Coriolanus* were inspired by similar riots in English during the pervious year. And Polonius was a knowing satire on Elizabeth's prime minister, Lord Burley. Yes, politics is what time erases from art; and the art must be well-enough constructed to stand without it, once it has been removed by historical ignorance. Still, without the political goad, often we would never have had the art in the first place. Honestly, *Sentimental Education* is a better novel than *Madame Bovary*, precisely *because* of its richer political concerns—the source of its richer esthetic elaboration.

When you stroll down the street at 4:19 in the morning, and you suddenly stop—to look at two crows playing in a pine tree across whatever suburban street fate has stuck you on for the last year-and-a-half, there's a history of crows, a tradition of crows, a discourse of crows that's stopped you, and because you've stopped and are looking at them *now*, you can never be wholly aware of what that discourse, that history, that tradition *was*.

Sure, a moment on you recall the pair in the *Neibelunglied*, but you *don't* recall the one you saw savaging a red cardinal carcass on the highway's edge when you were five, or the one with the bilious tongue your father's friend—Connie, I think his name was—split with a razor to make it talk, because he was under the mistaken impression that such cruelty would re-articulate the species and make of it a dusky parrot. Fiberglass curtains blew around the cage in the Harlem back window, while—its swollen tongue pink as a rose hip, holding apart its grey-black beak—the bird eyed me blackly, then looked down at the newspaper over the cage bottom, scattered with seeds and shit . . .

The really repressed, the inchoate, the *inconue* that one masks with public dragons and genre determined strong men and strong women, to whom one loans one's most cherished ideologies, one's most committed desires, to make them strong enough to possess and hot enough to be possessable, *they* just don't yield themselves up so easily as a pair of birds at play above the November sidewalk in Buffalo. That's why we turn to them through genre tropes—because we *don't* know what they're really about. That's what we need public symbols for—symbols that alone let us negotiate the unknown and the unknowable.

It's because we can't grasp, really, what they are to us, that, moments later, as the crows fly off above the green and orange alley, our throats suddenly fill and we are trying not to cry—

So then, angrily, we write about dragons.

RT: As you have added more autobiographical works to your *oeuvre*, you've also brought to the forefront matters of race and sexual preference, yet often in the most unpolitically correct ways—your books are unlikely to be accused of being "identity art." What does the culture at large need to do to more adequately discuss these most basic of subject-positions?

SRD: Fantasize—and fantasize in modes that allow our most cherished and forbidden inner worlds to peak out (and speak out) here and there. Fantasize. Analyze. The two are related by much more than grammar and rhyme. In order to negotiate the unknown with any precision and intelligence, analysis has to become speculative. That's where fantasy's role grows inescapable.

It's scary to talk about your own fantasies—to plumb that part of one's inner autobiography: the part we return to to initiate masturbation, the part that centers our reveries of anger or tenderness. Bring analysis—rather than blanket acceptance or rank dismissal—to *those* thoughts, and you'll find out how the world, dark or light, might figure itself under passion's stress.

RT: You have been adamant about the need to consider paraliterary genres on their own terms; indeed, the desire to make science fiction (or comics, or pornography) "literary" (i.e. more respectable) is probably reactionary at best. Yet isn't a genuine hybridization of genres possible? Your own work can easily be described in such ways: *Times Square Red, Times Square Blue*, for example, combines candid memoir with sociological analysis to produce a new kind of urban study. To take another example, your novel *The Mad Man* is a pornographic work—no question—yet it is also a serious erudite work, and serious erudite pornography is, we imagine, so rare that it might constitute a different genre, or at least warrant a different term.

SRD: To take the first half of your question first—about taking the paraliterary genres on their own terms: It depends on what terms you identify as "their own." If you mean only the terms that "literature" has set aside for them—and that now and then one finds the paraliterary genres have appropriated for themselves in an attempt to survive—then I think the idea is absurd.

An example: Paraliterature is just entertainment and is without further value.

Another: Paraliterature has no necessary history that helps us understand and appreciate it.

These are ideas about paraliterature you can find *within* the precincts of paraliterature today just as easily as you can find them—at their source—within the literary precincts, where they originated.

But the talk of origins is always distractionary and ideological. The point is, genres *are* never pure. Genres *were* never pure. The splits between them, while always noticable, always oppressively *there*, are most important, most valuable by virtue of what they allow to cross over (what has always-already crossed over)—and the speed or slowness with which they allow those crossings. When one is talking of a relatively slow speed (such as the time it takes for intelligent attention to pass across the boundaries set up in the 1880s and 1890s, when the provisionary notion of dismissing entire working-class genres out of hand laid the groundwork for the subsequent academic creation, momently after the Great War, of the genre collection we call, today, literature), it's easier to speak of impedances. That is to say, is the glass of water half full or is it half empty?

Above I spoke of the socioeconomic conditions that, until recently, informed at least one of the structures associated with patriarchy—the patrimony—with its pathos and glory: itself the pathos and glory of the family-anchored hero.

Well, the pathos and glory of the non-family-anchored hero is precisely the socio-economic situation that is growing more and more to replace it. The non-family-anchored hero in literature begins to come into its own with the hero of Knut Hamsun's *Hunger*, and, with Hamsun's disciple Henry Miller, spills out into the various tropics, onto the lush landscapes of Maroussi and the Sur. It also presses so close against the walls of pornography that we can't take it further without rupturing those walls and looking closely at what we find on the other side.

Both science fiction and sword and sorcery also tend to feature non-family-anchored heroes. (Personally, what I'm interested in is what type of *object* the family becomes when, within such a genre, you do turn and examine it with the appropriate modicum of fantasy and analysis.) As I've written elsewhere, the hero of the Sword-and-Sorcery tale is not the prince with his endless entanglements with various potential fathers-in-law in terms of the princesses to be rescued/won over/married. Rather, he is the unencumbered troll—Chyna, Hacksaw Jim Dugan, Luna, the Rock, Jacquelyn, Mankind, Booker-T, Conan, Saturn, Sable, Eddie Guerrero, Jr., or Goldberg—grown in human proportions.

RT: A term that's been used increasingly in the last decade or so is "slipstream." The term (like any) is used in various ways, now meaning literary fiction which adopts paraliterary techniques and tropes (as in some of the work of William S. Burroughs or Marge Piercy), now used to describe science fiction/fantasy which employs the tropes and techniques of literary fiction. As well, it's marked perhaps with a certain surrealism (for instance, some of the fiction of Jonathan Lethem or Stepan Chapman). You've maintained that what sets science fiction (or any paraliterature) apart from literary fiction is that it needs to be read according to a different set of conventions. How should one approach this "slipstream" fiction which seems to occupy a twilight region between the two genres? Are the reading conventions of either science fiction of literary fiction appropriate here, should readers mix conventions from both sides of the literary/paraliterary divide, or is "slipstream" developing its own way to be read?

SRD: You're imputing ideas to me which, while your expression uses a couple of terms that I've occasionally used, are just not mine. There are many, *many* ways in which a given text recognizable as belonging to a given *paraliterary* genre is likely to be different from a given text recognizable as belonging to a given *literary* genre. (You're not likely to mistake the ironic banalities in John Ashbery's *Three Poems* for the equally amusing ironic banalities in Alan Moore's *Tom Strong*. They come from two different traditions. Put bluntly, one's a comic book; one's a poem.) But there are many ways in which they can be the same. If the paraliterary text happens to be well written enough, and also the vessel of what Nabokov once referred to as "sensuous thought" (his particular description of art), then you might find yourself advantaged by bringing across the divide the kind of intense attention more typically devoted to literary texts. Now—and only now—can we get to the point I think you are trying to make, above.

Since what any genre actually *is* is a way of reading (or, more accurately, a complex of different ways of reading), different ways of reading constitute different genres—if I may risk a founding tautology.

One of the ways of reading that controls many of the parts of many of the texts usually associated with the literary genres might be characterized as "the tyranny of the subject"—that is to say, much of the information in these texts is organized about the concept the subject, the self, psychology.

This is not necessarily the case with texts usually ascribed to the paraliterary genres. Often, there, we find the subject given relatively little attention. We say, from the literary point of view, that the characters are shallower, or are not as richly drawn—though we are quite used to the flattening out methods occasionally used in literary comedy, parody, or satire. But there's also, in literary discourse, an always-already present disdain *for* the paraliterary genres. This can be shown by pointing out the above contradiction: While we praise the caricatures of a Dickens or a Mark Twain, we will quickly turn around and criticize a Kornbluth, a Blish, a William Tenn for using equally flattened characters in a story. But in such tales, the character level simply isn't the focus. In such stories, to read for such character depth is blatantly to misread the text—as it would be in, say, Thurber, although for different reasons.

Generally speaking, the kind of attention that we pay to the subject in literature—an attention that, in part, constitutes the way of reading that is literature—has to be paid to the social and material complexities of the object in many of the texts usually ascribed to the *paraliterary* genres—more specifically in those texts usually recognizable as science fiction.

Because literary critics are so used to talking and writing about the subject, often when they come to science fiction texts they simply are not comfortable yielding up their analytical attention in these new ways, to these new topics.

Now, if *that's* what you mean by reading paraliterature by a different set of conventions and reading it on its own terms, then—yes—I'm with you. Or, indeed, if you mean reading parliterary texts, with a sophisticated awareness of how the genre's history makes various rhetorical figures signify in their particularly nuanced way, then—yes—I'm *still* with you.

But even while no text escapes the mark of one genre or another (often a given text must bear several generic marks), no particular way of reading belongs ultimately and absolutely *only* to one genre. The genre field is constantly reconfiguring itself under historical pressures that cause ways of reading to move about and displace each other across what—only if we step way back and squint—can we make ourselves see, from time to time, as severing chasms.

As to slipstream: Well, I find myself smiling.

"Speculative fiction" is the term that once fulfilled that same job until it become so generalized that it no longer meant anything at all—or rather, meant almost everything, so that it was appropriated by all sorts of groups with some really bizarre agendas. I wonder if the same thing will happen to "slipstream"?

RT: The incidents talked about in *1984* precede your professional entrance into academia. The book offers a sometimes gritty look at the life of a writer trying to survive on writing alone. Aside from the financial stability, is the writing life much different as a university professor? And let's not forget that many people are . . . let's say "upset" that writers seem to hole up behind the ivy—is there merit to this complaint, or are there aspects of this culture they may not be considering?
SRD: "Aside from financial stability . . ."

Well, that's a pretty big one to put aside. It contours everything from your health to the time you have to write. It suggests you've never read a nineteenth-century-style novel.

One of the ideas that underlies much of what I'm speaking of here is, however, what might be called "the fundamental complexity of the recognizable." That is another way of saying that anything stable and enduring—or, indeed, iterable—enough to be recognized is bound to be complex. This notion is one of the few modern philosophical concepts, by the bye, that actually flies in the face of what old Pappa Plato thought: Plato thought that stability was a simple notion, related to the good and the beautiful. I say, rather, stability is always a matter of complexity. Anything that is stable must be involved in a complex of interchanging relationships—physical, electrochemical, mechanical, economic, social, psychological, or discursive—within the complex of the greater system in which it's embedded. Otherwise it would simply be destroyed and cease to exist. Solids are more complex than liquids, which are more complex than gasses. Universities, rocks, and solar flares are all complex phenomena, because they endure—or because they repeat. We're only beginning to realize what an incredibly complex system what scientists heretofore have called "nothing" is: that is to say, "pure" "empty" vacuum. For one thing, perfuse it with nothing more than gravitational force, and—besides bending— it starts spontaneously belching up pairs of anti-particles here and there throughout . . . ! No, this is not simple stuff. And its intricacy down around the level of quantum foam and six-dimensional Callabi-Yau shapes below the size of the Planck length alone can explain why there's so much of it and how it's lasted so long—that is, can answer Heidegger's question ("Why are there somethings rather than nothing?") in its most recently fascinating form (from novelist and North Carolina newspaper columnist David [*The Autobiography of My Body*] Guy): "Why, in an infinite universe, is there an infinite universe?"

This insight about the inherent complexity of stability is, of course, the joy and justification both of the material scientist and of the culture critic.

But I seem to be veering away from your question, instead of boring to its center.

What was Goethe's quip? As soon as a man does something admirable, the whole world conspires to see that he never does it again. For a writer to be in a university must mean that, at one time or another, she or he must wonder: Aren't they really paying me *not* to write?

The process is recognizable—but its ways of holding the writer within it *are* complex; and, indeed, recognizable. Maybe they could stand a little analysis too.

Reading/Delany

Matrix Magazine/2001

From *Matrix* Magazine, 2001. Reprinted by permission of the publisher.

1. *Postmodernism/Baudrillard*

There's something in Baudrillard's Marxist revisionism that I like very much—while there is something else in it that, as much as I like it, also feels *dead* off. And so far I haven't got the time or the energy to sit down and tease out what exactly it is, although I honestly suspect if I did, not only would *I* be a better person, but the *world* would be a better place.

> Delany, Samuel R. *1984: Selected Letters* (2000), p. 88

Similarly, Foucault had already been identified as the clear and present enemy by those who claim history is over, and that we have entered some posthistorical period (often designated postmodernism), where all discourses are homogenized and there are no discursive articulations to be found any more, thanks to the current invisibility of power; I mean, of course, the author of *Forget Foucault,* Jean Baudrillard.

> Delany, Samuel R. *Shorter Views: Queer Thoughts &
> the Politics of the Paraliterary* (1999), p. 35

Matrix: What are your thoughts on Baudrillard, in particular, and postmodernism in general?

Samuel R. Delany: I found the early Baudrillard—*For a Critique of the Political Economy of the Sign* (France 1972/Translated 1981) and *The Mirror of Production* (1975)—quite useful. My 1982 novel *Neveryóna, or: The Tale of Signs and Cities* is drenched in ideas from those works. But after *The Ecstasy of Communication* (1987) much of the work of his that I've encountered (and certainly I haven't encountered all of it by *any* means) began to seem like a species of delirious impressionism, some of it enjoyable but not of any particularly weighty theoretical import.

I think, in the transition from scholar to celebrity, Baudrillard lost—or perhaps was manipulated into losing sight of—more than most. We mustn't forget that he was substantially older than, say, Foucault or Barthes ever lived to be, when he was taken up by the American academic "theory" star system, and he had completed his work of a certain youthful energy long before. Put out in Australia, a chapbook-sized selection of eight brief essays, called *Seduced and Abandoned* (1984), discusses Baudrillard's enterprise and gives a remarkably good summing up of its strengths and weaknesses.

I only heard Baudrillard speak once—a very unhappy talk he gave, back in the eighties, at Columbia University. Its substance was that the current intellectual community suffered from mental AIDS, because our intellectual immune systems had broken down, and we now took in everything and gave it equal weight and consideration. First off, it was just a terrible—and highly angering—choice of metaphor, at that particular point in time (the mid-eighties), when AIDS itself, its treatment and the treatment of people with AIDS was so politically fraught, with cuts in research funds, public misinformation, and the tragedies of people ill and dying all around us. It fell on my ears and those of many others that evening as one of the more monumental pieces of bad taste we'd yet been exposed to in the academy. Several people got up and left in the middle. With that fascination one can experience when you observe someone doing and saying the absolutely wrong thing—and go *on* doing it and saying it—I stayed to the end. Only one person (probably whoever had invited him) posed a question, surely to defuse some of the pent up hostility the audience was feeling. But, by now, Baudrillard had *begun* to pick up, just from the atmosphere in the room, that he'd done something dreadfully wrong—though I don't think he knew, as yet, what it was. After all, he had just come from another country, with another intellectual tradition.

He gave the quickest answer, then cut things off. Indeed, I've often wondered if he ever did learn what had created the atmosphere of all-but-suppressed rage there in Columbia University's Philosophy Hall that night. I hope so.

Perhaps there was a valid social argument somewhere in his talk. But that night it was lost under his strategically disastrous choice of metaphor: Try to imagine a group of anti-Nazis in Germany, right before the war, many of them working to save Jews from the growing tide of anti-Semitism, who'd invited a speaker to address them. Now, imagine that speaker starting his talk by declaring (without a jot of irony): "Let's face it. We're all nothing but Jews; we all suffer from the Jewish outlook on life. As such, we deserve what we get." Really, it was *that* appalling.

A few years later, an editor of *S-F Studies* was very excited when he elicited a brief piece on science fiction from Baudrillard. An entire section of the journal was given over to it, with several respondents. But the piece itself turned out to be all too clearly by someone who hadn't read any science fiction since 1975—if not 1955. Certainly none of the ideas about it were either new or interesting.

Again, in that issue, you can read the respondents, in their own pieces, struggling to maintain even ordinary academic politeness and not just go, "Duh . . . ?"

Fredric Jameson reads science fiction and occasionally has things of interest to say about it. Terry Eagleton doesn't, and has the good sense to remain silent on the topic. Baudrillard could have written a piece, of course, in which he presented himself as someone who did not know the genre's recent production and thus talked, rather, of what the genre looked like specifically from the outside *to* such a reader as himself. That might have prompted an interesting discussion. But to offer up your own ignorances as exemplary of the general public's takes some intellectual daring—and "daring" is *not* how I would characterize Baudrillard's self presentation, so far as I've seen it.

If only for things like that, Baudrillard has never been for me a particular exemplar of postmodernism. Which is to say, he never struck me as up-to-date enough or "with it" enough to be any sort of postmodern icon. If he had been, he could never have delivered that talk.

A problem built into the academic star system is the laziness that it encourages, not in the star him- or herself, but in the administrative level that invites and presents him or her. Instead of organizers doing the work needed to familiarize themselves with the person's work and presenting him or her with questions and topics that might currently be of interest to the person, the organizers either invite the "star" to talk about whatever he or she wants—which is silly, if it's a conference that has a theme and a topic. Or they assign a topic about which the person knows nothing—or has only the most general awareness of—and then say, "But we want to know what *you* have to say about it." When coupled with a few thousand dollars' of honorarium, that's a hard one to turn down.

One way the first generation of French theorists managed to maintain their reputations was by rigorously refusing to speak about topics they knew nothing about. Since they were awesomely informed men and women, they had an impressive range of material about which they *could* speak.

It's something of an *ad hominem* argument, I know. Nevertheless, that's been my experience. *Forget Foucault* (1977/Tr. '87) always seemed to me basically a silly and exploitative book—that only has any value at all when you realize no one *is* going to take its main tenets seriously; Paglia sees Foucault self-destructing from the pressure of the outside; Baudrillard sees it self-destructing from what he takes to be internal contradictions. But both miss the mark wildly. *Simulations* (1983) and *The Ecstasy of Communication* (1988) are interesting now and again—but nowhere near as interesting as Spivak, Ronell, Lentricchia, Haraway, or Robert

Reid-Pharr—not to mention Fredric Jameson, Ernesto Le Clau, John Davidson, or Pierre Bourdieu.

As for postmodernism, I've been too close to it to offer any objective overview. When Ihab Hasaan coined the term in the early sixties, it was a much-needed period designation that simply referred to literary works published after 1960. It separated the enterprises of John Barth, Thomas Pynchon, Donald Barthelme, and Robert Coover from those of Joyce, Woolf, D. H. Lawrence, Steinbeck, and Faulkner.

Fredric Jameson's useful and powerful analysis of what was going on in the greater society (in *Postmodernism: or, The Cultural Logic of Late Capitalism* [1991]), from architecture, to the stuff on the museum walls, to his hard look at global capitalism, presupposed that a certain order of academic Marxist analysis could provide a ground and methodology from which the greater society (that Jameson designated postmodern) might be critiqued. (The elements he located in what is traditionally thought of as cultural production [i.e., art and literature], such as its recent reliance on pastiche, were wonderfully clarifying: the New Forty-Second Street in New York City really is *the* example of postmodern architecture.) But today I have friends outside the academy for whom in general the term "postmodern" means what is going on *inside* the academy—and specifically what goes on in terms of just that sort of critical theory. Because they don't understand it, they're rather unhappy with it, too: the "science wars" of a few years back and the know-nothing attacks it brought forth on "theory," which those attacks equated with "postmodernism," were an example.

The result—for me at any rate—is that "postmodernism" is a term I simply don't get much use from. It means too many things; and too many of those things that are dead on at loggerheads. Therefore I manage to do most of my thinking these days—and pretty much all my writing—without it. So far I haven't missed it.

2. Post/Marxist

... an awareness of that importance [the relativity of infrastructure and superstructure] makes me a marxian, rather than a Marxist.
                            Delany, Samuel R. *Time Square Red, Times Square Blue* (1999), p. 163

... I believe the real is synonymous with the political. That is, it's what you have to deal with, one way or the other.
                            Delany, Samuel R. *Silent Interviews: On Language, Race,*
                            Sex, Science Fiction, and Some Comics (1994), p. 163

All political action within a given political system perpetuates that system if only because that system has defined which actions are and which actions are not political.

Delany, Samuel R. *Heavenly Breakfast: An Essay on the Winter of Love* (1979), p. 34

Matrix: How would you describe your political position(s), and how do they relate strategically to your work as a writer, critic and academic?

SRD: Certainly *not* "post-Marxist." Regardless of what it says up there, I'm just a boring old Marxist. In some academic situations, occasionally it's worth making the distinction between Marxist and marxian: Marx made a number of predictions that simply didn't come true—nor are they going to come true any time soon. The state has *not* withered away. And—thank God!—there has been no dictatorship of the proletariat, as of yet. (I'm being somewhat disingenuous, of course. The megalithic republics of the current day seem to resist [some aspects of] the single-class "dictatorships" that Marx envisioned for the nineteenth-century style nation.) A current of what Karl Popper called "historicism" flows through orthodox Marxism, leaving its predictive abilities seriously compromised: Now and again Marx fell into a set of rhetorical tropes that promoted a belief that history can be treated as a hard-edged and predictive science. Sometimes, in Marx's writings, these predictions (like many of Freud's speculations) are simply a kind of metaphoric decoration. At other times, however, they control, as it were, from the wrong end, entire arguments, which have to be rethought. Those folks who acknowledge the problems (or "poverty," to use Popper's appropriation of Marx's term from *The Poverty of Philosophy* [1847]) of historicism in Marx, even while they still believe that the economic register is privileged and are comfortable with such basic tenets of Marxism as "The means of production influence the ethical, cultural, and social life of society," or the rule of thumb you can derive from it, "Infrastructure tends to determine superstructure—and *not* the other way around," without necessarily buying into Marx's predictions as to how the world was supposed to develop, can be called marxians. For most purposes today, though, that's a fine distinction, which, unless you're in the midst of a gathering of Marxist scholars discussing the history of Marxist critique *per se*, is not really needed.

A few folks will argue that Marx's predictions *did* come true, only in wildly distorted form: that, with consumer society, we *do* have a dictatorship of the proletariat (only the proletariat doesn't run it), and that states have withered to the point where they are simply individual big businesses among the many other big businesses making up the global economy. Well, if that's the way you want to look at it, I can only say that that *isn't* what Marx meant by "withering."

How does my Marxism relate to my writing? As a fiction writer, I still want to know how my characters (and the characters in the stories my students write) support themselves—how they make their money, and how that situation is related to their various anxieties and, in general, the little twitches that characterize the human subject—what our marvelous story teller Grace Paley called the *Little Disturbances of Man* (1973).

Few of those disturbances fail to return us to those earlier turbulences in Marx's privileged economic register—and the realization of which created not only Marxism but practically the entire nineteenth-century novel.

3. Auto/Biography

I usually tell people that I live in a world where Samuel R. Delany-the-writer doesn't exist. I've never really read anything he's written. I know a lot about him. I've even looked over his shoulder while he was working.

Delany, *Shorter Views*. p. 337

"Well," she said, "you've left out an awful lot about yourself."
The others laughed. They all agreed there.

Delany, *Heavenly Breakfast*. p. 116

But what would the ideal biography be?

Delany, Samuel R. *Longer Views: Extended Essays* (1996), p. 147

Matrix: How might a (unauthorized?) biography of Samuel R. Delany differ from your autobiographical memoirs, anecdotes, and examples? What remains in excess, or unsaid, or uncontrolled?
SRD: It fascinates me how many commentators on my essay about urban communes in the 'sixties, *Heavenly Breakfast*, have homed in on that particular exchange—as you have, above:

"Well," she said, "you've left out an awful lot about yourself."

—as though it hinted at possible revelations of great mystery.

I wouldn't focus on it this way if you weren't about the sixth person to have brought it up: At the time, it referred only to the fact that I hadn't mentioned in the book that I happened to be an award-winning science fiction writer while I was living with the Breakfast.

I didn't mention it for the same reason I didn't mention that I worked as a library page when I was fifteen, or that I wear briefs and not boxer shorts. It wasn't relevant.

It indicates no cache of sexual, experiential, or philosophical subjectivity or objectivity, however, that, once declared, will open up and wholly recolor the enterprise's meaning or truth value, start to finish.

I was twenty-five, and awards or no, writing wasn't (in Marxist terms) making me any money. I had all but given it up during that period for music. Thus I felt mentioning it in a book on communes would only have confused things.

Now, the fact was, to people outside the Breakfast who found the place interesting enough to talk about or to visit or to ask questions about, at least one thing that, yes, made it interesting was, "that young writer who wrote the novel that won that award lives there, too." But *Heavenly Breakfast* (the book) is not *about* me—nor is it about the "rep" our commune had outside the walls of the apartment where it was located. It's about the communal living process *per se.* As such, a mention of science fiction in the book, not to mention my place in the S-F field, would have been distracting and confusing.

There's no mention of SF or Nebula Awards (all "Lee" meant when she made the comment and all I meant when I recorded it) in *Heavenly Breakfast* for the same reason there's no mention of them in *Times Square Red, Times Square Blue.* That's not the topic of the books. To drag them in would have been unnecessarily muddling.

Now, what would an ideal unauthorized biography of "Delany" be like? A good one might correct a few odd dates I've managed to get wrong. It would probably give facts and figures when it tried to untangle my IRS problems.

A bad one, alas, through the writer's not having enough information as well as his or her simple love of scandal, would feel free to lie and distort and tell simple, exciting stories in place of the complex and duller ones that actually obtain.

The truth is, I've already written the most accurate *unauthorized* autobiography that I could: *The Motion of Light in Water*—and it won me a Hugo. An *authorized* biography—could there be such a thing—might be even more interesting and informative: one in which other people were consulted to find out what they thought was going on at the time. *I* might even learn something from that one . . .

were anyone interested in undertaking the grueling amount of research it would require to write it.

4. Over/Interpretation

Justice is a more complicated phenomenon than critique. . . . In the criticism of fiction we are, of course, fairly used to "exotic," if not off-the-wall interpretations.

Delany, Silent Interviews. p. 272–73

To say that interpretation (as the basic feature of semiosis) is potentially unlimited does not mean that interpretation has no object and that it "riverruns" merely for its own sake. To say that a text has potentially no end does not mean every act of interpretation can have a happy ending.

Eco, Umberto. Interpretation and Overinterpretation (1992), p. 24

Matrix: Does interpretation have limits? If so, how do you know when those limits have been crossed? For instance, when you critically engage a text, such as Hart Crane's poem, "The Bridge" (as in *Longer Views*), what guides your sense of being on or off track (or the wall)?

SRD: Well, a great deal of criticism is simply "intuition." Or, at least, that's where it begins.

What *do* we know about Crane and his poetic sequence *The Bridge*—to take an example where a certain amount *is* known, but where a certain number of gaps have to be filled in by logic?

Well, Crane began the sequence not terribly long after he read *The Waste Land* in the November *Dial* for 1922. (Letters and documents let us know he started it within weeks.) He began by drafting the poem—"Atlantis"—he would eventually place at the end of his series, although, for the first few years he worked on the sequence, he called that final poem "Finale." Five years later, in 1927, when Crane was twenty-eight, a couple of changes occurred in the poem. The text of "Finale," which had been already rewritten several times, suddenly got a new title: Instead of "Finale," it became "Atlantis." As well, Crane changed the title of the initial poem in the sequence, "Dedication to Brooklyn Bridge" to "Proem: To Brooklyn Bridge."

Now, the "Atlantis" title is particularly odd, because the poem itself is not about a city, sunken or otherwise. Despite the various revisions, it's still very much a poem about being on the Brooklyn Bridge itself, one night, while the bridge is flooded with moonlight. The poem contains no image of the city as seen from the bridge, which would justify the naming (or the renaming) of the poem after the mythical sunken island-city described by Plato in the *Timaeus* and the *Critias*. We have some record of Crane's reading during those months, and there's an Emerson essay that he very likely read sometime over those months which refers to the poet building "a bridge to the Atlantis," where Atlantis is a stand-in for a kind of Heavenly City or Utopia. Often it's assumed that this passage may have influenced him to change the title.

But what about "Proem"? The word's in the dictionary, certainly—it's an archaic term for an introductory poem. But did Crane just find it there? Usually Crane got his odd words (like "leeward," "spoom," "kelson," and "spindrift," which all came—directly or indirectly—from Melville) from other writers. (He picked up the oddly spelled "wrapt" from the late New York City poet Samuel Greenberg.)

Now, there's an extraordinary Victorian warhorse of a poem entitled *The City of Dreadful Night*, first published in 1874, by an eccentric Victorian poet and political journalist, James Thomson, who used to write under the pseudonym "B.V." (which stood for "Bysshe Vanolis," his first name borrowed from Percy Bysshe Shelley—day-to-day, all Shelley's friends called him Bysshe—and the second of which was an anagram of the eighteenth-century early romantic German poet Novalis). When it was first published, *The City of Dreadful Night* had a lot of fans, including George Eliot and the Rossetti brothers, the poet Dante and the critic Michael. (I don't know how Christina responded to it. Indeed, I'd love to learn.)

A young man of nineteen named Bertram Dobell befriended Thomson on publication of the poem, and fifteen years later, after Thomson's death, published a two-volume complete poems of his friend. As well, he spearheaded a campaign to move Thomson into the canon. But, one, Thomson was an alcoholic, possibly gay, an atheist, and also a flaming radical in his politics—all of which helped to keep him out of the center of the canon. Also, when all is said and done, most of Thomson's poems just don't quite have it. Save for two or three sections which are surrealistically vivid, the major interest, even in *The City of Dreadful Night*, is didactic. Thomson came from a tradition that, despite a few inspired moments (such as the *City*'s section IV, "As I came through the desert, thus it was, / As I came through the desert . . ."), sees poetry as prose put into meter and rhyme.

Having said all this, *The City of Dreadful Night* still holds some interest for a modern (and, indeed, postmodern) reader. What's more, the introductory poem in the sequence *is* entitled "Proem." If you're going to come across a writer using the term "Proem," Thomson is about the only one a relatively wide-ranging poetry reader is likely to run into—and this has been the case for pretty much most of the last century. So, it seems, that Thomson would have been the likely place for Crane to encounter the word.

When I started researching Thomson, I discovered that, much earlier, when he was twenty-three, Thomson had written another poem, with much the same feel to it, called *The Doom of a City*—a kind of twenty-eight-page dry run for *The City of Dreadful Night*. *The Doom of a City* is basically a retelling of the Atlantis story; what's more, the first encounter with the city, before it falls into the sea, is drenched in moonlight, with all the inhabitants turned into marble statues.

The relationship between *The Bridge* and *The Waste Land* we've already noted. But another creeping suspicion that has always haunted me, since I first read *The City of Dreadful Night* when I was twenty-three or twenty-four, is that *The Waste Land* itself was, in some way, an attempt to write—or rewrite—a poem of the same sort as Thomson's. Both are poetic sequences composed of shorter poems. Each shorter poem is an all but stand-alone work; yet they are thematically imbricated. Both are essentially city works, dealing with the modern predicament in its urban manifestations.

Well, that's where I was when I wrote my critical essay "Atlantis Rose . . ." But the autumn after I had first finished it, I found myself looking through the stacks of the library of the University of Minnesota, where I found a two-hundred-fifty-page edition of Thomson's selected poems, put out in the States by Henry Holt in . . . 1927! What's more, the editor's (Gordon Hall Girauld) introduction goes out of its way to rescue *The Doom of a City* from the section of juvenilia that Dobell had consigned it to, and claims that it is a work of genius. Further, that collected volume contains *three* poems by Thomson entitled "Proem," one of which introduces *The City of Dreadful Night* and two more of which Thomson wrote to introduce his own volumes—one of which editor Girauld placed at the head of his collection. During most of that year, Crane was living in Paterson, New York, but made frequent trips to New York City—specifically to buy books. (A book he read that year which we *know* had an influence on the subsequent development and revision of *The Bridge* was Spengler's *Decline of the West* [1922].) This means, in the year that Crane made those changes in *his* poem, a volume of Thomson hit literarily inclined bookstores and would have been readily available, highlighting precisely the poems involved. Just to add some icing to the cake, in Christopher Ricks's *Inventions of the March Hare* (a collection of Eliot's marginal writings: 1996) I found a passage from T. S. Eliot admitting to *his* adolescent fascination with Thomson's *City of Dreadful Night*, in which he claims that he "owes something" to Thomson (as well as John Davidson's "Thirty Bob a Week"). But just what, he says, he's not prepared to say.

Well, however reticent Eliot wanted to be about that influence, I think it's fairly obvious. To Davidson he owed all those little working-class vignettes, such as "when Lil's husband got demobbed" and "the typist home at tea-time" that pepper *The Waste Land* (vignettes that, before Pound's cutting, made up more than half the earlier version of the poem, "He Do the Police in Different Voices") and to Thomson he owed the whole idea of a highly intellectual, urban poetic sequence, observing moments of urban *civitas*—the spiritual problems of the city-bred/civilized sensibility: If anything, Eliot's proposed spiritual position is far less radical than Thomson's. Indeed, Eliot's suggests a rather adolescent reading of *The City of Dreadful Night*, by, indeed, a young man far more impressed with the form than with Thomson's content.

Anyway, we can see that what began as an off-the-wall hunch *now* has the heft of some historical evidence to support it.

Another critical contention of mine is that Crane's last poem, "The Broken Tower," has its textual origins in Lionel Johnson's sonnet "The Age of Dreams," a poem which describes in detail a broken bell tower and in which the phrase "the broken tower" appears. First, we know that from the time he was fifteen, Crane owned a volume of Johnson that he treasured and had read and reread since adolescence. Certainly it was the 1916 *Selected Poems* of Johnson, with the laudatory introductory essay by Ezra Pound—which, indeed, contains the poem in question. Second, "The Age of Dreams" is one of a pair of sonnets regularly anthologized throughout the teens and twenties, so that there is almost no way a conscientious poet of that time could *not* have encountered them.

Today Ernest Dowson and Lionel Piggot Johnson are by far the two best-known poets from a group that also included William Sharp, John Davidson, and John Arthur Symons, which, during the 1890s, called itself the Rhymers' Club (the L=A=N=G=U=A=G=E Poets of the 1890s). Dowson—the most tortured and (arguably) the most talented—is the only one read at all today. (The title of Margaret Mitchell's novel *Gone With the Wind* comes from Dowson's best known poem, *"Non Sum Qualis Eram Bonae Sub Regno Cynarae,"* whose title in turn comes from Horace's fourth ode.)

Still, the point is that all historical criticism starts as some sort of intuition such as mine, more or less "off the wall." But further reading, along with historical and/or biographical research, either does or does not provide supporting evidence. (No, we don't know for *sure* if Thomson figures in the story of Crane and Eliot in the way I have speculated. But now such speculation is at least a reasonable theory.) This is the way a more or less ungrounded "off the wall" hypothesis becomes a more or less supported theory—or, often, it doesn't.

5. Anti/Porn

> *Hogg* is a work of pornography—that is, it was pornographic for the writer at the time of writing.
>
> Delany, Samuel R., "The Scorpion Garden" in
> *The Straits of Messina* (1989), p. 1

> While the author's disclaimer that *Hogg* is not pornography *for* heterosexual women, *for* heterosexual men, *for* male homosexuals, or *for* Lesbians is accurate (But, if it isn't, who *is* it for? Another reason to call it "anti-pornography") . . .
>
> K. Leslie Steiner, " 'The Scorpion Garden' Revisited: A Note on the Anti-Pornography of Samuel R. Delany" in *The Straits of Messina* (1989), p. 31

> . . . we can probably describe pornography as those texts which arouse, either by auctorial intention or by accident—if not those texts which can be assumed to be arousing, either to the reader currently talking about them, or to someone else . . .
>
> Delany, *Shorter Views. p.* 292–93

Matrix: What guides (legitimates?) our assumption that another (ideal?) reader would find a particular text arousing if we ourselves do not? Couldn't all sorts of texts be assumed to be pornography for *someone*? Are other genres to be described in terms of a physical response they are assumed to evoke in the reader?
SRD: What guides our assumption that another reader will find a particular text arousing? Only some hopelessly misguided notion of an "average" sexuality—a notion that, just stating it, I would hope, reveals its poverty, banality, and inadequacy.

In a better world, we'd all be far less shockable—and far less concerned with the deleterious effects of someone else becoming accidentally sexual aroused.

Now, you're right. People can sexualize anything. I knew a perfectly straight man who explained to me that the women in his masturbation fantasies all wore eyeglasses. The first women he'd had crushes on as a child had all been teachers or librarians—thus women who did not wear glasses just were not, as far as he was concerned, the proper sex. I've known another man whose sexual interest was pretty much limited to other men's shoes—specifically their sneakers and running shoes. Leather shoes were not particularly of any interest to him. And still another man of my acquaintance, back in San Francisco, was turned on largely by beautifully colored fabric. The age and physicality of the person wearing the cloth was quite secondary.

I've written before about my own sexual make up. By the time I was five, six, seven, I realized I was extremely attracted to men with large hands who bit their nails badly. It's a highly gendered preference. Women who bite their nails do nothing for me. (Often I've wished they did. On several occasions it would have made my sexual life much easier.) I never bit my own nails. Neither did my father—though he had slightly clubbed fingers, which may or may not have had something to do with my own development:

For me personally, one of the most extraordinary few minutes of my life was some thirteen or fourteen years ago, when I got on the 104 bus coming north up Eighth Avenue and happened to see a big, strapping fellow, in his forties, who had extraordinarily large hands, and—indeed—had the same sort of enlarged fingers and finger nails as my father had; but, unlike my father, this guy *was* an inveterate nail biter. Really, it was downright galvanizing. He was talking to a woman friend, and I learned his name was John—I doubt I shall ever forget it. (When I got off the bus, I was literally dizzy.) Now my best friends in elementary school were the boys who were the class nail biters. But were they the cause of this overtly sexual obsession? Or did the obsession make me pick them out to be friends? At this point I couldn't tell you.

I enjoy—and indeed seek out—the sort of sex that many gay men enjoy.

But, as I said, this particular "perversion," if that's what you want to call it, was certainly fixed—hard wired, if you will—into me by the time I was seven. By the time I was eleven, I knew it was sexual. My tastes in pornography are overwhelmingly for the written sort. Rarely do pictures, films, or videos get more than a single going over from me, while a written account of sex between the proper men—even if hands are never mentioned—I can come back to again and again.

The exception to this is photographs of the hands of men who do bite their nails.

Odd, isn't it?

Though I have found ways to satisfy myself, I've never physically attacked another man—I'm not a "hand rapist." Still, I know all the movie stars and entertainers who bite their fingernails. (Ben Affleck, Guy Pearce, Andy Gibbs, the late Brad Davis . . .) With my life-partner and mate of the last thirteen years, often we will sleep holding hands; and I must tell you, it gives me a positive joy I can only call luminous and an active contentment that, bluntly, most people will never know.

That sort of complexity of response, I suspect, underlies the sexuality of most people—women and men. That is the complexity level on which sexuality needs to be envisioned and analyzed.

Now, *you* tell me?

How should society deal with *my* particular perversion?

What laws does it have to institute to restrain me from running wildly amuck? What curbs must it put on my behavior to protect children, parents, the social contract itself from unraveling under the assault of me and people like me? The point is, of course, I've managed it quite well, without the help of laws or what have you. It's meant from time to time I had to explain to various guys that I was different. The vast majority of those conversations have been very good things, both for me and for the person with whom I was talking. When I was thirteen or fourteen, those conversations were desperately hard for me to initiate. But by the time I was twenty-five, I realized that I just wasn't going to be able to find much contentment if I *didn't* learn how to articulate them. Not all of those conversations were happy, of course. Some of the saddest were, however, with guys who said: "Gee, I wish I had met you ten, fifteen years ago, when I was still a kid. Maybe I would have grown up feeling better about myself—what I've grown up thinking of as nothing but a deplorable habit that no one could possibly see anything positive in. But I spent so much time learning to think of my hands as ugly—sliding my fingers under my thighs when I sit on a park bench, folding my hands up in one another when I'm sitting on a subway train or a bus, so no one will see that I bite my nails, keeping my hands moving when I'm talking to people or pointing at things, for the same reason. The idea that someone finds them bearable, not to mention beautiful, by this point is just too much for me. I don't think I can deal with that."

My heart goes out to these guys, when I think of how unnecessarily they've suffered. But I've met half a dozen men—and two women—who share my perversion, which just goes to show you.

There's a much larger tradition of talking about men's sexuality than there is of talking about women's. But I don't think any of this—my personal experience as a gay man—will really mean much, outside of a kind of already-extant discourse of sympathy-for-the margins, until the variety of women's sexuality gets an equally clear and clarified examination, and establishes itself in people's minds as equally complex and gets an equally inflected hearing and nuanced understanding. That context-related interrogation—economic, social, psychological—cannot even begin until the initial myth ("women's sexuality is somehow much less intense [but nevertheless unspeakably more wild/dangerous] than male sexuality") gets wholly jettisoned from the discourse. It's simply criminal that, at this point, there is as little evidence as to whether the HIV virus can or cannot be transmitted to or from women vaginally as there was, in 1950, on the existence or lack of existence of the vaginal orgasm—though the reasons for both, fifty years apart, are much the same.

Still, it's genocidal.

Recently I wrote a letter to the Margaret Sanger Planned Parenthood Association, suggesting they do some monitored studies of HIV transmission vectors in women. They take women's sexual histories all the time. Certainly, they are the institution best set up to run such "cohort studies." If you want to write them and follow up my suggestion, please do.

6. Reading/Writing

Take the fundamental notion governing most of my SF criticism for the last fifteen years: that science fiction is—as are *all* practices of writing, as are all genres, literary and paraliterary—a way of reading.

Delany, *Silent Interviews. p. 273*

Smiling, I said: "You know, you should shelve some copies of that with science fiction."

She look up startled, frowned at me, then smiled: "Oh, no," she said. "Really, this is a very good book."

Delany, *Shorter Views. p. 208*

Matrix: When you finish reading a book such as Burroughs's *Cities of the Red Nights*, Acker's *Empire of the Senseless*, or *Infinite Jest* by David Foster Wallace, do you feel you have read a work of science fiction? Why?

SRD: No, not particularly. I feel, rather that I have read literary works of differing levels of experimentation.

Why? Because that's how those works register on a mind with my particular range of literary training.

I have no particular desire to expand the boundaries of SF or of literature . . . as long as I'm allowed to write both—and, indeed, to experiment with both. That's simply another way of saying that I don't think the *boundaries* (which, finally, are set in place by critics) are the proper concern of the writer. Jane Austen—that most formal of novelists—changed the boundaries of fiction by bringing an intense formality that had been suggested but, till she wrote her books, had never actually been achieved, into fiction for the first time. *Mansfield Park* (1814) and *Emma* (1816) are, of course, just as formally complex as *Ulysses* (1922)—indeed, careful readers intuit they are likely a good deal more complex than Joyce's account of a Dublin day in June, with its intertwining of the lives of Leopold and Stephen, Ulysses and Telemachus. But even more important, Austen's formal invention allows Joyce's to be visible, if only through the differences.

7. SF/Speculative Fiction

The editors have tried to display the finest work of new and established authors, whatever its imaginative substance, structure, or texture.

Delany, Samuel R., and Marilyn Hacker (eds.). *Quark/4:*
A Quarterly of Speculative Fiction (1971)

SF: Speculative Fabulation. A satisfactory solution at last for my abbreviation-in-search-of-an-extension?

Merril, Judith. *SF 12: New dimensions in science fiction,*
fantasy, and imaginative writing (1969), p. 11

By the end of '69, "speculative fiction" meant "any piece that is experimental *and* uses SF imagery in the course of it." . . . At about the same time, various academics began to take it up. Most of them had no idea either of its history or of its successive uses; they employed it to mean something like "high-class SF," or "SF I approve of and wish to see legitimated." . . . I simply won't use the term in that way. It's uninformed, anti-historical, and promotes only mystification—all three of which I feel are fine reasons to let this misused term die the natural death it actually came to fifteen years ago.

Delany, *Shorter Views. p.* 346–47

Matrix: Doesn't the term "speculative fiction" still contour for many readers a particular set of expectations, conventions, and interpretative codes (so that, for instance, when buying an anthology such as *POLY: New Speculative Writings* [1989], the reader isn't surprised to find Disch and Bradbury rubbing shoulders with Arp and Tzara)? Must the term be terminated?

SRD: While I'm delighted to see such juxtapositions (and think there should be many more of them), I don't think you have to come up with a new term for every resultant convocation.

Like "postmodern," "speculative fiction" is not a term I find very useful personally, at least today (for the reasons you cite in the heavily abridged passage above)—although, as your quotations above show, there *was* about a four-year period ('68 to '72), when, indeed, I used it. Signifiers slip around and over various signifieds. When that slippage gets too great, or when the word begins to cover almost diametric meanings, however, writers who aspire to a certain sort of clarity and precision often let such terms—especially if those terms are neologisms—go.

In writing manuals, this manifests itself as the often very good advice: "Avoid neologisms." And "speculative fiction" was definitely a critical neologism of my youth.

Certainly I'm not into terminating *any* term—including the "n"-word.

Sheree Thomas, who recently edited the anthology of African-American science fiction, *Dark Matter*, has revived "speculative fiction" and uses it in its specific pre-1972 meaning, the same way Marilyn Hacker and I used it in our brief-lived journal *Quark*. Thus I know what Thomas means. Whenever Thomas lectures, she tells people what she means by the term. Thus, a few informed readers will know as well.

Ms. Thomas is also a great deal younger than I am, however—and she hasn't seen the word slide off into uselessness once already, the way I have. If, under informed and intelligent use such as Thomas's, the older meaning resurfaces and remains stable, however, I shall be delighted.

8. SF/Criticism

In 1975 I gave a talk on the theme "The Embarrassments of Science Fiction," in which I developed a notion I had first advanced in 1970, in the bulletin of the Science Fiction Writers of America: that science fiction should be accounted, and can best be understood as, a branch of children's literature.

Disch, Thomas M. "Big Ideas and Dead-End Thrills"
in *The Atlantic*. Vol 269, No. 2, February 1992, p. 87

America is a nation of liars, and for that reason science fiction has a special claim to be our national literature, as the art form best adapted to telling the lies we like to hear and to pretend we believe.

Disch, Thomas M. *The Dreams Our Stuff Is Made Of:
How Science Fiction Conquered the World* (1998), p. 15

I selected the stories for *Fundamental Disch* as I would for a reader who might someday find Disch important in some of the same ways I do. . . . Three of Disch's brief non-fiction pieces make up a first appendix because it's interesting to read what writers who are important to you have written about their own writing, other people's writing, or writing in general.

> Delany, Samuel R. *"Starboard Wine: more notes on
> the language of science fiction* (1984), p. 153

Matrix: What's your take on Thomas Disch's science fiction criticism? Is his work still important to you?

SRD: Disch's work has been important to me for years; I suspect and hope that it always will be. In criticism, especially criticism of SF, largely he takes on the position of gadfly or devil's advocate. Sometimes I think this is a *bit* limiting, because it requires that the reader be familiar with the thrust of the criticism of the genre in the years before any particular piece of Disch's got written—in order to appreciate thoroughly the context that informs what he's saying. But this is also true of much of John Milton's critical prose. It's not an ignoble failing.

Faddish, flighty, and changeable critical theory has brought home to a number of writers what is, finally, a paradox: What any culture considers universal, self-evident, and subject to objective-standards-that-do-not-need-to-be-explained tends to revise itself pretty much every decade or so—at least in literary criticism. I mean, consider just how much society itself has changed. To take only the most flamboyant of examples: The tragedies, say, of critics F. O. Matthiessen at Harvard and Newton Arvin at Smith. In 1951 Matthiessen killed himself, because it was discovered he was gay. For the same reason, in '60, Arvin was shut up a mental hospital, his career in ruins, because police had raided his apartment—on a tip from a friend—and discovered that he owned some gay pornography (a cache of magazines of a sort that would be thought quite mild today). Both feared they would be jailed. This was the beginning and the end of the "Happy Days" decade of the fifties. Today my gay graduate students busy mastering "queer theory" find the inner workings of such tragedies all but incomprehensible. Matthiessen's and Arvin's stories are signs of such students' inability to conceive of the ninety-degree turn the world was to take in a decade—and the close to 180-degree turn it would have undergone in just two, on some of the most fundamental issues of how life was to be lived and pursued. Those twenty years, more over, from 1960 to 1980, were the years of Disch's—not to mention my own—maturity.

Those writers who aspire to write about the universal often find that their own critical texts, twenty or thirty years down the pike, make particularly hard reading and require the greatest amount of historical context to make those texts make sense to a modern reader. Alternatively, those writers who conscientiously wrote about this critical fad or that new critical notion took the time to explain what those new notions were and their underlying principles—because, at the time, they were writing about something new—ended up producing texts that, while today they are no less old fashioned and odd than those of more conservative writers, are nevertheless easier for a modern reader to follow if only because the underlying precepts were more clearly outlined.

In the fifties, it was self-evident that the purpose of poetry was and had been throughout eternity to provide the populace with models of heroes, which the people could then imitate . . . today a perfectly lunatic and clearly limited conceit. But unless you know this, anything but the [then] new and radical "new criticism" and/or Richards and Ogden's highly eccentric "practical criticism" written about literature is all but incomprehensible. But that's because the New Critics (and Richards and Ogden) could take far less for granted when they were setting things up for *their* readers.

Often, I suspect, Disch saw himself appealing to a higher set of literary universals—which, alas, are not so rigorously in place today as they were when he wrote *some* of his best criticism, even ten or twelve years ago.

(A piece like Edmund White's "The Gay Philosopher"—literally too radical to be published when it was first written in 1968, a year before Stonewall, and which today introduces his collection *The Burning Library* (2000)—strikes most of my gay graduate students as politically troglodytic, thanks to its reliance on the suppositions of identity politics. Yet I don't think it would be a waste for them to spend a term trying to revivify for themselves historically what made it once such a dangerous piece.)

One of Disch's best known essays, that you cite above, "The Embarrassments of Science Fiction," first appeared at a time when science fiction scholarship was first getting itself together, so to speak, and when scholarly writing about the topic had reached a density where an attitude of celebration could reasonably be taken for granted. Disch felt there were still many self-evident generic flaws that it would be fatal to lose sight of. However much I was a part of the celebration, I still feel, fundamentally, he was right.

It's all too easy, however, to read his piece today not as a necessary corrective to the late seventies' and early eighties' academic new optimism (the time it was actually written), but rather as a holdover of pre-sixties prejudices (in which case it just seems unnecessarily crabby). The fact is, Disch's criticism, not only of SF but also of drama and poetry, tends to be reactionary in the strictest—and often *most* salutary—ways. He writes with wit—and, reading him, you always learn something. Usually it comes at you from a direction you don't expect. But that means to appreciate it, you have to have a firm historical grip on what it's reacting against. That makes him, yes, a difficult critic. But the the rewards are well worth the difficulties.

In the book you cite above, the wittily titled *Dreams Our Stuff Is Made Of,* Disch does say one wholly untrue thing about me: That I do not believe that HIV is the cause of AIDS. (He claims I shared this notion with Michel Foucault.) Well, I have the science fiction writer's general faith in the scientific method, and, from the April 23, 1984, announcement of the Gallo discovery of what was then called HTLV-III on, I was fairly certain that the virus had been located. That announcement formed the climax of a novel of mine, *The Tale of Plagues and Carnivals,* which came out in '85. There was a period of a few months, where, personally, I said to friends, that it was important we be very sure. But this is *because* of my faith in scientific method; it doesn't contravene it, and certainly it's not the same thing as disbelief.

Given that blood tests for the antibodies were not available for another couple of years after the announcement, to make such a statement about Foucault is lunatic. He died from AIDS complications six weeks after the announcement was made, on June 25 of that year. While, over the last months of his illness, he wondered aloud several times to friends if he had been properly diagnosed and actually *had* AIDS, that says nothing about his belief or disbelief in a theory of causes.

Now, I would certainly not like to believe Disch himself is one of his own "licensed liars," as he calls them in his book. I have much too much respect for him. I think the problem is, rather, one of reporting, research, and possibly nuanced interpretation of what I can only assume reached him, in both cases, as gossip. There's nothing in print to substantiate such a claim about about either Foucault or me. Certainly, if, at any time he'd been writing his book, Disch had phoned me up and asked, "Do you believe HIV is the cause of AIDS?" I would have replied, "Yes. Of course I do. Moreover, I think any other belief is lunatic, such as the position Charles Ortlieb holds onto or that the current President of South Africa endorses—positions that, in a field already rife with so much fear and misinformation, even today, do a great deal of harm. They can't even be justified as promoting healthy scepticism." Could I make a stronger statement? I don't know how. But that's precisely what's wrong with Disch's reductive enthusiasm to label folks, as he does in that book, "licensed liars." It's a brush that, if you're consistent, must be applied to yourself whenever you make what I would like to assume, in his case, was an honest error.

9. Stars/Cities

> *Stars in My Pocket Like Grains of Sand* is the first in a diptych of novels. The concluding novel, *The Splendor and Misery of Bodies, of Cities*, will be published by Bantam Books in fall, 1985.
>
> Delany, Samuel R. *Stars in My Pocket Like Grains of Sand* (1984), back flap

> Throughout, certainly, the enterprise has constrained me to an acknowledgement of the splendor and misery of cities, of bodies, as assent to the vast background of negativity against which finally arises the success of *Les Fleurs du Mal.*
>
> Howard, Richard. Translator's "Foreword" to *Les Fleurs du Mal* by Charles Baudelaire (1982), p. xxi

> Four Walls Eight Windows plans a 500,000 print run of Samuel R. Delany's *The Splendor and Misery of Bodies, of Cities.*
>
> Locus Online (April Fools Day, 2000)

Matrix: What relation, if any, exists between the long-anticipated *The Splendor and Misery of Bodies, of Cities* and the Richard Howard translation of *Les Fleurs du Mal*? Does the motivation behind the novel and the selection of title still have relevance to you? Does *1984: Selected Letters* somehow respond to the non-appearance of this novel after sixteen years?

SRD: Well, I took the title from the translator's foreword to Howard's version of Baudelaire. Baudelaire was, of course, after Blake and Wordworth of the London and Paris sections of *The Prelude*, the first major poet of the city—or, perhaps one could put that more accurately: the first major poet of the *modern* city, the city conceived of as housing more people who were strangers than people who, as in small towns, largely knew who each other was, even if they didn't regularly associate with one another.

The book was conceived of as a city novel. For the bulk of it, the main characters, Rat and Marq, try to make their home in a city on the other side of the planet Velm from the one Marq was born and raised in. Then they have to journey back to Dyethshome, in an educational trip across Marq's world. In the course of it, a number of things that once looked pretty fair in volume one turn out not to be so pleasant in volume two.

Right now, I have three books—two novels and a nonfiction project—I want to finish before I get back to it. But, yes, *1984* pretty much details the forces in my life that brought the project to a halt, more than a decade-and-a-half ago now.

A Conversation with Samuel R. Delany

Jayme Lynn Blaschke/2001

From *Voices of Vision: Creators of Science Fiction and Fantasy Speak.* Nebraska: Bison Books, 2005. Reprinted with permission of Jayme Lynn Blaschke.

JLB: Like so many other authors over the last couple of decades, you have suffered through the extinction of the midlist. Now, however, it appears you're coming back in a significant way with Vintage Books' re-release of *Dhalgren.* Why now? And why *Dhalgren* in particular?

SRD: The factors controlling a writer's popularity are as mysterious and ultimately as unknowable as the number of stars in the sky or (to quote Sir Thomas Browne) the name that Achilles used when he hid himself among the women.

But, as Browne also suggested, even such unknowable questions are not beyond all speculation. When a significant number of reasonable answers have been marshaled, however (the topics of the books still, to certain readers, seem of interest; still others may remember the writing as having a vitality they liked; the book was commercially successful twenty-five years ago; and Vintage's marketing department feels they may be able to reduplicate that), the greatest and the most humbling one remains: I've been lucky.

JLB: When it was first released in January 1975, *Dhalgren* caused quite a stir with its racial and sexual content. Stylistically, it was daring as well, and today is among a handful of works considered "landmarks." Does the book hold up today? Has it aged well?

SRD: I'm the last one who would be able to answer that, of course. You'll have to ask a reader far less involved with the book than I am.

JLB: After *Dhalgren,* a large portion of your back catalogue is scheduled for reissue as well—*Babel-17, Empire Star, Nova,* and *Driftglass.* How involved have you been in the reissue process?

SRD: No more, I'd guess, than any other writer having a book reissued. I've suggested what editions Vintage should use to set from, given them lists of typographical errors to correct that, over the years, various readers have brought to my attention. Like many writers, I keep files of old reviews and articles that have appeared—and I gather Vintage's publicity folk have found some of that documentation helpful.

I don't believe, however, I've been any more involved in the process than any other writer having a book reissued by a major publisher.

JLB: Midlist problems aside, how is it possible for a writer as influential as yourself with as many critically acclaimed books as you've produced, to fall so badly out of print?

SRD: Again, you'd have to ask the people who worked at my previous publishers. Sometime in 1987, Bantam Books—then my major publisher—started putting my books out of print, basically one every two weeks. That term I was a Senior Fellow at the Society for the Humanities at Cornell University's Andrew D. White House. Every couple of weeks I'd get a call at my office: "Just wanted to let you know, we're putting *The Fall of the Towers* out of print. Sales just don't warrant keeping it alive . . . Hey, we just called to let you know that, because of sales figures, we're putting *Nova* out of print . . ." And I'd say, "Um . . . Uh . . . yeah. Okay . . ."

Over a few months, my baker's dozen Bantam titles, some of which had been in print for as long as ten, fifteen, even twenty years, disappeared from the shelves. At the time, I thought: Well, my hour in the public eye is over. It's happened to writers before. It'll happen to writers again.

I did think it was strange how the sales of title after title had fallen off like clockwork. Later, of course, I learned that, under all sorts of economic pressure—from rising paper costs to new tax laws to the myriad mergers that transformed the publishing industry over that decade from some eighty or so competing businesses to five corporate monoliths—Bantam had instituted a new policy, where everything from publishing slots to advertising budgets to catalogue space was being taken away from midlist writers like me and given to far fewer projects with a shot at becoming low-literary-quality bestsellers, along with a few slots reserved for brand new writers, who were to be given—exactly—three chances each to make it as a bestseller. They were paid low advances, though often a fair amount of promotion went with their books.

If, however, after three tries, these new writers didn't produce something that could be fed into the bestseller machinery, they were dumped—and were often very surprised (and unhappy) men and women: Up till then they'd assumed that, as writers, they'd had a supportive publisher behind them. Nobody ever told them they had only three chances. Presumably they'd look around and figure it out for themselves. Some—the John Sauls, the Dean Koontzes, the Clive Barkers—actually did, and made the transition. A lot, however, didn't.

You say "midlist problems aside," but that's what the problems were. Nor was I the only victim. Not just from science fiction and mysteries, but dozens of writers fell out of the mainstream as well. Science fiction—however—has a particularly vociferous and relatively organized fandom, so that calls for reissues and attempts to throw some attention back on worthy writers from the past can come with a bit more force—another way of saying I've been lucky.

JLB: Are you now coming back into favor?
SRD: You make it sound as if I'd been dismissed from the palace in disgrace for a tasteless joke I'd let slip about a powerful courtier; then, because she missed my quips and dinner table repartee, only now has the Empress passed on an approving nod at a mention of my name that's allowed me to return.

Would that it were like that!

Of course I'd like to think a few people remembered the reading experience my work represented for them, readers who felt that experience was worth making available again to others. Probably, though, that's too utopian. More likely someone I've never met and whose name I'll never know decided that there was money to be made—either from nostalgia or whatever. Thus the decision to bring Delany back into print.

JLB: So are you now getting the credit due to you?
SRD: But what credit is due anyone? The only sane thing any writer can say to such questions Thomas Mann said, many years ago: "As to the worth of my own work, I cannot know, and you cannot tell me."

A half dozen years after *Dhalgren* appeared, someone sent me a recently written grammar book, for people learning English, in which—among the various examples of American writing scattered throughout—two or three paragraphs of *Dhalgren* were quoted as an example of economical and informative prose. The writer talked a bit about the structure of the sentences, made one or two points about their arrangement and internal form. At the time, I remember, I was overwhelmed.

Works by many classical poets and writers have survived from Greece and Rome—in fragmentary form—because some grammarian used a quotation from the work as a particularly effective example of one grammatical figure or rhetorical trope. The 124-odd fragments surviving from the pre-Socratic philosopher

Heraclitus come to us pretty much this way. So does most of what survives of Sappho and the even more fragmentary work of Achilocus.

After that book showed up in my mailbox, I recall thinking: There's nothing more a writer can ask. That someone might choose a sentence or six of mine to teach others how to read, write, and think in this extraordinary language, American English—well, when set beside questions of "attention due," I feel that honor simply dissolves those questions.

JLB: With so many reissues coming up, what original projects do you have in the works?

SRD: A lot of my energies of late have gone into nonfiction: *Times Square Red, Times Square Blue*, the essays in *Longer Views* and *Shorter Views*. At this point, I've always got two or three nonfiction projects going. They relax me and allow me to get away from the toils of teaching, the worry of workshops, and the general *agita* of academic administration.

Fiction—at least for me—requires long, relatively uninterrupted time stretches in which to bring it to fruition. I've never been a two-hour-in-the-morning writer, who could put in another six hours on Sunday afternoon. For me, a novel requires weeks of living in a largely mental and wholly internal landscape. Everything else has to be relegated to the odd hour here, the bit of time there. Sadly, however, uninterrupted time blocks are not what life doles out today to any of us with regularity.

JLB: Have you made any progress on the long-awaited follow-up to *Stars in My Pocket Like Grains of Sand*?

SRD: I have real hopes of getting back to it someday—though, no, currently it's not on the front burner.

JLB: You first made a name for yourself in the sixties, when science fiction was in the midst of the "New Wave" renaissance. Has the genre fulfilled the promise and potential of that era?

SRD: In the arts, people are always waiting for someone or some movement to "fulfill her/its/his promise." Then, half-a-dozen or a dozen years on, others begin to realize that, really, something extraordinary was actually happening: That's what all the talk of promise was about.

From the teens and twenties, there's a whole sub-genre of embarrassing reviews, which explain, in effect, that poets like T. S. Eliot, Ezra Pound, William Carlos Williams, H.D., Hart Crane, or Wallace Stevens really do have quite a bit of talent. As soon as they learn how to write "real poetry" and stop all their experimenting, they just might fulfill their promise and produce something worthwhile . . .

The New Wave had some extraordinary writers: Disch, Zoline, Ballard. And, yes, they wrote what they wrote back then. Well, *Camp Concentration*, *334*, *On Wings of Song*, *Neighboring Lives* (this last, Disch's collaboration with Charles Naylor) . . . these were—and remain—extraordinary. I'm hoping soon people will begin to rediscover the range of Joanna Russ's work—and the work of the late Roger Zelazny, through *Bridge of Ashes* and *Doorways in the Sand*, before he became trapped in the downward commercial spiral of his Amber series.

JLB: Currently, what writers impress you?

SRD: What writers do I like? Richard Powers, certainly. Guy Davenport, and William Gass, surely. In science fiction, Lucius Shepherd, Bill Gibson, Karen Joy Fowler. Ethan Canin (to return to the mainstream)—though I'm not sure what happened to his control of the sentence in his most recent novel *For Kings and Planets*—is a spectacular writer. I like the work of Robert Glück and Edmund White—as well as David Markson of *Reader's Block*.

JLB: Several years back, on an episode of *Deep Space Nine*, Avery Brooks portrayed a black science fiction author for a Campbell-esque magazine in the fifties, whose race was concealed from the readers. The episode has distinct Delany overtones, although the circumstances of this character appeared quite different from yours.

SRD: I never saw it—though people have been mentioning it to me on and off for years. Once, even before that, I got a call from an old high school friend of mine, whom we used to call Chuck. He was at a sports event out in Seattle, I believe, and calling on a cell phone—before everybody and his brother had one. "Just a second," he told me, "I want you to say hello to someone." Sitting next to him, apparently, was Brooks—who, I learned, to my surprise, was something of a Delany fan. Chuck and he had ended up on the same national committee to promote libraries—and, at one of their Seattle conferences, had all gone to a baseball game together. My name had come up, so Chuck had decided to give me a call and introduce us. A few years later in 1998, at a publication party for Octavia Butler, I actually met Brooks—and we had our mutual friend to gossip about for a while. Brooks is a very pleasant, if somewhat shy, man. Since that time, I've managed to catch half a dozen of his *Deep Space Nine* episodes in rerun. He's an impressive actor.

But, no, I've missed the one you mentioned.

Certainly, though, the situation of that character was different from mine!

My race was never concealed. From 1968 on, I was pretty much "the black gay SF writer."

JLB: You've quoted Joanna Russ before, that the science fiction clubhouse door has a sign upon it saying, "Girls stay out. Minorities stay out" as an explanation of why white males dominate the field of science fiction and fantasy. While that's changed significantly for women, three decades after you broke through the barrier, progress has been negligible for minorities. Octavia Butler and Nalo Hopkinson (both women, interestingly enough) generate a flurry of attention whenever they release a new book, but after them . . . Is that sign still up on the clubhouse door? Or is there something else at play?

SRD: Things, when they get better, often get better in spurts—and get better for different subgroups at different times. Because we're going through a period of social solidarity among women, and black women especially, there's been a much-needed surge of improvement in the visibility of black women writers that's even reached into the science fiction precincts. Octavia Butler was my student at Clarion back in the late sixties. Nalo Hopkinson was my student at Clarion only a handful of years back. I had the honor of recommending Hopkinson's first published story to editor Ellen Datlow—something I can be proud of for the rest of my life. But I hope things will get even better—as they need to, for women black and white; and for black men; and for Asians; and for the range of Amerinds; and for Hispanics—writers, readers, and just plain folk.

JLB: Science fiction/fantasy generally prides itself on being broadminded and all-inclusive. Do you feel your race or sexuality hurt your success?

SRD: No. I think a much better argument might be made that both have added to what success I've had. I don't mean through any reverse prejudice (the cherished fiction of the politically conservative). But both have provided me with a great number of life experiences, many of which do not often make it into fiction. While publishers are convinced fiction readers are only interested in reading about what they've read about before, the reality is, I suspect, more sanguine: People want new stories and new materials to explore and interrogate and have adventures in. The world—particularly the academic world—has been changing with a rapidity that, while astonishing, is still just slow enough to escape the eye of, say, the university student who has only been in school for four years, or even the graduate student who stays for eight or ten.

Today, there are gay studies programs in every university worth the name. Forty years ago, not only was there no such thing, there were no women's studies, no African American studies, no film studies. Moreover, if you'd proposed any such ideas, for most of them you'd have been laughed out of the department meeting, and for one or two, you could have ended up incarcerated.

In 1996, I gave a talk at a conference at Yale on postcolonialism, in which I discussed ideas and experiences I'd had that reflected on the postcolonial situation, but which had come to me largely because I was a gay man traveling about in the world.

The Egyptian novelist and psychiatrist Nadaal El Sadawi was also at the conference, and when a bunch of us went out for pizza between conference sessions, Dr. Sadawi remarked: "You know, Chip, if you had given that talk at my university in Cairo at noon the way you did here, by four o'clock you'd probably have been in jail." It was a sobering thought.

It has only been these changes in the academic culture of the United States that have, of course, allowed my personal situation to function in a positive manner.

JLB: Do you feel your writing has ever been overshadowed by your persona? Whenever your name is mentioned, it's almost always in the context of "SF's first major black writer" or "SF's first openly gay writer," or both. Do those tags unfairly, or fairly, distort the perception of your work?

SRD: Whenever a writer begins to garner a reputation, various "biographemes" (Roland Barthes' term, I believe) begin to sediment out. They're all ridiculously restrictive. But they give us something to hang the reading experience from. Robert Frost is that New England rural poet. Gertrude Stein went to France and wrote silly sentences, such as "Suppose to suppose suppose a rose is a rose is a rose is a rose." Edmund White is that radical gay novelist. Chester Himes is that black literary writer who ended up writing detective fiction. Jackson Pollock was a loud drunk who did drip paintings. What ridiculous summations for any artist's work! Nor do I think it's an accident that of the writers I've mentioned, the one who's had the greatest influence on the development of the course of American literature—Stein, without whom there would have been no Hemingway or anyone else who ever aspired to an accuracy beyond the standard sentence—gets the silliest.

Most people only know my "persona," as you call it, through my writing. I already do a fair amount of lecturing, but even there I'm reading from lectures I've written down. So I wonder, indeed, if your idea above—that my "persona" overshadows my work—isn't something of an illusion, produced by the work itself. The fact is, the fat, forgetful old man, who walks with a cane and stutters a lot when not reading from a prepared text, just isn't that interesting.

JLB: Running a search for "Samuel R. Delany" through several online booksellers turns up as many—if not more—books about you and your writings as by you. What does that say?

SRD: Alas, I've never run such a web search. I can't really comment. Having said that, I mention that, a couple of years ago, my daughter told me she was going to sweep the web for me and print out a bunch of stuff—and sent me some thirty pages of bibliographic material various people had gathered. As I recall, there was about one error every fifth entry in most of it—which seems par for the ratio of information to misinformation on the web. Still later, I stood at the shoulder of a professor in his study up at SUNY Buffalo, while he showed me this and that reference to me on the internet. I admit, I didn't think they were terribly exciting—though, somewhere up in Vermont, a fellow named Jay Schuster has put together a careful and accurate few pages on his website. Such attention is very warming. But since I simply haven't seen it all—or even most of it, if there's really as much of it out there as you suggest—I can't tell you what it says.

JLB: Since the late eighties, much of your writing has been for academia. Essays, articles, and papers are obviously a different thing to write than short fiction or novels. Do you, as a writer, find fulfillment in that form?

SRD: Yes I think the writing of other writers about writing can produce a kind of stabilization process—and, as a window into various traditions, it's helpful to other young writers. Books like Stein's *The Autobiography of Alice B. Toklas, How to Write,* and *Lectures in America* were wonderfully inspiring to me when I read them as a seventeen- and eighteen-year-old. So was Forster's *Aspects of the Novel,* as was Pound's *ABC of Reading.*

> *Stand close around, ye Stygian set*
> *With Dirce on one barque convey'd,*
> *Or Charon seeing, may forget*
> *That he is old, and she a shade.*

I memorized that Walter Savage Landor quatrain ("Dirce") out of Pound's cantankerous and contentious meditations ("In his time Samuel Johnson was the best mind in England—except for those months Voltaire was visiting London.") on what was good and what was bad poetry, back when I first read it. When I can't remember the year *Heart of Darkness* first appeared in *Blackwood's* or in which library the earlier manuscript version of *The Time Machine* is on store, that still stays.

Jorge Luis Borges's lectures from the famous Charles Eliot Norton series at Harvard for 1967, *This Craft of Verse*, form another of those extraordinary books—Borges is as humble in his suggestions about literature as Pound is arrogant and iconoclastic. Yet both are wonderful turn-ons for the young writer contemplating the range of enterprises that (as they might say in current critical jargon) constitute the literary.

JLB: Has your joining academia changed perceptions of your fiction? Nonfiction?
SRD: Other people's or my own? Perhaps a few people find me more of a curiosity now and so are willing to give some of my work a look. If anything, though, I find my encounter with academia only confirms me in my own sense of what literature (and literary activity) is. First of all, it's not and never has been a consensual enterprise.

Concepts of what constitute good writing form a conflictual field—highly so, and they always have. That is the only reason why, say, simplicity and clarity are just as much aesthetic virtues as ornamentation and rich ambiguity. It's also why either one, out of control, can become an aesthetic failing—dullness and banality in the one case, and overwrought clutter in the other.

JLB: Do you feel your most significant contributions to the field have/will come from a university setting, or as an author of fiction?
SRD: Writers write what the world compels them to write; and the university nudges you strongly toward writing nonfiction. Significance is not a factor in that—because it's the one thing the writer him- or herself has no access to. The eighteenth-century playwright Thomas Otway very probably died more or less sure he would go down in literary history as the greatest English playwright of all time. During his lifetime, his work was regularly compared to that of Shakespeare, and it was a critical given of the time that his play *Venice Preserved* was a better play than *Hamlet*.

Today how many people remember Otway? Or have read a line by him? If he survives at all, it's as a canonical example of just how wrong-headed an era or a local and provisional set of literary opinions can be.

JLB: As a writer, what are you capable of now that you weren't thirty years ago?
SRD: Your question puts me in mind of Goethe's quip: "A man of fifty knows no more than a man of twenty. They just know different things." Indeed, I'm far more aware of the mad things I did at twenty, things that, today, I simply wouldn't have the gall to try—I mean, even if, through whatever dumb luck, I came close to pulling them off or a few readers were kind enough to refrain from pointing out the number of times I fell on my face.

Really, though: A writer's talk about what he or she is capable of, like a writer's talk about the worth of his or her own work, is a pretty good way for that writer to start sounding like a pompous poseur.

Above all things, the story, the poem, the text is—and is only—what its words make happen in the reader's mind. And all readers are not the same.

Any reader has the right to say of any text: "But I didn't think it was that good."

Only this morning, I talked to one of my graduate writing students, whom I'd suggested read Flaubert's *Un coeur simple*—one of the greatest pieces of French prose by one of the giants of early modernism. It's a tale that, the first time I read it, struck up tears in my eyes; as well, I felt that I had been exposed to—no, I'd been struck to the center of my writerly being with—illuminations of the structure and texture from this single woman's life in the French provinces a hundred-fifty-odd years back. It's as close as work from a human hand can bring you to that imagined moment where the Judeo-Christian God pulls back His hem to reveal, beneath it, a moment of starkest suffering and the human redemption into which the heart can recreate it.

"So, what did you think?" I asked.

Frowning behind his glasses, my student told me: "It was an okay story. But there was just so much description . . ." The most carefully observed and meticulously organized account of lived provincial working-class life in any language in the world, I'm thinking: and to him, it's "so much description." While he went on to ask me: "Was all that description supposed to be symbolic or something . . . ?" It was enough to make you start quoting Heidegger on "the forgetting of Being" in our day.

But the point is, when the writer turns to address the reader, he or she must not only speak to me—naively dazzled and wholly enchanted by the complexities of the trickery, and thus all but incapable of any criticism, so that, indeed, he can claim, if he likes, priestly contact with the greater powers that, hurled at him by the muse, travel the parsecs from the Universe's furthest shoals, cleaving stars on the way, to shatter the specific moment and sizzle his brains in their pan, rattle his teeth in their sockets, make his muscles howl against his bones, and to galvanize his pen so the ink bubbles and blisters on the nib (nor would I hear her claim to such as other than a metaphor for the most profound truths of skill, craft, or mathematical and historical conjuration)—but she or he must also speak to my student, for whom it was an okay story, but with so much description.

This second—and far more important—task requires, however, some humility.

An Interview with Samuel R. Delany

Adam Roberts/2003

From *Argosy Magazine*, vol. 1.1 (January/February 2004). Reprinted by permission of Adam Roberts.

Adam Roberts: You've written in a wide range of modes: SF, general fiction, criticism amongst others. I was reading something by the philosopher Mary Midgeley that put me in mind of your writing. She talks about "the desire to have values located somewhere" and asserts: "In an age of change it becomes increasingly difficult to locate them in the past; people could no longer confidently say, 'it's good because our fathers did it.' So they began to say, 'it is good because our descendents will do it.' Hence the bizarre cult of the Future itself as a kind of mythical subsistent realm enshrining value—a cult invented by Nietzsche, filled out by Wells and the Futurists, and still very influential."

In a work like *Atlantis: Model 1924* you explore what your father did (and in other writing, both critical prose and fiction, you have examined in a more general sense, what "our fathers" did); and you have written hugely influential science fiction about what our descendants might do. One of the things that fascinates me in your writing is the multiplicity of ways you explore the relationship between values and cultures. How would you respond to Midgeley here?

Samuel R. Delany: Quoted out of context (and possibly in context as well—as I don't know the text it comes from), Midgeley's statement suggests to me a rather troubling deconstruction, one of whose sides or clines is distressingly conservative. It hinges on the second half ("located somewhere") and just how restrictively we want it to function with respect to the first half. Do we desire to have values located *somewhere* (have them fixed, unchanging, not subject to drift and reinterpretation, i.e., they are assumed to be universal, stable, unchanging) as opposed to *nowhere* (that is *nowhere in particular*, i.e., they happen to be located one place and not another, i.e., any old where: the values are provisional, situational, context dependant); or do we desire to have *values* located somewhere, as opposed to our actions and thoughts, which, as long as our values are fixed to a position—a theme, a positivity, a place—are then relatively free to circulate where they will because of some ineluctable bond between those placed values and actions and ideas in general, no matter what new realms and unknowns our ideas and actions enter?

As well, there is what I might call the "quodlibet" problem in the "somewhere" part of the statement, the problem Giorgio Agamben has brought most recently to the forefront of current intellectual thought (in *The Coming Community*, University of Minnesota Press: Minneapolis, 1993). Is that "somewhere" to be taken as somewhere in general, i.e., wherever? Or is it to be taken as somewhere in particular? That is to say, among those places rich in anchoring possibilities, in hospitality to the concept of value itself, in their ability to make values flourish, grow, and proliferate?

Finally, then, the deconstructive move: how do these multiple and contradictory—even mutually exclusive—interpretations of Midgeley's statement depend on and necessitate one another? Is that "somewhere" somewhere chosen (i.e., we choose our values through moral agency) or somewhere unchosen (i.e., history, tradition, discourse choose our values for us)?

The whole interconnected argument that seems nested *in*, that seems unpackable *from*, that seems intrinsic *to* such a statement is one I'm pretty distrustful of—since it seems to me to contravene a situation that someone of my leaning is likely to take as self-evident.

I assume that we all have values, including—say—the guys who tortured gay student Matthew Shepard to death on that frigid Wyoming highway, or the three fellows (two of whom met in jail where they had been enthusiastic supporters of a group of felons, the Aryan Brotherhood) who dragged black Texan James Byrd, Jr., by a chain fastened to the back of their pickup truck, till his body pulled to pieces along Huff Creek Road outside the town of Jasper. I also assume that many of them are not very nice or profitable values for the greatest good for the greatest number (and certainly not for my personal happiness), and that a constant vigilance turned toward these values with an eye to revamping, rethinking, and revising such value systems is a Good Thing. I also think that looking for *new* places and ways where values might be grounded is also a Good Thing.

What I hear in Midgeley's statement is a laudable desire to reform values, in the sense of a *return* to something—somewhere. But, by the same token, it seems a far cry from Nietzsche's "transvaluation of all values," which might be taken as the radical version of such an enterprise and the rubric under which much modern reformation might be said to occur—that is to say, I also see a kind of abuse built into the revamping process Midgeley's statement suggests, where somehow those of us with values that we like are seen as good people and those of us who have any other sort are seen as somehow deficient in values—or seen as people who have no values at all.

This is not the way either to reform or to transvalue values in a democracy.

Indeed, if you had told Bill King, Lawrence Russell Brewer, and Shawn Berry—the three Byrd murderers—that they had to get back to basic values, doubtless they would have told you that's what they had already done, back in jail, where they had learned about the natural superiority of whites and the subhuman status of blacks, which they felt justified their post-release action.

Values have histories, even the ones we don't like. That is to say, they are lodged in discourse.

Here's a tale of values:

In 1920, when black All-American football player and Phi-Beta-Kappa scholar Paul Robeson entered Columbia University Law School, he was the first black law student at that graduate school and had to be given special clearance by the Dean to attend. Many of the faculty and most of the students were hugely indignant about the whole thing. In his class, whenever Robeson would try to speak, all the students would stamp their feet loudly, so that no one could hear him. What's more, the faculty member who led the class approved of this, and encouraged it among the students—until Robeson himself had to accost the student ringleaders of this activity outside the class and threaten physically to beat them up if they persisted. Now, this is pretty difficult for us to conceive of, today—to conceive of as something that happened eighty-three years ago, a single lifetime in the past, in liberal New York City, between the wars, within walking distance of the apartment I currently live in. To understand the indignation, however, you have to understand that the discourse still largely in place at the time said that blacks were not human beings but were rather a species of animal—specifically a species of domestic work animal, akin to sheepdogs, donkeys, and horses. You have to realize that this general consensus extended back to scientists such as the anti-Darwinian Louis Agassiz (1807–73), among the many who thought this.

A kind man, who (paradoxically) opposed slavery as cruel treatment, Agassiz died believing his greatest contribution to science was the sentence "Ontogeny recapitulates phylogeny," a phenomenon that can appear to be the case but that, finally, is as wrong on scientific grounds as his contention that blacks and white were different species, as different as cats and dogs—or his contention that the ability of blacks and whites to mate was biologically the same as the lion's ability to mate with the tiger—that, indeed, lions and tigers were, themselves, as different as cats and dogs: thus, the great chain of error.

The outrage and indignation of the law students and faculty was much the same as if, in an experiment because of recent scientific finds, the Dean of the Law School had decided to enroll a goat in the law course. The Dean had hoped for quietly amused tolerance on the part of his teachers and students—and since Robeson was a brilliant young man, who had already been valedictorian of his class at Rutgers and a notable public speaker, who had won oratory contests at his university year after year, perhaps they would be surprised by the experience and even learn something. But what the Dean got was outrage.

Now, let's leap ahead to that Jasper, Texas, murder in 1998, when King, Brewer, and Berry offered a ride in the back of their pick-up to forty-nine-year-old James Byrd, Jr., who was coming home, somewhat inebriated, from a party, then, after driving for a few minutes, stopped, got out, pulled him from the truck-bed and beat him all-but senseless, sprayed his face with black spray paint, then chained him by the ankles to their truck bumper and dragged him, still alive, down Huff Creek Road, till his nose and genitals were rubbed away and pieces of his body, including his arm and his head, came loose over two miles of highway.

A year or so after the murder had made national news, I saw an interview on Public Television with the family of one of the young murderers. It was fascinating. First of all, they were bewildered by what had happened. "My boy," said King's adoptive father, "didn't learn to hate in *this* town." Listening to their grieved bewilderment over their son's fate, as the conversation moved on to talk about the racial relations in Jasper, I realized that these people were nevertheless sunk in and deeply inhabited the same discourse that had obtained in the classrooms of Columbia University Law School in 1920. Even by their own understanding, their son and his friends had not killed a human being. His act was of the same order as that of a group of boys taking a dog and tying it to the back of a truck and dragging it to its death. All were aware that fifteen or twenty years ago, such an act would have been unlikely even to reach adjudication. It was a high-spirited unthinking thing country boys might do when they've drunk too much beer. Indeed, it must be the virulence and intensity of this particular instance that alone made it so vicious. They were trying to rearrange their minds to accept, as it were, *this* as the kernel that made it murder.

Explaining the history of a discourse does not excuse an action. Probably Byrd's murderers were particularly unaware of the discourse they inhabited as an historical construct—that is, they thought of it as self-evident common sense and ordained by God. One of them carried a lighter embossed with the KKK emblem and had a tattoo of a lynched black man on his flank in one quarter of an Aryan Brotherhood shield. Certainly the political pressure under which advancing liberalism had put them, as they perceived it, had made it imperative for them to act as they did. But I am discussing the discursive template to which the act belonged, that made it conceivable (thinkable, reasonable) for them. Still, if we—you and I—are to make any progress with sedimenting new discourses that promote new understandings of the relationship between groups of people, we will have an easier time if we approach it with a sense of the history and development of such discourses.

Values are among the most persistent parts of discourse. Now, the values here have to do with the value of human life versus the value of animal life. The fact is, I too value human life over animal life—if it comes to a choice. Thus, I suspect that's a value I share with the murderers. My conflict with them comes over where I—and people like me, who are black—get entered in the discursive matrix. Am I a human? Or am I an animal?

Less than three years after Robeson went to Columbia Law School, my Aunt Bessie entered Columbia Dental School. Whenever she handed in a paper to one of her instructors, it came back with an "F." A young white woman, who'd befriended my aunt in the class, compared her paper with my aunt's, and found that often they'd given identical answers. My aunt's had been marked wrong; the white woman's had been marked right. The young woman proposed an experiment to my aunt: For the next assignment, they would exchange papers and would hand them in with each other's names on them, then see what the results were. When the papers were returned, the paper with my aunt's name on it was failed, while the paper with the young white women's name received an "A." I grew up hearing this story, and the white dental professor was characterized simply as "a bastard." But the fact is, just as much as we have to understand what happened three years before, we have to realize that we are dealing with people who almost certainly felt it was wrong and outrageous for a black to be a doctor or a dentist—probably very much in terms of the discourse contoured by the same or similar ideas held by Agassiz. The value that my aunt and the young white women shared, however, was what might easily be called "a respect for truth." And, apparently, so did the professor: When they confronted him with what he'd done, he ceased to do it—and passed my aunt with the marks she had actually obtained. Notice though: He was not chastened or censured by the university in any way. Neither my aunt nor the young woman considered that a possibility, any more than Robeson had, three years before at the law school of the same institution. That's a sign we are *really* dealing with another discourse. In American schools today, even conservative students, who don't approve of affirmative action or who believe that the homeless are all lazy and just don't *want* to work, are often surprised—occasionally to the point of disbelief—to learn that such things were a regular part of academic life a lifetime ago—even if it was a lifetime of eighty-three years: or to learn that, here and there, parts of such discourses still persist. That's a sign of just how much discourses have changed; just as much as the Byrd and the Shepard murders are signs of how other discourses have remained stagnant in certain localities: Billy the Kid took part in over a dozen passing and sometimes playful murders of "Mexicans, niggers, 'n' injuns," whose names were never even recorded and who are not included in the famous roster of the twenty-one murders he committed before his twenty-first birthday. At the time—i.e., during the 1870s—they were not considered human beings.

In a very real sense, all values are located in the past—even those that basically say the future is valuable in itself just because it *is* the future—an idea Wells was trying to question in *The Time Machine*, published in the same year—1895— as Wilde's *Picture of Dorian Gray* was questioning the fetishization of youth (a highly related topic) from a different position. What's truly interesting, of course, is how both Wells and Wilde are as complicit in the fetishization of the decaying body *per se*, and the decaying world, and by extension the decaying body politic, as they are critical of it.

Now the problem with starting off from what the Greeks called *zoë*, or, as Agamben translates *zoë*, "bare human life," as your grounding value in a discourse, has its problems too. Very quickly we find ourselves with no way to separate it from animal life in general (that's why today zoology is zoology). Half an hour into the argument, we've all agreed to become vegans and never swat another mosquito. In taking up this argument, Badiou (in *Ethics: An Essay on the Understanding of Evil*, Verso: London, 2001) has explained that such an argument, grounded on such a value, tends to define human beings only in terms of their victimhood. As well, there are far too many discourses around that *blame* the victim for what occurs: humans eat animals because animals deserve to be eaten. The weak deserve to be beaten and eaten by the strong. That soon becomes a self-replicating process that ends with the vast majority of humans pretty much on the bottom of the heap—under a *very* few self-declared lords of the universe.

The other thing I hear in the fragment of Midgeley's text that you quote is a question about the form of our self-justifications that we pick. When we feel we are in oppressive situations in the present, yes, we turn to the future: because this or that freedom is not yet universal, we look forward to a future time when it *will* be—for our children.[1] People have always done that. But in just that sense, very little of my work, science fiction or pornography, is *about* the future. Rather it's an attempt to present images of freedoms, options, and the discourses that stabilize them that I see operative about me in the present—i.e., in the recent past, months or a few years back, or as the case may be, at the time of writing. I simply tend to look outside the usual social boundaries for their expression. But most of my work—even far-future extravaganzas such as *The Fall of the Towers* (1963–65), "The Star Pit" (1967), or *Nova* (1968)—are concerned with describing, in heightened form, things I saw about me at the time. The science fictional elements are there largely to foreground some of those things with particular vividness. If the reader doesn't recognize things from the actual world in their presentation—if only a desire *for* them, or an anxiety *about* them—then I doubt she or he will likely enjoy those books.

AR: I'll confess I'm particularly interested in this question of "values" in particular as it relates to SF. The issue of race, for instance: almost all the futuristic SF I can think of assumes a level of blandly utopian racial integration: from the rainbow society of *Star Trek*'s Federation to the world of *The Matrix*, where the bad guys are all white and the good guys a range of hues. Even somebody as reactionary (i.e., somebody whose values were as past-defined) as Heinlein seems to have assumed racial integration as one condition of the future: I'm thinking, for

---

1. Really, the trope can not be laid at Nietzsche's feet. It's expressed just as strongly, if not more so, already full blown, seventy or eighty years earlier, in Hölderlin's famous letter of 1792, to his half-brother, Karl Gok: "My affections are now less directed toward particular individuals. The object of my love is the entire human race, though not, of course, as we so often find it, namely in the condition of corruption, servility and inertia . . . I love the race of coming centuries. For this is my deepest hope, the faith that keeps me strong and vital: our grandchildren will have it better than we, freedom must finally come, and virtue will better flourish in the warmth of freedom's sacred light than in the ice-cold zone of despotism. We live in times when all things are working toward better days. These seeds to enlightenment, these still wishes and strivings of isolated individuals for the development of the human race, will spread and grow strong and bear marvelous fruit . . . [T]his is the sacred purpose of my wishes and my activity: that I might stir the seeds of change that will ripen in a future age." The point, of course, is that "the better tomorrow for our children, our grandchildren" is an eighteenth-century Enlightenment trope, not a nineteenth-century late romantic one. It was smelted in those same rhetorical furnaces in which all those travel books—Georg Foster's *Journey Around the World 1772–75*, Admiral George Anson's *Voyage Round the World 1740–44*, and even Oliver Goldsmith's distressingly provincial *Citizen of the World* (c. 1759)—were changing the concept of "la raza," the Spanish term for a great and powerful old family into the specifically Enlightenment concept of "race": a social unit indeterminately larger than the family, initially thought to be coextensive with the nation, but mediated by heredity rather than geography.

instance, of the Filipino protagonist of *Starship Troopers*. So: should we say "the last 150 years have seen steady progress in the area of racial integration: we extrapolate that into the future and, bingo, we're all living in a happy melting pot by the twenty-third century"? Or should we say the opposite, that this tendency in SF is a wish fulfillment precisely fueled by the palpable lack of racial justice in the world around us? That, for instance, the society that murders a Martin Luther King is precisely the society that projects fantasies of a multiracial future onto primetime TV? You say "if the reader doesn't recognize something from the actual world" in the SF s/he reads, then it won't work: is this the kind of recognition you're talking about?

SRD: It could be, if that discrepancy between fiction and reality were one I'd written about. Sadly, I haven't, yet.

But let me back up for a moment. I think there are at least two problems that trouble, say, the overall problem of making progress on the racial front. (What I shall be working up to is the part values play or don't play in the solution.) Most of us are intuitively aware of these problems, even if, without some prompting, we might have trouble articulating them.

First we don't remember our history.

Not so long ago, in the lobby of an Atlanta hotel, during a citywide Black Arts Festival, a group of young black students interviewed me. They were college age, and they began their questions by saying, "Since the racial situation is just as bad today as it was forty years ago, and there has been almost no progress . . ." Well, I had to laugh—and, indeed, had to say, "In no way do I think this is the best of all possible worlds. Certainly vast amounts of change need to be made. But if you think there's been no change in the racial situation in forty years, you're out of your mind. I was *here*, forty years ago. You weren't. The fact that we're meeting in a hotel in Atlanta where there are both black guests and white guests—that would not have been the case forty years ago. There are both black and white waiters in the dining room, here. Atlanta has a black mayor—as do half a dozen other cities in the country, including," at the time, "New York City, Washington D.C., and New Orleans. This was *not* the case forty years back; and what's more, if you had suggested that, in forty years, it might be, people would have thought you were crazy."[2]

2. My friend Josh Lukin writes: "Here's my attempt to cast the Atlanta students' conduct in a charitable light: some people would also have been pretty incredulous if you'd suggested that young black men would be several times more likely to spend a good number of years in jail than any in college (that only became the case in the eighties) or that, once the then-raging struggles to allow black Americans to vote had met with wide success, many states would enact laws denying the franchise to

What, I'm afraid, most militates for the lack of change in the racial problems of *present* Atlanta is precisely these students' "forgetting" of the specific strategies, energies, and activities that so many *other* students, two and three generations before, worked so hard at, to bring about the current situation. The obliterating of all sense of the trajectories along which the present situation has arrived at its current place is a major discursive barrier—even barricade—against change.

When we forget the historical provenance of some discourse that we and the people around us inhabit—the scientific ideas or the philosophical theory a discourse developed in response to—that discourse becomes even more powerful and more difficult to eradicate or revise. When the historical details go, what remains is a set of feelings, habits, expected behaviors, annoyances and discomforts whenever behavior strays from these expected norms. The discourse becomes naturalized. It moves out of the area of considered response into the area of common sense and the self-evident. I don't feel and behave like this because at one time people thought and felt and observed and decided. I feel like this, I behave like this because everybody feels and behaves this way. It's simply the way things are—*especially* if such feelings and behavior happen to stabilize any material or even psychological benefits for me or my particular social group.

Forgetting a discourse's history simply closes off one more door to interrogating and critiquing that discourse—when someone else complains, hey, but *I'm* not benefiting from it; or when someone else starts feeling hostile to such behavior.

Traditionally this sort of historical forgetting is blamed on the brief attention spans and faulty educations of the young—the classrooms full of kids who aren't sure of the difference between World War I and World War II. But, deeply, I believe *that* phenomenon is fallout from an outdated discourse, which, today, does *not* cover the problem. Rather, the deployment of information itself is to blame for this historical amnesia.

In his general linguistics lectures from 1906 to 1911, Saussure is usually credited with first articulating the difference between the synchronic and the diachronic;

---

ex-felons and work tirelessly to assign that status to an unprecendented chunk of the black population. To understand the claim of the students you mention, you have to see that it comes out of the dissonance between those facts and the liberals' doxa that things get better, reforms stay with us, etc.—or indeed the comfy centrist conviction that injustice is a thing of the past. Young people like the students you mention are told those kinds of things but see horrors to which such claims are meant to blind people, then end up making hyperbolic statements on 'the racial situation.' Things are bad enough that it's very difficult to maintain the diachronic perspective." I agree. In that sense, the need here is not for charity but for wholehearted support in which such insights as you might find in my statements above are only the smallest additions to the mix—accents that merely inflect the greater materiality with insights.

such have been the two axes around which, more and more, information has been organized, with greater and greater concentration on the synchronic. This went on to climax, in its most productive moments, with the kinship work of Lévi-Strauss just after World War II, the *Annales* School of historians with their histories of everyday life—Ariés, Ladurie, Veyne, and preeminently Fernand Braudel—and perhaps most spectacularly with Foucault's three early "Archaeologies," 1961's *L'Histoire de la folie*, 1963's *Naissance de la clinique*, through 1967's *Les Mots et les choses*. But what is problematic for the great minds of the century becomes simply a problem when it turns into the form of knowledge for everyone. Human beings can only hold so much in their heads. There is simply so *much* to know about *today*, that it displaces more and more the possibilities of a sophisticated knowledge of the past.

Much of what today we call "globalization" is simply the hyperinflation of the synchronic. How many large cities do you know how to get around in comfortably? London, Paris, Athens, Rome, San Francisco, New York, Buffalo, Philadelphia, and half a dozen smaller towns where I've summered or wintered for two or three years—that's *my* list. How many cities did your father know well? How many cities did Dr. Johnson know? Or Shakespeare? Believe me, nowhere *near* as many as you, I, and our students do.

But *that's* why we know so little Latin, Greek, and history. In order to survive, in order to talk to each other, we have to know too many other things.

The second problem is the increased granularity of the data that we do have to master. How much of my intellectual capacity is taken up with the lyrics of forty-year-old commercials and popular songs from the forties and fifties, not to mention outdated computer operating systems like DOS and CPM? Think of the technologies we must learn and abandon every two or three years. In one form or another, these are the problems that drove Foucault to give up his discursive elaboration of the épistémès for *dispositifs* (or apparatuses) and a theory of genealogies, as spelled out in *L'Archaeologie du savoir* (1970)—a move that must be taken into account if discourse as a strong theoretical concept is not to be lost.

It's impossible to speculate on precivilized society without such speculation becoming a projection of our own desires and fears. But one of the earliest Roman legal concepts, from well before the Republic in the most primitive days of Rome, was the *vitae necisques potestas*, which designated the father's power of life and death over his male offspring. Much early family law is about establishing wife and children as property who were subject to the father (to sell, to make work, or to kill)—which suggests that such murders were common enough that they had to be exempted from more ordinary dealings among peers. By the same token, one of the earliest problems of slowly congealing sovereignty was that when a man was tried by the state court and found guilty, often the populace simply rose up and took it upon themselves to slaughter him—so that one of the first acts of power from the king was to declare the judged criminal "holy," that is, a "homo sacer," a sacred being who could *not* be killed, so that he would survive long enough for the state to visit whatever punishment it saw fit to deal out—whether death or imprisonment.

The fact is, in times and situations we might risk calling less sophisticated and less civilized, it is not the ego and the id that run wild, seeking innocent or even ignorant pleasure. (Innocence is a value if there ever was one; so is guilt.) Rather it is the super-ego that runs amok (through which, as Freud knew, the id and the ego try blindly to live). Paradoxically, the cultivation of pleasure and all those conditions where the ego and id are allowed to express themselves, whether through art or action, with minimal hurt to others, requires leisure and affluence, as well as many intersecting discursive traditions.

In historical terms, freedom of speech, is, alas, neither a basic nor a primitive value—as much as I wish that it was. (Neither is that revolutionary American right to the pursuit of happiness, with which it is closely allied.) It's a relatively new one, eminently civilized, and highly fragile. It only thrives when there is a general philosophical awareness of the distance between word and object; and a general psychological awareness of the distance between the feelings that impel words and those that impel actions. We maintain it only by a complex of infrastructural stabilities along with interacting discursive mechanisms in delicate interplay. Upset any one of a dozen infrastructural elements and it crumbles—almost instantly. In strained times, people are ready to see it go with frightening ease, as we have experienced so recently with our national Patriot Act.

The vast majority of the violence and brutality committed in the world, whether it is the horrors of war or an urban gang of adolescents boys, in muddled imitation of the adult gangs of organized crime, committing murder and mayhem over their "rights" to a square block of cracked, weedy, and otherwise meaningless urban "turf," are acting on the *most* rigid notions of what's right and what's wrong. They are fixated on values such as honor, bravery, right. As such situations become more and more strained, all aggression becomes a matter of respect and disrespect—down to the point where disrespect is indistinguishable from disagreement.

Pride, respect, dignity, right, wrong—this is the cosmos of value, the cosmos where offense takes place, the cosmos where no slack can be cut for ignorance or difference.

Even those overtly antisocial acts of burglary and assault are committed in the firm conviction that, "I should have . . . In reality I deserve . . . The greater scheme of things allows me to . . . In a better world I *would* have . . ." First and foremost, those too are statements of value. Greed is just as much a matter of values as altruism.

Well, you can't go running around just blowing up everything you don't like. There are too many discourses extant to catch up the resultant increased hostility and reshape it into precisely what was there before, often in stronger form. Pretty soon *you're* more into the sound of the bang than the results, anyway—and somebody comes along, sees that your guard is down, and the next thing you know you've destroyed yourself. While a few people manage to change places, nothing fundamental has been reshaped.

In the past certain cultural programs have been bent on changing the structure of discourses: both Buddhism and the part of Christianity that isn't just Platonism for the masses (as Pater and Nietzsche both knew most of it to be), for two: You can't exchange hostility for hostility if your goal is to change the *structure* of the hostility—as every parent who manages *not* to kill his or her offspring eventually learns. But that takes affluence, leisure, and a tradition of structured thought—discourses, if you will.

Other programs have been bent on obliterating discourses. The initial treatment by the invading Europeans of Native Americans and, shortly afterwards, of African slaves are examples. Then Germany tried something like it with the Jews. Obliterating a discourse often means obliterating a people—but not always. By far the most successful of these programs was the program to squash all traces of African language, family forms, and culture in its imported African labor. Because three generations of slaves endured with all vestiges of African language, African family forms, and African discourses systematically and brutally smashed (it began in the slave pens of the Florida barcaroons and the markets at New Orleans, with no two Africans who spoke the same language penned or sold together; with brutal beatings administered when any words other than English were uttered at all; and nothing resembling a family allowed to endure through a sale), America has been paying for that, white and black, over the last three hundred years.

For the first three generations of slavery, 90 percent of us were raised in pens. Even the recent term "African American" is drenched in a hunger for the coherent cultural discourses we were never permitted to maintain.

It is precisely their unawareness of the history and the nature of the changes—both as it means their unawareness of how Robeson and my aunt were treated, or the equal unawareness of how systematically and brutally we were cut off from

everything African through the entire period of slavery (despite some acciden-
tal homologies, the sources for the "Uncle Remus" stories are not African, but
rather American Indian and Irish, coupled with the [dare I use the metaphor]
native genius of a black ex-slave story teller, filtered through the writing skill
of a white Georgia journalist, in his books of 1881 and 1883, whose own white
family had lived, in the previous decades, about as close to slavery conditions as
was possible)—that leaves the kids open to all the conservative strategies that get
foisted off on them, in the name of something new and radical, like the shut-
ting down of affirmative action programs, as it leaves them incapable of understanding (I didn't say forgiving; I said understanding) what occurred on Huff
Creek Road.

Thinkers like Alain Badiou have already all but equated ethics themselves
with evil. Agamben has certainly considered a similar move with morality. Even
the ancient philosophical plank on which so much of ethics and morality stands
("The greatest good for the greatest number") has to be rigorously localized if it
is to be a useful ground for deciding right action: Still, we have to remember not
to overdo it. In the situation of a war, for example, we must make sure not to limit
ourselves only to one side or the other. Yet how hard it is for most people to extend
such generosity to even something like the Second World War with Germany.

Again let me bring up an instance of the persistence of values—in this case
on a *Jerry Springer Show*, which I happened to catch a few days back. A working class white fellow had married a young black woman. (Paradoxically, today
there is a far higher percentage of interracial marriages in this country among the
working classes than in the upper middle class.) The conflict came because his
brother vehemently insisted that she would never be part of their family: He be-
lieved that blacks were not as good as white people and the races should not inter-
marry. There was the usual *Springer* yelling and screaming. The largely integrated
audience was very much on the side of the young black woman and her husband.
But one of the epithets that was constantly bandied about—one you don't hear
on Springer a lot—was "ignorant." The brother's objections were based on ignorance, everyone kept accusing him: He hadn't gotten past the tenth grade. Finally, Springer asked the angry brother where he had learned all this about black
people.

The answer was both surprising and instructive: In reform school.

There blacks had regularly beaten him up, and that's where he had learned
from the other white kids with him, certainly as some sort of compensatory
morality, that blacks were less civilized than whites, and were not fully human—
were, in fact, animals. (He used the word several times.)

His understanding of the reality of race had come to him largely from the same penal-style environment which had fostered Bill King and Lawrence Russell Brewer, the two ex-felons among the three in Jasper, Texas, who had murdered James Byrd and who had passed their notes back and forth in jail, after their arrest, congratulating each other on their deed, from which notes it was clear that they actually expected not only to be declared innocent of any crime but to be proclaimed heroes. (The highest IQ available among the three belonged to Bill King: 107.) At the end of the Byrd murder trail, when Berry was given life and King and Brewer were sentenced to death by lethal injection, the oldest, Lawrence Brewer sobbed, "We didn't mean to kill Mr. Byrd." Myself, I wouldn't be surprised if they were right: They had *not* intended to kill a "Mr. Bryd." Rather they had intended to fuck up a nigger, and show the other niggers and the whites how things should be. Doubtless the court proceedings themselves had made clear to them that "killing a Mr. Byrd" was what, indeed, they *had* done—or, to use Foucault's language for what happens when one discourse gives way to another, the proceedings had provided them "a new outline of the perceptible and the statable."

Given the violence the young ex-reform-school inmate on Jerry Springer had been subjected to, the acceptance of such a discourse might well have been necessary for his ego to survive—there in reform school. But he was no longer *in* reform school, and the historical persistence of these (dare I call them) values was breaking up his family. And he was not happy about it. But this is where, in various social margins—in pockets in the rural south *and* north, in gang and penal situations—such discourses endure today. Indeed, it is arguable that today such penal establishments do more to feed and support overt racial violence in the country than any other single institution, as they remain the seat—there—of a materially supported and active discourse.

Values are one kind of social object discourses create. The notion that unchanging permanent values are ultimately good and that fleeting, transitory values are ultimately bad goes back to Plato—though earlier Heraclitus had already identified the human condition with the understanding and negotiation of flux and change: *"Change alone endures"* (as Plotinus reports him writing). Heraclitus's advice on how to negotiate this was:

Hen to sophon. Epistasthai gnomen hohi kuvernesai panta dia panton. In my own translation: "One thing is wisdom: the knowledge of how all things are steered in their courses by all others." We have to remember that the animalizing of humans was not uniquely endured by blacks: it had been liberally doled out, as it were, to peasants, workers, and indeed criminals for several thousand years. What was unique to slaves—and criminals, once apprehended—was the legal prohibition on any movement from such conditions: their legally enforced lack of liberty.

As his last book, in 1893, Walter Pater published a set of Oxford lectures for undergraduates, *Plato and Platonism*, which, while rigorously managing not to say anything that would impugn Plato's genius, still manages to let the careful reader know that Pater is far more in sympathy with Heraclitus than he is with the author of *The Republic.*

We are now at a point where a good part of the population would probably say that rigidly inflexible values are a Bad Thing and that responsive, pliable values are a Good Thing—and not just a gay thinker who almost got canned from his nineteenth-century Oxford position at Brasenose for his irreligious ideas and behavior. (At an Oxford dinner, a younger Pater had scandalized a visiting minister and his wife, who got up and left after Pater declared: "For me to base my entire notion of good and evil on what a man said and did who lived two thousand years ago and three thousand miles away is absurd.")

Indeed, following the kind of moves already effected by Badiou and Agamben, in their critiques of "ethics" and "morality," it probably could be argued, starting off much the way I already have, that in Western discourse "values" themselves imply an order of rigidity that cries out for abuse in such a way so that "values" themselves might be declared an evil *per se.* But even as we consider such an argument, without following through on it, we have to remember that the values of permanence and change are themselves discursive sediments going back to Plato and Heraclitus.

In order to get the benefits values are assumed to give, what we must do is cultivate *not* values, either as ends or as beginnings, but rather cultivate the ability to think through situations in their complexity, deciding who will suffer and who will benefit, and what are the optimum intervention points that will effect the changes we want, after giving careful thought as to why we want them. Fiction is particularly good training for this—particularly the large-scale nineteenth-century social novel. That quality is what *I* find of value (a metaphor that means no more than important) in the nine non-SF novels Philip K. Dick wrote in the 1950s (which, in my opinion, are worth ten times the totality of his SF) as well as the recent science fiction of L. Timmel Duchamp—even though until recently she's worked largely in the short story form.

I think we have to give up on the idea that one atomic fact, be it social or material—whether gold or human life or imagination or freedom or innovation or genius or whiteness or blackness or tradition—is more valuable than *anything* else. Yes, some things *are* more important than other things. In different situations, it might be different things. If I am dying of dehydration, water is the most important thing. If I am starving, it's food. But by the same token, we have to realize that the things that are particularly important—like freedom of speech—are always complexes, historical and intricately maintained. That's *why* discourses have produced/reduced them *as/to* single social objects. But we have the responsibility to understand the workings of discourse and the nature of that production/reduction, even if it goes against the self-evident—as we have to know that the earth is round (even if it looks flat), should we want to travel from London to Chicago and arrive with our clocks correctly set.

All too often an appeal to a preset value—whether it is located in a Victorian idea of the family or a biblical idea of nature or of God (values that have little necessary relation with families, nature, or contemporary life as it's actually lived)—is an attempt to short circuit the analytic processes out of a misguided nostalgia for Platonic permanence.

AR: I'd like to ask a really basic question about the business of your writing, one of the most distinctive things about which is your style, the expressive and poetic compression of your prose. To take a sentence more or less at random as an example (from *Dhalgren*, 1975): "In the cups, one after another, glistening disks rose, black without translucence." I love that sentence, but (if you'll excuse me putting this with a deliberate naivety) I'm wondering: why is it better to write that sentence than to write, say, "he poured two cups of black coffee"?

SRD: You yourself have just given the reason. Because you love it. A possible reason to love it is because it makes two things pop up in your mind's eye more vividly than does the sentence "He poured two cups of black coffee." (The poet Robin Blaser has written "language is love." I suspect this is one of the things he means.) One is what specifically happened at *that* particular time when those particular two cups were poured; it has been described. In some light, in some venues, when you pour black coffee, the coffee *is* translucent. In others, such as this one, it's not. The second thing that pops up is your awareness of the hand pouring and the table on which the pouring is done (even the sound of the coffee going into the cups is suggested: ". . . glistening disks rose . . . without translucence")—because they're *not* mentioned, but are so strongly implied. The combination of careful description and strong implication is one that, to a statistically large sampling of readers, affords a more vivid reading experience than the simple "statement of information."

Now, such combinations of presentation and withholding are a trick—though it's one used by writers from the J-Writer who wrote all the good parts in the early books of the Bible (like the story of Adam and Eve in the Garden of Eden or the interrupted sacrifice of Isaac by Abraham), through Homer, through Shakespeare, through Joyce, Woolf, and Nabokov—which is to say, it *doesn't* work for every reader every time. But it works for enough for us, enough of the time, to keep writers like G. K. Chesterton and Djuna Barnes in print, when aspects of the political (or, in Chesterton's case, of the religious) content of their work have become highly out of favor if not downright repellent. We love a sentence not because of *what* it means so much as the manner and intensity with which it makes its meaning vivid.

People whom the trick tends not to work on include people who are just learning the language and/or who have no literary background in any other language before they start. It tends not to work on people who know the language well enough but also know exactly what they're reading for, and who are not interested in getting any other pleasure from a book except the one they opened the first page expecting.

The vividness comes pretty much from a kind of surprise, the surprise from meeting a series of words that, one by one, at first seem to have nothing to do with the topic—the pouring of two cups of coffee—but words that, at a certain point, astonish us with their economy, their accuracy. Again, some readers will find it will work, whereas others will find it only affected. But it's managed to remain part of literature so that we find it employed as a technique in the works of Thomas Middleton and Sir Thomas Browne, in Alfred Bester and Theodore Sturgeon, in Katherine McLean and John Updike, in Guy Davenport and Gene Garber, in Charlotte Bacon and Lucius Shephard and Rikki Ducornet.

Now: "He poured two cups of black coffee" has a precise economy that projects its own beauty. We can enjoy that, too. But the other—through that combination of specific statement and withheld implication—puts a higher percentage of readers closer to the pulse and texture of the incident. Rhetorically, it makes more readers feel there's a shorter distance between words and occurrence.

If an early nineteenth-century essayist had written, "The true and the beautiful are largely the same and often entailed in inseparable ways. That is one of the few self-evident facts of the modern world. Indeed, I believe if you have understood that, you can pretty much negotiate the whole of modern life," I doubt if anyone would remember it today.

But Keats wrote:

Beauty is truth, truth beauty,—that is all
Ye know on earth and all ye need to know.

The economy, symmetry, and specificity here—the performance of its meaning through implication, accuracy, and bodily rhythm—raises it to a level of immediacy that won't shake loose from the mind. "Beauty is truth, truth beauty," is, of course, in the same rhetorical mode as "He poured two cups of black coffee." But "—that is all / ye know on earth and all ye need to know" is a spectacularly huge bit of implication. If, as I unravel those implications, I can allow myself to hear its tragic declaration of the limits on what, indeed, *can* be known—you really *don't* know anything else, and its bare sufficiency is our world's great gift to us, for it is that from which all law and science and art have been constructed (behind all we presume knowledge, whether correct or incorrect, some correspondence between elements in the world was once noted that someone must have assumed beautiful, fascinating, or at least interesting before it could be judged useful, efficient, or functional—those three categories already fundamentally aesthetic constructions themselves)—it can make me weep in the same way as does the tragic knowledge we took with us on our expulsion from Eden: *Lord, we chose the wrong tree!* Such implication is so broad that, today, most of us would probably figure, "Don't even *try* it!"

But it works.

And when one approaches it through the historical set-up of *Ode on a Grecian Urn*'s previous six stanzas, it can take the top of your head off. Keats is, after all, *the* master of accuracy and implication among the English romantic poets, working toward vivid immediacy. Indeed, as are Cather's "My Mortal Enemy," Joyce's "The Dead," Russ's "The Other Inquisition," and Lawrence's "Odour of Chrysanthemums," Keats's poem is one of the gentlest, one of the most powerful retellings of the tale of the Edenic expulsion implicit in knowledge itself.

Again, not everyone is affected by it in this way. Nor is each reader affected by it in the same way each time she or he reads it. But enough readers find that it works enough of the time to preserve it as a valued technique of the literary, both in prose and poetry. Writings that employ it generously often seem, over the long run, more immediate, more protean, and more vibrant than works that eschew it for a safer rhetoric and more distanced affect.

AR: Do you write poetry?

SRD: No. But I'm a poetry reader. Recently I've had a few opportunities to teach poetry—they've been wonderfully revivifying to me as a prose writer. I enjoy getting a chance to run on about things. And one can run on about poetry forever. But, no, I don't write it. The difficulties of prose are quite enough.

AR: Do you have a favorite work among your novels or critical endeavors?

SRD: That's a hard question to answer. Writers often compare their work to children, and it's like someone trying to choose a favorite child. You don't want to play favorites.

Having said that, I can perhaps give a provisional answer.

Not too long ago, I was paging through an ordinary commercial gay men's porn magazine *(Inches,* ed. Doug McClemont, January 2000, Vol. 14, No. 5), when I found an article, "The Best Gay Smut of the Last 1000 Years." Turning over the page, I found myself staring at a reproduction of the cover of my novel *The Mad Man,* beside a mini-review that began "The filthiest book I have ever read, hands down . . ." and whose closing sentence contained the word "triumph." In between fell the sentence "It made me feel both strong and healthy and terrible about myself—as most great smut should do." Other items covered in the article were Alan Hollinghurst's *The Swimming Pool Library,* a video called "The Bigger the Better," Maerten Van Heemskerck's painting from 1550, "Man of Sorrows," depicting a working man's Christ, crucified with an erection, and Michelangelo's *David.*

For all that review implies, I should have to answer, yes, right now I think *The Mad Man* is the book of mine I prefer—not for the book itself so much as for the nature of the response the book gets. For a variety of reasons, I'm pleased with the tone people seem to adopt when they talk about it.

But, of course, I'm busy writing another.

AR: In a 1996 collection of critical essays dedicated to your work, James Sallis praised not only "the scope, ambition, and achievement" of your writing, but also "the discomfort it causes us personally." Do you consider it a writer's job to make her or his readership uncomfortable?
SRD: No. I never begin with the idea of troubling or discomforting my audience. While, from time to time, I realize probably some readers will be troubled, I also assume they won't get far enough through the book even to discover those parts.

Each epoch has a number of discourses in place that help define the human. By the end of the eighteenth century, and all through the nineteenth and early part of the twentieth, they included the literary convention—for example—of never describing directly what the genitals did: pissing, shitting, sex. You can read through all the novels in Leavis's Great Tradition, including D. H. Lawrence, and find no mention of the fact that human beings are creatures who, between once and five times a day, take a piss or a shit—and while there is much in them that can only be explained *by* sex, save in a few paragraphs of *Lady Chatterley's Lover,* sex itself is not mentioned, whether onanistic or with others. While we build bathrooms, bedrooms, sewers, and brothels to accommodate these functions, not to mention double beds and chamber pots, genital functions were basically considered animal properties. Our humanity—especially our literary humanity—resided in remaining politely silent about them. (It's that "bare human life"

problem again.) Among his endless innovations, Joyce violated this convention—
and his great novel *Ulysses* was declared obscene because of it.

What can happen when a writer enters one of these areas of silence is that, instead of defining the human by a reticence, sometimes we can bring readers to the
notion that articulating what actually goes on within such silences—especially
if we do it with sentences of the sort that you so enjoy—can reverse the process
and start expanding the definitions of the human by including the material up
till now excluded. The sexual—and especially the large areas dismissed as "deviant
sex" and/or "public sex"—is simply another area of silence. But in order to do it
so that it works, you must carefully and observantly follow your characters into
those spaces, and record dispassionately what you see. If you get carried away by
your own sense of transgression or your own daring, the effect is majorly spoiled
and aesthetically marred. Yes, I think some people are going to be troubled by a
writer following the thoughts and actions of a thirty-two-year-old Irish laborer
as he masturbates along with a stranger, while the two stand at the last couple of
urinals at 6:12 in the morning in a loo at Golders Green, or in which a secretary
compresses her thighs to give herself pleasure, under her denim wraparound, at
her desk when, during the second half of lunch hour, no one but her is in the office. But if you start off with the idea of shocking people, all you do is confirm
such readers' conviction that such is not to be articulated and that such behavior
reduces us, rather than shows us as larger beings with greater capacities and inge-
nuities for pleasure than has been assumed.

AR: I very much take that point. Still, the idiom that was once called "the obscene"
has a wide range of registers, doesn't it? The sex in *Dhalgren*, for instance, doesn't
(I'd submit) read as especially shocking nowadays, or not as shocking as I'm sup-
posing it did in the 1970s: most novels now contain sex-acts described at that level
of detail. *Hogg*, on the other hand, did shock me when I read it (and I don't think
of myself as especially shockable); less the specific things described, more the precise and careful tone of the writing, the leveling of affect that rendered "straightforward" sexual encounters on exactly the same level as let's say, a father sexually
abusing his child and so on.

SRD: *Hogg* is an angry book—one I think it's hard to understand outside its historical context. Despite the subscription place-date at the end, *Hogg* was first
drafted, in longhand, in four notebooks in San Francisco during 1969, from the
end of March through the last days in June. Probably within a day or two of its
completion, the Stonewall Riots occurred in New York City. Within months,
within weeks, even, a sense rose all over the country, at least among gay men and

women, that we'd entered a new era, and there was a possibility—an actuality—
for a Gay Liberation movement.

Had gay men and women tried to effect a betterment for themselves before?
Of course we had. But these efforts did not make headlines in the newspapers.
The idea of "coming out" was not conceived and promoted in the press as a basic
political strategy to end oppression.

Though the book was rewritten and stylistically polished over the next four
years, all the plot elements and the incidents were in place, however, by the time
Stonewall happened. Thus, even though the book had to wait twenty years to
find a publisher, it's not too far afield to say that *Hogg* is the last, or among the
last, pre-Stonewall gay novels written within the United States. It was written by
a twenty-seven-year-old black gay man who was as furious and as outraged by
the sexual condition of the country as any of those black queens back on Waverly
Place.

Hogg himself is my emissary of destruction—and Dennis Harkner is his
apostle. Both were white, but at least one reason for that is because I couldn't
conceive of a black reaching the age of sixteen with anything like the potential
for that sort of action, without being killed first. (An early reader once told me
that what she would have really liked, was to see Maria, the fifteen-year-old Hispanic girl, prostituting for her brother and her father, take the part of Denny, the
seventeen-year-old mass murderer—she would have found that politically more
satisfying.) But I see Hogg and Denny as the avenging angels for all the "spies"
and "niggers" and "freaks" gathered in the cellar during the first chapter.

AR: In essence I think I'm asking a question about degradation. The old Puri-
tanism ("sex is bad!") has very largely gone out of fashion, at least away from
the centers of religious fundamentalism. In its place we live with a new "official"
value: "sex is good providing it isn't degrading sex." Of course the discourse is actually couched in terms of "consent" ("sex is good provided it's consensual"), but
I suspect it really involves notions of "clean sex: good" versus "dirty sex: bad."
One of the things that works so well in *Tales of Nevèrÿon* is the way it dramatizes
"sexual degradation" not only as a function of general social degradation (we
might say: of course) but as an attractive and even necessary part of sex itself.
Nevertheless it seems strange to me to talk of your writing in terms of "degradation": Its mood is so completely the opposite of degraded.

SRD: Degradation is, of course, a discursive effect. So are objectivity and dispassion. The discourses that create them also create the first as a warning that something is amiss. Discourses praise and value the latter two.

I wouldn't be surprised, however, if the dispassion with which I have always tried to write about sex isn't eventually seen—that is, if anyone pays any attention to it at all—as some kind of crippling aesthetic limitation. Today, a writer like D. H. Lawrence, with his Victorianly rigid notion of where everyone is supposed to fit on the sexual and gender schema—I mean, it's something he fundamentally fetishizes—seems a far greater prude to me than, say, Jane Austen, with her group of late adolescents in *Pride and Prejudice*, coming in happily from an afternoon spent watching a soldier publicly flogged. The fact that—and, yes, it *was* a breakthrough—Lawrence employed the occasional four-letter word, which people actually used all over the place, seems quite a small step, now that—post 1968, when the obscenity laws changed—it's a commonplace.

Discourses (the structures of understanding, of reading, of response), which are the results of thought and language under material pressures, are the stabilizers of civilization. But we have to understand that they are as much at work when Klansmen ride out to burn their crosses and the SS erupts in the violence of *Kristallnacht* as when the Supreme Court overturns, as it did last year, an evil and inhuman decision from 1986, *Bowers v. Hardwick* (for a decade I kept the newspaper account of it taped up to the back of my office bookshelf, so I could be reminded that this inhuman precedent obtained in my country), by upholding Lawrence and overturning the Texas Court of Appeals decision, in *Lawrence v. Texas*.

Things that are forbidden, especially in childhood, are often sexualized—and that includes words and acts that traditionally degrade. As long as that's the case, many folks will come to find what degrades sexually exciting. I've always suspected that the sexualization of forbidden, despised, rejected acts, substances, language, and symbols represents an order, even a useful, necessary order, of social memory. That's certainly one of the ideas weaving through my *Nevèrÿon* tales.

AR: Whom are you reading now? Whom do you rate in terms of contemporary writing?
SRD: Waiting to be read, two book piles sit on my bedside table. One contains some research volumes, which I hope will feed my current writing project. Some of the titles are Arna Bontemps's 1936 novel *Black Thunder*, about a slave revolt in Richmond, Virginia, in 1800, when one slave, Gabriel Posser, decided to revenge the death of another; then there's Sidney Monz and Richard Price's *The Birth of African American Culture* (1972); still another is *Before the Mayflower: A History of Black America*, by Lerone Bennett, Jr. (5th edition; 1984); and finally Darryl Pinckney's *Out There: Mavericks of Black Literature* (2003).

Then I have another pile—my pleasure reading for when I need a research break. That includes Karl Sabbach's *The Reimann Hypothesis* (2003), John Derbyshire's *Prime Obsession* (2003), Marcus du Soutoy's *The Music of the Primes* (2003), and Robert Kanigel's *The Man Who Knew Infinity: The Life of the Genius Ramanujan* (2003). Somewhere between them falls the bound galleys for Paul West's new novel, *The Immensity of the Here and Now*, his story about 9/11.

As for what rates, well—about forty years ago, I stopped rating what I read and started reading exclusively for the sake of the exploration itself. Some of what I started to find was wonderfully fun and interesting. All of it was informative— though more times than not, the lesson was a negative one: This is what you don't want to think; this is the kind of argumentation you don't want to let yourself get caught up in; here's a sentence I'm glad I didn't write.

But my life became a lot more interesting.

If I made a shelf of those books that really hit my G-spot—a handful of novels by Balzac and Flaubert; the fiction and essays of Davenport, Nabokov, Woolf, and William Gass; a solid "reader's" volume each of works by Borges, Beckett, Bester, Sturgeon, and Sir Thomas Browne; a pile of comics by Alan Moore; Hugo Von Hofmannsthal's *The Lord Chandos Letter*; Chesterton's *The Man Who Was Thursday: A Nightmare*; Richard Hughs's *A High Wind in Jamaica*; Djuna Barnes's *Nightwood*; John Keene's *Annotations*; a block of the ten Pater volumes; some Foucault, some Derrida; Christian Bök's *Eunoia* and Lucien Goldmann's *Philosophie et les sciences humains*; my Keats and my *Keats Circle*; Eric Auerbach's *Mimesis*, John Livingston Lowe's *Road to Xanadu*, Spencer-Brown's *Laws of Form*; Silliman's *Ketjak* and the rest of *The Age of Huts*; Saintsbury's *History of English Prose Rhythms*, Lessing's *Laocoön*; story volumes by Denis Johnson, Alice Munro, and Junot Diáz—well, it would be neither representative (of me or anyone else) nor historically very interesting.

Though it would be a shelf of wonderful reading.

As I've already said in another context, however, producing such responses is a trick. It has only a statistical reality. While names on them often repeat and overlap, no such lists can remain stable. (Isn't literature—not to mention its avatars and epigones in the paraliterary wilds—finally a statistical illusion through which we try to make a gorgeous, illusory, and impossible discourse cohere?) Next week a sweep of my forearm may clear that shelf and I'll plunge into the remaining novels of W. G. Sebald I've yet to read, the truly wonderful later Michael Moorcock, the next volume of John Crowley's *Ægypt* tetrology, or go back and re-read Wescott's *Pilgrim Hawk*, Tsypkin's *Summer in Baden, Baden*, Russ's *Souls*, or L. Timmel Duchamp's *Alanya to Alanya*, or perhaps I'll retreat into some adolescent love, like Merezhkovski's *tour de force* about the years of Giovanni Beltraffio's artistic apprenticeship, *The Romance of Leonardo da Vinci,* one of my and Sigmund Freud's favorite novels.

But the lists are just that—lists; and all their choices are wildly unrated: Intellectually they're "triple-X," every one. Every one transcends some category you might want to put it in. That's why it's up there.

TK Enright interviews
Samuel Delany about *Hogg*

TK Enright/2004

Previously unpublished. Printed with permission of TK Enright.

Enright: One of the few things that's comforting about the book is that there seems to be a real acceptance of human beings—the narrator accepts them young or old, fat or skinny, hung or not. And not just every kind of human but everything that comes out of them. In addition, no one seems ever to get jealous—Hogg never tries to claim the boy solely for himself or anything. Since this attitude prevails in *The Mad Man* and from what I know of your autobiography, it strikes me that you might be endorsing this as a utopic vision of love and sex. Would that be accurate?

Delany: I feel a little odd talking about a novel as "endorsing" anything. Always, I've felt that novels were fundamentally records—and necessarily distorted records—of things observed in the world. It would be disingenuous not to admit that some things I observe I like and some I don't like, but the basic enterprise is to portray them—with all the distortions—in some sort of aesthetic pattern. My like or dislike of them should be of secondary, or even tertiary importance.

Because, with jealousy, you feel majorly disrespected, jealousy is different from the simple sadness of not getting what you want. With jealousy, you feel you *should* have what you lack—as a man, as a woman, as a wife, as a husband, as a worker overlooked for a promotion, as a child who has not received a present some other sibling has gotten, as a friend who hasn't gotten a phone call thanking you for a gift you gave or a dinner check you picked up at a restaurant.

Fundamentally, jealousy is a social emotion. People are jealous because they are brought up to feel that they have a right to certain treatment—to other people's attention, to other people's work, to other people's sexual fidelity. When they don't get it, they feel diminished, insulted, and cheated out of something they believe society marked out as their due. Jealousy is not particularly "natural"—or, for that matter, "unnatural." Nor do I think it's necessarily "healthy," or "unhealthy." I think it's learned. When it's extreme, often it's a pain in the butt, both for the person feeling the jealousy and for the person who is the object of that jealousy, as well as the world around both persons. Once we learn what it is, however, in some cases—if we live certain kinds of lives—we can unlearn how to be jealous.

The vast majority of us live in our superegos, rather than in our ids or even our egos. It's much easier to do something we think is right (even momentarily) than it is to do something *only* because it's pleasurable (and, even trying, we cannot think of an ethical justification). Indeed, it takes a highly civilized person with a highly cultivated aesthetic sensibility to do something just because it's pleasurable. And most of the time, the necessary prior cultivation has been the setting in place of a discourse that says a certain amount or type of pleasure is itself good, moral, right, and beneficial to the individual and promotes the greater good.

Only the strongest egos can occasionally break through this mental stricture—at the behest of sex, say—and even that usually leads to a restructuring of an ethical discourse. The vast majority of the "evil" perpetrated in the world is perpetrated in the name of the superego, through which, as Freud showed us, the ego and the id try blindly to live.

In your question up there, basically you're right as far as my own feelings are concerned. I've never thought of myself as a particularly jealous person. But because I'm a gay man who's lived a relatively active sexual life, in many places the idea of sexual jealousy is so self-contradictory that I simply couldn't tolerate it in myself. So I've worked—not terribly hard, when all is said and done—to eradicate those feelings. I'm glad I did. Yet once in a while a surge of it flares up and surprises me. Today, rarely do I feel jealousy for sexual reasons. Social attention from a friend—or its lack when I'm expecting it—is far more likely to set me off and leave me feeling the painful, angering deprivation that's what jealousy is. Frankly, today even that's pretty rare for me.

Still, I work on it.

A few people—often ones who have never thought of themselves as particularly deserving of anything in the first place—are astonishingly "non-jealous." Certainly this is the case with the narrator of *Hogg* as well as Hogg himself. But, yes, such a lack of jealousy is one of the things a sexually active life may actually be able teach you.

It was Blake who said the Road of Excess leads to the Palace of Wisdom. I always suspected this was one of the things he had in mind.

Fundamentally, I don't think there's anything necessarily healthier about monogamy than there is about promiscuity, either. Or vice versa, for that matter. But, yes, if you lead a promiscuous life, putting some curbs on your tendency toward jealousy is the only reasonable way to do it. Only extremely powerful—and dictatorial—people can afford to be *both* promiscuous and jealous.

Enright: The most disturbing element of the book—aside from particular scenes of especially gruesome depravity—is the utter passivity towards the pain of others (when that pain isn't being actively inflicted). Even the characters who ostensibly provide contrast to Hogg and his crew exhibit a stunning unwillingness to intervene in the suffering of others. Red, Rufus, Mona, and Harry all at least suspect Big Sambo of abusing and raping his daughter, but none of them does anything about it. Then there's the narrator who seems almost completely indifferent to the suffering of the women—he seems aware of what they're enduring and, at the urging of others, helps assault them. Is he supposed to be too young to be able to think these things out for himself? One reviewer was under the impression he licks a girl to ease the pain of the rape—but to my eye that's a misreading of a pretty straightforward text. He prepares to lick her and as he does so, it occurs to him it might ease her pain—but they weren't cause and effect.

Delany: I think you're perfectly right in that particular reading. But just as I believe jealousy, even sexual jealousy, is a fundamentally social emotion, I also believe identification with other people's suffering is almost entirely an aesthetic emotion. When we watch real suffering occur, out on the street, perhaps, the fact is, most people don't feel very much. The offers of help may be real. The shows of concern tend to be a variety of emotional miming. Sometimes people feel fear—and sometimes that fear can even linger. But that's about all. To watch real suffering causes our emotions—unless we've had a particular kind of education—immediately to clamp down.

Think of the young people in *Pride and Prejudice*, girls and boys of eighteen, nineteen, and twenty, who come in, laughing and chattering, from a pleasant afternoon watching a sailor publicly flogged—a sailor who, as happened in three out of five such floggings at the time, probably died over the next couple of days.

We learn compassion for others through works of art. It's one of the ways art civilizes—it's something narrative art really *can* teach. The *major* thrust of Aristotle's argument on tragedy—pity, terror, and catharsis aside (they're only the machinery through which it happens)—is that tragedy promotes compassion in the public audience for that public's leaders, leaders who often, however inadvertently, make terrible mistakes. This compassion in the people is politically advantageous to the greater society, Aristotle argues. If they feel this compassion, they are more easily governed. (The fact that *Hogg* starts to make people feel some compassion for people both like Hogg and the narrator is, I suspect, what readers find *most* unsettling.) Aristotle also argues, in effect, that to have such compassion for ordinary men and women—the working classes, say—would be silly and socially counterproductive. There's far too much suffering in the world and no practical way to relieve it. It would only gum up the social workings—and, for fourth century BCE Greece, he was probably right.

But the fact that my *characters* don't feel much compassion for each other—people who are being really hurt—only means that they haven't spent a lot of time at the movies or watching TV.

That's all.

Even by the end of the eighteenth century, there was probably less compassion for the working classes among the bourgeoisie and aristocracy than there is today for the run-of-the-mill child molester. While people were proud of their own country's soldiers killed in the line of duty, nobody felt sorry for them—unless a casualty happened to be a personal friend. Even the working classes themselves, while often they felt severe family loyalties, had little compassion for one another, as individuals or as a class. The general wisdom—which the working class itself shared—was that 95 percent of them were thieves and layabouts, when they weren't retarded. Unless they were under strict supervision from overseers or army officers, they would probably rob you blind and, with half a chance, rape your daughter. (Think of all those scheming peasants in all those Balzac novels!) This was the life Hobbes described as "solitary, nasty, brutish, and short," and thus a relief for everyone else when you were finished with it—and nobody gave much thought at all what losing it might mean to you.

In *Sentimental Education* (1858) Flaubert's portrait of Dussardier is a mid-nineteenth-century analytical attempt to bring a member of the urban working class into the circle of middle-class compassion, through the aesthetic strategy of revealing what happens when that compassion is withheld, dissembled about, faked, and the bourgeois characters continue on in what at the time was their traditional manner. Dussardier's death on the blade of Sénécal (the coldly calculating politico, Frédéric's truly terrifying "bad consciousness"—and by implication what would be left of Frédéric were all his wishy-washy romanticism stripped away) is the moral and intellectual climax of the novel. Frédéric likes Dussardier, certainly. But he accuses him falsely of thefts to justify Frédéric himself borrowing large amounts of money (ineffectually to run after his pipe dream of an affair with Madame Arnoux), and generally abuses him shamelessly. The twin things Frédéric lacks for Dussardier are respect and compassion, and the result is that Dussardier is the character for whom the reader feels the *most* compassion—at least, by the calculus of nineteenth-century melodrama that was alone available to even such an innovator as Flaubert, however flat it falls for readers today. (How could one person, for the coldest and most inhuman political reasons, Sénécal, run through with a sword someone who once so good heartedly invited him to a party he gave in which he went out of his way to impoverish himself so that Sénécal might have a bottle of decent beer—that's the question the novel asks in effect, as though writer and readers were all cousins of Nick Carraway, the narrator of *Gatsby*. The argument is finally one about the value of pleasure, as are finally all arguments about compassion—its poetry, its ubiquity.)

For thousands of years, people have been saying war is a terrible thing. There have still been wars. What there hasn't been, however, is "war movies." Starting with *Battleship Potemkin, Napoleon,* and *Intolerance,* up through *The Grand Illusion, Paths of Glory, The Battle of Algiers, Apocalypse Now, The Big Red One, Saving Private Ryan,* and *The Pianist,* those are what, in not quite a century, have helped stabilize the idea that war is terrible in a world economic order where it is far more profitable to take over a country's functioning industrial system already in place rather than to first smash its infrastructure with bombs and troops beyond the point where it can function. Wars are relatively reasonable for conflicts between agricultural countries. Replanting a battlefield is not particularly difficult. For conflicts between industrial nations, it's extraordinarily wasteful. I hope this awareness keeps growing.

In France the working classes weren't even expected to marry with full church ceremonies until 1875, four years *after* the Paris Commune—when the *first* laws facilitating church weddings for the working classes came in!

In John Gay's *The Beggar's Opera* (1765), from 110 years before the Commune, in England, when the first possibilities for working class marriage are being considered, the bone of contention is that Polly Peachum wants to *marry* Macheath. Polly's parents are *not* married. And while Mr. Peachum thinks it would be a fine idea because then his grandchildren would not be bastards the way his daughter, Polly, is, and many of the better off artisans are trying out the new socio-legal arrangement, Polly's mother thinks it's a terrible idea, because then all a legal wife's assets are entailed to her husband. That is just not a good plan in a social milieu where women are regularly abandoned and betrayed—especially by shiftless hustlers such as Macheath.

Finally, why *is* life pleasant enough so that most people really do want to live it for a long time? What is the basis of pleasure which is the positive measure (after the negative measure of freedom from pain, hunger, ill health, and discomfort) for general compassion—that is to say, the yearning to relieve the suffering of others. Shockingly enough, I suspect masturbation is the one truly self-administered and self-regulated pleasure central to well over half the world's positive pleasure—along with its attendant fantasies. (Since masturbation is such a large part of people's lives—and has been since primates' arms reached their current length—I really believe that the reason it has been all but repressed from political and even most public discourse is that the moment it is politicized as a positive pleasure men and women have a right to, it redefines the relationship of individual to the group from the bottom up in a way we might never recover from; today, we might not even recognize what some of those new discursive definitions of humanity could look like.) Then comes sex with other people. The pleasure of sociality, work, accomplishment, and others talking and socializing with people probably comes next. Finally the pleasures of nature fall in there—which range over those of children, small animals, greenery, good food, fine weather, beautiful landscapes, and flowers. Somewhere in there is, I'm sure, art itself—music, dancing, singing, painting, sculpture, literature, architecture, as well as history and philosophy (even though the last, as Benjamin points out, has no muse). The pleasures of love are really quite wonderful—though I suspect they are rather a luxury and require a certain level of socioeconomic stability to be anything other than a mode of suffering. But certainly I feel privileged to have had thirty years of them with my daughter and fourteen with my current partner, as well as a briefer stint, now and again, with various friends, with some of whom I had sexual relationships and with some of whom I never even considered it. How these pleasures finally map out in terms of which are more or less important to us, is, I'm sure, different for each individual. But most of us will recognize the basic areas. In short, pleasures are everything the poet celebrates, directly or indirectly.

As to the characters' leave-it-alone attitude toward Big Sambo's relationship with children, *Hogg* is a historical novel after all. Specifically, it's pre-Stonewall. As is still largely the case—and it was even more so thirty-five years back, when *Hogg* was written—you don't interfere with how people raise their children. Honey-Pie is a deeply depressive and wounded kid. I'm almost certain she doesn't attend school. I doubt she has any friends her own age. Add to it that her out-of-work father uses her as a sexual plaything, and I think that's a truly bleak existence. There's nothing there I'm endorsing. But the fact is, at the time, the Rufuses and Reds of the world had to protect the Sambos from the otherwise well-intentioned eyes of the Harrys and the Monas in order to protect their own practices.

Today, Rufus and Red would probably have a support group with monthly meetings and trips to play with other S&M groups in near-by cities, with whom they kept in regular on-line contact—at least I'd like to think so. They might even put out some considerable effort to get both Big Sambo and Honey-Pie some *serious* counseling. Failing that, they might well call the police. Certainly I wouldn't fault them if they did, even as I would prefer them to start with the former before resorting to the latter—for the child's sake.

As far back as the middle 1950s, I first heard, on television, a noted child psychiatrist, a Dr. Schimmel, explain to the public that, in his considerable experience, in the vast majority of actual cases, however harmful sexual relations were with children, the way the police and other social institutions brought those relations to an end was far more painful and emotionally scarring *to the child* than the relations themselves. There was no way for the child to read his or her subsequent removal from home and other family members, the subsequent incarceration in an institution, the new lack of freedom of motion and general harshness of how, from then on, he or she was dealt with, as anything other than punishment for what she or he had done, no matter how little he or she was actually to blame. Despite the sentimentalities of post-primetime TV (when the *controversial* programs are aired), rarely can you prevent a child from eventually saying: "I would have been better off if I'd kept my mouth shut or at least if I'd managed to get away and no-one had ever known." You can dismiss this as "silly childishness" if you like, but that contravenes the entire subjective set of measures by which one acts to bring the situation to an end in the first place. One of the terrible things about our society, even today, is that, in five out of six cases, the molester who threatens the child, "If you tell anyone what we're doing, they will do awful things to *you!*" is usually, in the long run if not in the short, right. And that was far more the case a quarter of a century ago.

To repeat, in no way does citing such a contradiction mean that I approve of such child/adult relationships themselves. But counseling and gentler intervention *is* the direction that the world is going in—it just hadn't arrived there, yet (as in only a few cases has it today), when I wrote the novel.

In the scenes on the docks, the narrator sees (with just a little *Nachträglicheit)* that the garbage men's protection of Sambo is also fundamentally *self*-protective. Because of it, it also facilitates what he himself desires, so Rufus and Red get points in his book for it.

The novel presents the thinnest cross-section of everyone's experience. The real test of the extremely delicate moral structure the book is trying to set up would be for the reader to come back to Crawhole after three weeks, after two months, or after a year, *then* see how things are going with them all.

Do you think the narrator will still be there, with Rufus and Red? Or will he have grown tired of their S&M shenanigans and run off once more?

There is just the possibility—and I think the narrator, to the extent his fantasies ever run in this direction, probably would like it in theory—that Red and Rufus will provide him with exactly what he wants as well as whatever he needs that he himself has little way of knowing in any detail. (He *is* eleven!)

And, who knows, they might.

But if you, as reader, tell me that you feel it's highly unlikely, I, as writer, am certainly not going to argue with you. I know what the world is like. I think it's pretty unlikely too.

Enright: I read an interview where you were saying that one of the deliberately unsettling parts of the book is that even the brutalizers have sympathetic qualities. Is the passivity of the other characters the inverse of this—that they are basically sympathetic with terrible flaws? Or would you disagree that it's a moral flaw not to intervene in the unequivocal suffering of others?

Following from that, what's the significance of "Nothin'"? How does the word link Honey-Pie and the narrator? Is it an argument for the sexual agency of children—that they are content with their situations? Maybe it's that contrary to all appearances the subs have been controlling things all along, and both knew they could leave anytime they wanted? Honey-Pie lingers in the doorway; the narrator plots his escape—different destinies informed by a common awareness of their autonomy. Maybe that's why you go out of your way to use chess to establish that the narrator—and maybe that other little kid Hogg kicks—are of high intelligence. Or maybe I'm way off-base? And if not, would you still, thirty years later, posit that most children that join in these relationships do so out of choice?

Delany: That's a lot of questions, and I don't know whether I can tease them apart, into their respective suppositions, which is probably the level this should be addressed at. By and large, I think most children—i.e., those under sixteen—should stay out of sexual relations with people more than five years older than they are. They don't, always. But it's far too easy to abuse the power differential, especially when the people involved, child and adult, are part of what is called the civilized world. But it doesn't *have* to be abuse; abuse is easy to fall into, but it's not inevitable. (It's been my experience, when they are a part of a non-civilized *world*, rather than hidden from view, these relationships are less likely to be abusive, because they are accessible to social policing.) But that doesn't change the statistical leaning.

We have compassion for others not because *they* have compassion. We have compassion for them because they suffer—and suffer in ways we can recognize.

Although the narrator is not too concerned with the way Hogg is going to suffer over his coming absence, the reader is. The reader can recognize the kind of energy that Hogg has put into rescuing the narrator from Big Sambo on the docks—and what it says about Hogg's feelings for the narrator, even though (or, especially though) jealousy is not particularly evident among them.

Enright: I've thought about this quite a bit. Probably from pubescence on I would have been happy to be in a sexual relationship with an adult. But a kid's desire to please adults and his fear of them, to my mind, probably robs him of the ability to exert his will when an adult wants sex but he doesn't. To my mind—and I get the sense we differ here—statutory rape laws are meant to protect children who, while not without their own desires, are often powerless against adults. They aren't just senseless, old-fashioned adherence to primitive sexual mores, like anti-sodomy statutes.

Delany: Your supposition about statutory rape laws is one of those painfully ahistorical statements that ends up grounding vast amounts of pain, harm, and injustice. Statutory rape laws have been around in this country from before the Civil War and go back in their basic form to late medieval times. As with most rape laws, they have nothing to with protecting children (or, indeed women). "Rape" means theft. Traditionally what is stolen in rape is honor, sexual purity, and marketability. Traditionally the plaintiff in a rape is the father, husband, or brother of the woman violated—who can now no longer swear to the woman's purity to intending suitors. In historical terms until fairly recently, rape "victims" were killed (without penalty from the state) by their families because they were subsequently useless in the cementing of family bonds, as they were no longer marriageable. I don't see how you can defend a law that says if, unknowingly, I give a lift to an under-eighteen-year-old and take her across a state line, thinking she's twenty or twenty-one, I am now guilty of the crime of rape, even if we did nothing in the car but chat—nor do I see how such a law protects children. Myself, I think that all rape legislation needs to be reconceived in terms of assault and coercion legislation; the way sexual elements can figure in assaults and coercions must be rethought without recourse to notions of honor or purity. But that's to get away from the thrust of our argument.

I don't think we would necessarily differ in our judgments of various relationships in the book—if you can find anything in *Hogg* you like at all. But we might well differ in how each of us feels such relationships ought to be prevented, policed, intervened in, or punished.

As it is in all situations where major power differentials fall between two people in a relationship, I think the margin for abuse depends largely on fear—as you seem to, above: in the case of child and adult, how afraid is the child of the adult? Children are terrified of adults precisely to the extent they feel themselves dependant on them. We've all watched the scene: A mother becomes frustrated by a two- or three-year-old who wants to stay and do something that just happens to be wholly inconvenient for the mother at that point. So, finally, the mother announces: "All right, Jimmy. Mommy's leaving now," and starts to walk away. Little Jimmy screams in fear and, crying, runs after his retreating mother, who finally catches up his hand and leads him off.

Well, precisely that fear of the parent's abandoning the child—which I'm sure is hardwired into most children at that age—is precisely the index to how frightened the child is—and must be, if it is to survive—of the parent.

But even with such an evident example, it's still hard for people to understand the way love and terror can cohabit in one subjectivity.

In *Hogg*, the narrator doesn't feel particularly dependent on any of the adults he's with—which is why he's not frightened of them in the same way that a more middle-class child would be. Yes, one of the "troubling" parts of the book is that, through a set of preposterous circumstances, we don't see Hogg really abusing the narrator—at least in any way the narrator doesn't actually enjoy. (The exception is Jimmy's murder. Even there, though, so many of the separate elements have already been established as relatively ego-tonic for the narrator, other than the death shot, that the whole incident finally falls outside everyone's conception— the reader's as much as the narrator's.) One has to remember that the narrator and Hogg are together for not fully seventy-two hours. Because the narrator hasn't been afraid of Hogg, that's why the relationship doesn't *feel* abusive to most readers who actually engage the text—and, indeed, the fact that it doesn't feel abusive is *why* it feels so uncomfortable. Right now the reigning wisdom is that all such relationships *must* be. Well, all I'm doing is saying: Fine. Take a look at this one—and see what you think. But through aesthetic manipulation of the plot, I've limited it to a very small period of time. Extend that time even to a full week, or two, and the relation, both to the reader and to the narrator might start to look very different.

By the end of the three days the novel chooses to examine, the narrator has decided rather sanely that, even with the kinds of things he likes to do and have done to him, he'd probably be better off with Red and Rufus than with Hogg. Almost certainly, he's right: He *will* be better off if he can manage to get back to Rufus and Red without Hogg's knowing. Red and Rufus don't beat up and savage people. They don't kill people. They have socially acceptable jobs on the proper side of the law.

But I'm not eager to think about what might happen if the narrator *isn't* successful in his escape plans. Given who Hogg is, and given the angle at which the tale is told, we *don't* know whether, should he catch the narrator trying to escape, Hogg will say, "Aw, get out of here—good riddance to you, then!" (remember he is not *sexually* jealous: but his response to attentional jealousy is still a mystery) or if he will erupt in murderous hostility when he learns the narrator himself wants to leave. Consider: Hogg has already outlined an immediate future in which the narrator is to be beaten just for fun, chained up, and sexually abused by a whole series of not very savory adults. He's done this thinking the narrator will enjoy it. But clearly Hogg will enjoy it too. The question is, how far are their desires mutually congruent? Even our perverse narrator is likely only to find this enjoyable for a *very* short while! One assumes that, indeed, it is the unpleasant side of this he wants to get away from.

If you were to tell me that, in reality, an hour after the book closes, the narrator tries to escape and Hogg catches him, and still an hour after that the narrator is in a ditch by the side of the road, beaten to death, I couldn't—and wouldn't—tell you you were wrong. It's not a nice book. I don't think you should try to make it into one.

But if you told me, rather, that, when Hogg realized the narrator wanted to leave, he said: "Hey, you've given me a lot of pleasure, kid—more than anyone else your age has ever done. So I want you to go off and give other guys like me that same pleasure. I'm not unique. I know I'm one of a group. Because you are valuable to the group I belong to, however angry I am at you personally, I want you to be free," I'd believe that too—though I'm not sure to what extent that, itself, is a post-Stonewall reading; although there is nothing post-Stonewall that doesn't have its traces, its multiple roots, its disseminated origins pre-Stonewall. That's one of the things I know from living so long on both sides of Stonewall *per se*. Fundamentally that's the form of Humbert Humbert's statement to Dolores Haze, when, years after the fact, he encounters her, age seventeen, married, and pregnant after her escape from him in *Lolita* (shortly before they both die). Indeed, it's the novel's bid for moral responsibility.

Still, the angle from which the story is told—the attitudes toward jealousy and autonomy and even children in general—makes that sort of projection finally undecidable.

Only the fact that the narrator *is* narrating the novel (rather than Humbert—or Hogg) suggests that he survives his escape from Hogg (as Lolita survives hers—however briefly). How easy or how difficult that escape actually will be, I have no way of knowing. It's outside the book. It's not part of the pattern the book asks you to observe. But, through what it excludes as much as by what it includes, the pattern there *is* one that promotes our compassion.

Often, what makes us feel compassion for characters we read about is the fact that other characters, represented in the story, *don't* have compassion for them. In the end, it's the narrator's *lack* of compassion for Hogg that makes the *reader* feel some compassion for him. Hogg has fed him; Hogg has protected him; Hogg has come after him when he's been unscrupulously stolen and sold among the fishing boats; and Hogg has battled for him and won.

Do I *want* the narrator to escape? Yes—*however* momentarily sorry I feel for Hogg.

To the extent that I identify with the narrator sexually, which, to some extent, I certainly did when I wrote it (and still do), I want the narrator to move into a more stable *social* condition: that's how, as perverts, we grow up and mature in this society—moving from a socially untenable fantasy, such as Hogg's actions represent for most of us, to a more socially tenable reality, such as Rufus and Red's way of life represents. Although the criminal aspect of Hogg's activities is what makes those acts socially available, the narrator is beginning to learn that it is the acts themselves, and *not* their criminal aspects, which he fetishizes. A different kind of pervert might have to grow along a different psychological trajectory. (The book where I first learned this was, of course, Theodore Sturgeon's brilliant *Some of Your Blood* [Carol and Graff, 1961].) Now, to get back to the ending of the novel, with the narrator sitting in the truck, contemplating his escape from Hogg: *Do* I think such an escape is likely?

When I wrote it, thirty-five years ago, I thought the narrator had a fifty/fifty chance. Today, with what I've seen of the world, I think it's closer to twenty-five/seventy-five: one out of four. But, of course, he *is* still speaking . . .

But here we've already broached that area of inevitable distortion.

Having said all the above, I think you'd be surprised how much we *do* agree on, in terms of what's right and what's wrong about relationships across major power differentials, whether of age, or of physical strength, or of economic clout, or of intellectual abilities. But the point is, all social relationships happen across such differentiating boundaries, more or less. The question becomes, how do we police them? What, actually, are we policing them for? And is there a better way to do it? Look at the amount of child abuse that happens in ordinary families—much of which, but by no means all, is sexual.

I think most people will agree: Social censure itself *is* a pretty good policing process—certainly not the *only* one or necessarily the *most* effective one. Still, it's a good one. By suddenly declaring a whole category of relationships illegal, how-

ever, you set up a situation where such relationships do not cease but rather become clandestine. And because they are never seen by others, talked about by
others, and the people involved in them never get to relate to others about their
relationships, they are far more likely to become spaces of abuse, through the secrecy alone.

In his monograph on masochism, *Coldness and Cruelty*, Gilles Deleuze points
out that "The sadist is in need of institutions, the masochist of contractual relations. The middle ages distinguished with considerable insight between two types
of pact with the devil: the first resulted from possession, the second from a pact
of alliance. The sadist thinks in terms of institutionalized possession, the masochist in terms of contracted alliance. (20)" I suspect that, once the stressed situation is over, we all expect the relationship of Hogg and the narrator to fall back
into this relatively "healthy," or at least "traditional," or predictable pattern, because, however excessive its elements, given what Hogg and the boy enjoy, they've
gone about obtaining it in such a logical manner. But that's precisely what we
can't be sure of, because the level of, yes, I'll call it psychosis in both is too high
for even that to remain predictable. The things that would make such a predic-
tion probable are the narrator's articulate speech, of the sort he seems capable of
in the *narration* of the novel, how many years after the fact; and Hogg's ability to
think and listen—which is precisely what the book undercuts by the narrator's
silence-at-the-time and Hogg's concomitant "unattended monologues" (as critic
Ray Davis has characterized them), a kind of pseudo-logical speech about which
Deleuze makes the telling point for sadists, at least sadists such as Sade:

> [T]he intention to convince is merely apparent, for nothing is in fact more
> alien to the sadist than the wish to convince, to persuade, in short to educate.
> He is interested in something quite different, namely to demonstrate that rea-
> soning itself is a form of violence, however calm and logical he may be. He is
> not even attempting to prove anything to anyone, but to perform a demon-
> stration related essentially to the solitude and omnipotence of its author. The
> point of the exercise is to show that the demonstration is identical to violence.
> It follows that the reasoning does not have to be shared by the person to whom
> it is addressed any more than pleasure is meant to be shared by the object from
> which it is derived. The acts of violence inflicted on the victims are a mere re-
> flection of a higher form of violence to which each testifies. (18–19)

However true this might be for Sade's garrulous bishops and procuresses and
libertine aristocrats, for Hogg we waver a moment before committing ourselves
to such a judgment (as we do for Humbert Humbert): One thing *Hogg* tries to

accomplish, both by making its sadist definitely working class and by setting up a situation where what that sadist (Hogg) does and what the masochist (the narrator) does are so actively pleasurable to both, in such a mutual way, it suggests that the dissociation Deleuze finds between logic and practice in the sadist is actually there in more normative mutually pleasurable relationships as well: the contingent nature of their mutual ego-tonic support alone allows us, in the normative situation, to (mis)read the relationship as coherent. (Similarly, we might waver in assigning such rhetorical cascades as this one the same sort of place as we would assign Sade's or Hogg's diatribes a place in such a schema: Is all *this*, for instance, to be taken as issuing from the masochistic educator or the haranging sadist?) Is it only the reader's desire to "learn about the book" or his/her resistance to a belief in the possibility that there is really anything to learn that contours the reading one way or the other? (The person who cannot conceive of liking any of these acts—or of finding any of them ego-tonic—can only find an argument for them, even this one, an example of sadistic violence. The person who *can* so conceive may find the argument masochistically educative.) Is it only the ego-dystonic disjunction of one kind of pleasure with another that allows us to see the dissociation/disjunction in the first place? When all is said and done, such a vision of the "normal"—which, yes, at however many removes, the book suggests—may be even more unsettling than the nature of the illusory content of the pleasurable association/conjunction.

Remember: for most of the past five thousand years, even the joining of a man and a woman was considered the joining of two people from vastly different sides of an unequal power relationship—quite as unequal, in most people's minds, as the joining of child and adult: they were perceived to be of unequal physical strength, unequal educations, unequal money-making economic potential. And women—and sometimes men—were frequently married off at eight, nine, ten, and eleven. (I've suggested in "Sword & Sorcery, S/M, and the Economics of Inadequation" [*Silent Interviews*, Samuel R. Delany, Wesleyan 1996, 2nd printing, pp. 127–63] that only such power/functional differentials *can* be sexualized; and the idea that "normative" sex, however one describes it, somehow avoids these differentials is an easily demystified fiction.) Once we leave those cultural periods when men simply owned their women, the Enlightenment way of dealing with unequal dyadic relationships was (and remains) that the weaker partner must agree to obey the stronger; and the stronger should agree to protect the weaker. While, in social milieus such as large extended families and/or village societies where such relations can be regularly and socially policed practically hour by hour, such relationships may indeed work. But writers like George Sand were pointing out, at least since Sand's first novel of 1830, *Indiana*, that the moment such a relationship becomes in any way privatized, either by money or physical isolation or urban anonymity, the same structure of obedience and protection becomes a locus of the most easily instituted and appalling abuses, psychological, physical, and economic.

This was Aurora Dupin's (Sand's) take on marriage itself.

Fourteen years ago, I became the life partner, by friendly mutual agreement, of a man named Dennis, who, at the time I met him, had been homeless for six years and living on the streets of New York City, among the city's several thousand other homeless citizens. Dennis sold books from a blanket he set up daily on 72nd Street and did sweep-up jobs now and then for the merchants in the area. We knew each other for three months before we discussed the possibility of sex; we tried that out first, over a weekend at a motel, before we moved on to discuss the possibility of living together, which we tried in a subsequent six-week trial. Only then, after talking about how we both found it, did we decide to make it permanent. If only because he was the less "socially powerful" partner, Dennis had *more* doubts about the initial situation than I did, even though he also had more to gain. A couple of years later, with artist Mia Wolff, I wrote a graphic novel about how Dennis and I first met and eventually came to live together. The book is still available in some bookstores. It's called *Bread & Wine* (Juno Books, 1999). To draw its forty-six pages, Mia also spoke at length with Dennis. He took her (and me) on a tour of where he used to live and sleep in the city, before we got together. Though I wrote the actual words, Dennis was a co-producer of the book and still refers to it as "our book"—as do I. We both took photos of where we lived in Amherst, Massachusetts. Mia had us pose for a lot of the pictures that she drew.

I mention this particular book for two reasons: First, because there *are* several major power differentials between Dennis and me. And, second, because just a few days ago, on the web I read a review of the book that was kind of interesting.

Apparently the reviewer found the book almost as upsetting as you might expect people reacting to *Hogg*. The reviewer found the book "really creepy." He was somewhere between appalled and disbelieving that, fourteen years later, Dennis and I were still together and happy. His basic two worries were (one) how can two people who are so different in their experiences and educations even like each other, much less have anything to talk about, and (two) because Dennis had been homeless for six years and living on the street, he assumed Dennis must be crazy and psychotic and "wouldn't be surprised to learn that he had murdered Delany in his bed some day!"

Well, the answer to the first one is: Yes, I have a fairly high IQ: in spite of my dyslexia, when I was eleven or twelve it tested out at 169. I've written and published some forty books, twenty-three of them fiction (my first novel appeared when I was twenty) and the rest nonfiction, some of them scholarly; when Dennis and I met, I was a professor of comparative literature and the head of my department at the University of Massachusetts. Dennis stopped attending school when he was thirteen, and when we met, though he was a regular newspaper reader, he had never actually read an entire book end to end. (He has since read two, *Shogun* and one of mine—*The Motion of Light in Water*.) Dennis is also twelve years younger than I am. (Today he's fifty; I'm sixty-two.) I find Dennis endlessly fascinating—and I think he finds me interesting, if not equally fascinating. Also, we really do like each other and enjoy each other's company. Though I don't always agree with them, I find his takes on the world endlessly interesting and always informative. And he is sincerely tickled, I think, to discover that someone as smart as I am and who has a fair amount of social recognition can be so absent-minded or confused and befuddled by the small mix-ups of life—which he is much better than I am at keeping straight. (He is an obsessive organizer and knows where everything is; I can keep track of almost nothing.) Dennis enjoys social attention and likes people in general, as do I. When he's occasionally mentioned in a newspaper article, usually one about me, he finds it a gas. Our day to day life is relatively private: not a lot of social or extended family "policing" goes on to make sure power balances aren't abused—though there is some, both from family (specifically my daughter, a number of my cousins) and friends (a housemate, three or four other friends). And, in words of one syllable, the sex is still good.

As to the reviewer's objection (two), he seems wholly to have missed something Alan Moore cites in his "Introduction" that appears in *Bread & Wine*: Dennis was the one who was initially worried that *I* might be the psycho, "cutting me up in little pieces and burying them every which-where." As Moore points out, if you look at the Dahmers and the Nilsens, not to mention the Gilles de Rais's or the Countess Bathory's, whose fears—the middle-class reviewer's or Dennis's—are more grounded in actuality?

A major organizing principle by which Dennis and I live—and it seems to work—is that I make most of the major decisions having to do with money and general living arrangements. Dennis is pretty comfortable with these and goes along with them pretty easily. But perhaps to one in twenty of these, he takes exception. When he does, without question I back off. This is not something that I learned I had to do from experience, or from conflicts with him where I insisted on doing it my way and the results turned out badly. No. The first time he ever said, quietly, "No, I don't want us to do it that way," I just frowned, thought a moment, then said:

"Okay. We do it your way." And we did. And everything was fine.

So that's how it works. And it works well.

I can figure out 150 reasons why this has stabilized the relationship *per se*, starting from the fact that Dennis knows he has "veto power," as it were, on anything we do; he doesn't abuse it, and I try hard not to abuse the "primary decision making" power he has agreed, even urged me, to take. (As he's explained, he doesn't want it.)

Now Dennis is not a child—nor was he ever a child, in the course of our relationship. He was thirty-five when we met. I was forty-seven. He turned thirty-six a couple of weeks before we started living together.

But one of the things that I think people are coming to understand more and more is that there is a politics to *any* sort of relationship: that is to say, there are always rights and responsibilities on both sides. What is far more important than that they are "equal" in any objective manner is that both sides are comfortable and pleased with them and with the inevitable inequalities; and that the inequalities contour to the picture both partners have of themselves and of each other. Certainly once both sides are relatively linguistically competent, these have to be negotiated, and—in the case of parents and children, say—renegotiated regularly, year after year. Again, lack of fear is a large factor. Although I'm sure he doesn't particularly want to, Dennis knows how to survive on the street—of which, between once every year and once every year-and-a-half, (jokingly) Dennis reminds me. In no way are we afraid of each other.

Now, nowhere in the seventy-two-odd hours that *Hogg* covers do you see Hogg and the narrator—or Hogg and Denny for that matter—negotiating the rights and responsibilities that each has. (You do see [some of] it in *Bread & Wine*.) But finally that's why I would say that the lack of negotiating space, perhaps under the pressure of the immediate situations that they are involved in, which pretty much takes up all their time, leaves *Hogg*'s characters in a high-stress situation for the duration, which occludes any such negotiations. This is what finally places the characters in a relational space in which its "health" simply *can't* be judged. That's another of the novel's aesthetic distortions.

Part of this is, of course, the project of the novel—that is, the absence of any view of such a space (and its absence in a story where you don't miss it; at least not right away) is part of the novel's art. (*Hogg* is structured as an adventure novel, and one of the reasons people like adventure novels is because, in the relationships presented, often there isn't time to negotiate them: people are more or less stuck with the ones that fall into their laps. Because of the stress of the "adventure" *per se*, people [i.e., the characters] put up with behavior in a partner they would not think of putting up with in an ordinary situation.) Certainly the implication—which controls at least *some* of our judgments on it, however— is that Rufus, Red, and the narrator *will* probably do a better job of negotiating these political decisions than would the narrator and Hogg—so that, again, the narrator's decision to quit one situation for the other is finally, no matter the pathos entailed, a good one.

But, we need to point out, this is a bit of novelistic sleight-of-hand. We're talking about a purely relative situation here, whose relativity the writer has maneuvered to appear in just such a light. Hogg has his monologues; but has he ever really *listened* to anyone in his life? Save for that final word, the narrator has never spoken. We have no idea if he *would* be able to negotiate his own side at all. If this were reality, rather than fiction, that would be a very serious problem indeed, no matter how understanding Red and Rufus turned out to be.

Because I'm a bit of a utopian, I'm a great believer in education. All three major sexual relations I've had in my own life have been open relationships— one with a woman, two with men. For my particular psychology and temperament, I find open relationships preferable. I'm not interested in a monogamous relationship, and I wouldn't be interested in getting involved over a long term with someone who wanted one. Now open relationships are very specific kinds of relationships. They require as much thought, care, concern, and—yes— commitment as monogamous ones do. But, so far, I've never seen a book on how to have a good one. Lots of people are in them, but they're always having to re-invent the wheel, as it were.

Certainly there are principles that, if you follow them, are likely to reduce the strains of relationships with people across major power differentials, for both opened and closed relationships. But neither partner can be afraid—indeed, fear seems so often to be the major lever in closed relationships (the ones that break up because of infidelity), which is one of my large criticisms of them. There *are* many very satisfactory relationships between older and younger adults—and there are things to remember that the people involved need to know in order to make them work. Less than seventy-five years ago, in this country, however, in the rural areas, marriages between twelve-, thirteen-, and fourteen-year-olds and forty-, forty-five-, and fifty-year-olds were common enough not to raise an eyebrow. But even those relationships are going to be happier if certain principles are considered, interrogated, and adhered to than if they are not.

Now having said *this*, not much of this relates to *Hogg* directly as a novel.

Frankly, I don't believe that Honey-Pie is happy in her relation with her father, Big Sambo, anymore than the narrator is happy in his relation to him. But the narrator does learn something from her, which, at the end of the novel he uses: That language can be used to dissemble—and particularly to dissemble to adults who, at the moment, would seem—like Hogg himself seems, just then—to be sincerely concerned for you.

It may seem paradoxical from my statement that generally speaking I think sexual relations between children and adults are likely to go wrong and that most of them are likely to be, start off as, or quickly become, abusive, that I also support a group like NAMBLA—which I do. But that's because I feel one of the largest factors in the abuse is fostered by the secrecy itself and lack of *social* policing of the relationships. A little history helps:

For thousands of years, relations that today we assume are abusive by definition (child marriages, slavery, child labor, etc.) were the social and legal norm. They were institutional and ubiquitous. As well, behavior that we would find wholly unacceptable—flogging for slaves, wife beating in marriage, and child beating (in the family, in the school, and at the factory)—was regularly recommended by experts *and* clergymen as the most efficient and least disruptive way to maintain order and the necessary disciplined hierarchy for these institutions to function efficiently. More lenient ways were to be avoided, ran the general wisdom, because, while they might be attractive in the short run (as novels and melodramas welcomed more and more social types into the circle of compassion), in the long run they produced only further troubles.

Born a slave in northern Georgia, my paternal grandfather beat all ten of his children regularly—with switches he made them go and cut themselves, then bring back to him. All ten remembered him as a wise and loving father. He was a minister, a scholar, and the vice principal of a black religious college in North Carolina. His beatings were wholly operationalized: "He never hit us when he was angry," all ten of them agreed. As well, all agreed that the real punishment was the torture of having to go cut the switches with which you would be beaten—next to which the actual beating was, if anything, a relief. All ten agreed that, without this discipline, it would have been chaos. All ten remembered as a comic mishap the single incident when, once, this operationalization broke down: in an uncharacteristic rage, he chained one of his boys to the water pump and, in a fury, beat him bloody with an orange crate until the wood was in splinters.

Presumably, it was funny because it *only* happened once.

Ten years younger than my father, my mother, who was born and grew up in New York City, several times said that, to her, my father's father, whom she never met (in the last years of his life, he separated from his wife and sent her to live with her daughters in the north so that he himself could live, unhampered, with a woman who had been his housekeeper, so that grandfather and grandmother were not together when either of them died, a situation none of his children would ever discuss), sounded to her like a monster and that, in her opinion, from the stories all ten of his children constantly told about him (they were a very close family), his children's love for him verged on the insane.

Indeed, if anyone wants to see *Hogg* itself as an attempt on my part to work through the contradictions that swirled around the image of this grandfatherly figure who, while he was long dead at my birth, nevertheless dominated my childhood and my growing up, they are certainly free, and even encouraged, to do so.

All of these institutions changed, nevertheless, only when they were no longer economically feasible or beneficial to the greater society. My mother's take and my father's (and his siblings') take on this family institution, which my slave-born grandfather represented, represents as well a conflict among discourses, northern and southern, rural and urban, slave and free, male and female, and probably many more.

The pain or strain on the participants was, in all such cases, absolutely and totally secondary—although in all these cases, once the laws *were* changed, in the extant public discourses about them those subjective reasons were allowed to displace the material and political reasons, almost totally. By the same token, the socioeconomic reasons that brought on the actual changes were allowed to drop out of the discussion. The reasons that these relations worked as well as they did in terms of the subjectivities of the subalterns involved (i.e., the intersecting discourses, the social relations that previously had stabilized such situations) were also forgotten, discourses that were initially set in place through that social policing. Privatization and criminalization remove them from any such social surveillance and increases the possibility of abuse by major factors in all but the most priorly socialized persons.

Enright: One disturbing argument of the book is embodied in Hogg's speech to Ray the bartender, about the difference between normal people and sexual outlaws, where he equates subs/doms, gays, etc—with "babyfuckers" and professional rapists like him. Hogg, as I read him, is supposed to be intelligent and, in his way, moral—he tells the guys to ease up occasionally and even muses they'd be justified in turning him in to the cops. So his failure to distinguish between those whose sexual tastes are merely unconventional and those who hurt others is all the more perplexing, especially since many of his arguments—that women

should revolt, that the warmakers and downsizers are at least as evil as him—
strike me as cogent.

Delany: Do you know Terrence McNally's first play, which he wrote when he was
twenty-five, *And Things That Go Bump in the Night*? I saw it when it was first performed on Broadway, with Eileen Heckart, many years ago—and at least four
years before Stonewall. It very much impressed me, and, I think, when all is said
and done, *Hogg*, which I wrote, after all, only three or four years later, pretty much
shares its overall theme.

Briefly, in a post-holocaust landscape, a family is managing to survive—a
monstrous mother, her late adolescent son, and her somewhat younger daughter.
Each day, before sundown, the brother and sister go out and lure someone back to
spend the night with them; and each night, this person is both emotionally and
physically destroyed. In the course of things, we learn that, one night when they
did not have someone to destroy, they turned on one another and almost killed
each other, so that they now know this nocturnal ritual is a matter of their own
survival. Truly, they are an unsavory and monstrous lot. But, in a reversal that occurs perhaps twenty minutes before the last act's end, once we have watched them
drive their victim for the night to suicide, as they prepare for sunrise to get ready
and go out to find another, the mother turns to harangue the audience directly:
The substance of her dithyramb is that, while she and her brood destroy one person every twenty-four hours, by our lack of care and simple ignorance of the way
in which the world works, we, the audience, destroy thousands on thousands of
people unknowingly and produce the carnage among which only such people as
she and her murdering offspring can survive.

It was a pretty devastating argument, when I saw it. Heckart's monologue is
another sadist's harangue, but it left a lot of people squirming.

This is not the primary "theme" of *Hogg*, but certainly it's a secondary motif.

Enright: I'm neither gay nor a minority nor female. But I've always felt like an
outsider—a misfit. One reason why *Hogg* and *The Mad Man* are important to me
is that they really present things from the outsider's perspective—albeit a very
particular outsider. Still, to me, the books are so great especially because they
avoid that same boring, middle-class, average guy perspective. Almost all the big
characters are marginalized by society—and now they have their own book. It reminds me of how excited I'd get when I was in grade-school and some periph-
eral Archie Comics character like Dilton or Moose would get their own comic
book. They've even encouraged me to be more experimental in my private life.
(The books, that is—not the Archie comics. Though I suppose Jughead might be

an appropriate model for asexuality and eating-as-sublimated-desire.) My point? Thanks for writing them.

Delany: You're most welcome.

Enright: Mr. Jonas and Jimmy both meet deadly fates (as I guess all fates are eventually)—and I can't help feeling that their deaths are morally instructive. Is commissioning abuse, in the case of Mr. Jonas, somehow worse than inflicting it? Or in the case of Jimmy, is rationalizing misogyny and violence somehow worse than merely practicing it? In one interview you describe Jimmy as "morally loathsome"—well, sure, but in comparison to Hogg and Denny *et alia*, who inflict a lot more pain than he does? More prosaically, why would Mr. Jonas be in the driver's seat of his limo?

Delany: By and large, the commissioners of abuse have not yet been brought into the circle of compassion. (My elementary school-mate Ariel Dorfman, in his most provocative play, *Death and the Maiden*, has made perhaps the most intelligent first steps in this direction.) Mr. Jonas drives his own limo because most of Mr. Jonas's power is show. Not only does he drive his own limo, he also answers his own front door bell. As well, having to pay out relatively small amounts of money, given the services he wants to purchase, really bothers him. He wants the services themselves because it makes him look important. He's a man—a racketeer—living way beyond his means, so that his death at someone else's hands is almost inevitable. Yes, that it's a motorcycle accident Hawk is responsible for is ironic. But it follows—at least I hope it does. Also, while it's an ironic coincidence, it's one that doesn't register with anyone else except the narrator, for whom, finally, it's just *not* that significant.

Enright: As an author who's received no shortage of critical lauding I'd be curious to know where you think *Hogg* stands in your *oeuvre*. I'm sure it's hard for you to make these judgments, but do you see the book as important as some people do? (One site listed it and *Dhalgren* as among the 100 most important books of the century.)

Delany: I suspect that you've seen more criticism of *Hogg* than I have. I've read less than half a dozen reviews—probably only four, or even three.

I simply don't put any energy to speak of trying to work through such questions. That's for someone else's critical enterprise, someone who feels it's worth the time and thought. That someone might feel that way is complimentary. But it's not a question I'm inclined to take up on my own.

Enright: Denny's spree: why is it important that it take place off-stage? Are you, as one analyst suggested, drawing a line between rape and murder? And is the spree—which only begins once he finally feels his erection—a metaphor for suppressed desire? This seems like an apropos interpretation of events to me—especially as you say the book would have been impossible following Stonewall. Almost like you were saying, "if society insists on stifling us, that energy will come out in ways much less constructive than a little reckless sex."

Delany: I certainly don't have any problem with the reading you've just proposed. I've discussed some of this in two essays, one called "The Scorpion Garden" and another called "The Scorpion Garden Revisited" (the second as by K. Leslie Steiner. You'll find both collected in a book of my essays called *The Straits of Messina*, Sarconia Press, 1987.) I'd hoped Denny's off-stage murder spree would function like the fourth act of a Shakespearean tragedy. During those famous Elizabethan fourth acts, the major characters are off stage, resting up for the final fifth-act sword fight. It's both structural and ironic. It's there to worry you—"Why, when the whole thing is suddenly distanced like this, do I find it so funny? What is the endless sentimentality and sensationalism of the media through which it comes to the reader (and the narrator) doing to my perception of it all?"

You've just spent almost a hundred pages with Denny. You know, yes, he's a nut case. But what you're learning about is the kind of nut case you thought he was up till now. And, of course, what does this all make of the last thirty-odd pages of the novel, when Hogg is trying to rescue Denny—both from the police and from Denny's own self-inflicted insanity? Is what Hogg does logical? Why does it seem so, if it's not? Can you buy the implicit explanation for his behavior, at least in terms of the novel? Or is this just an implied ratiocination of the narrator's that's mostly a function of his own immaturity? We are back at those distortions of presentation we began with, I'm afraid.

One of the most important of those distortions is simply that the book is pornography. Its action takes place in Pornotopia—that is, the land where any situation can become rampantly sexual under the least increase in the pressure of attention. Like its sister lands, Comedia and Tragedia, it can only be but so realistic.

One of the most unrealistic things about the literary precinct of realism is that it is situated *so* far from the other three. Though I am happy to label the books with the despised term, finally they are works of the borderlands.

Hogg is another of my stories that takes place in the city of Enoch.

But these are all textual questions—and put us in contact with the discursive formulations that, I suspect, allow the novel to signify.

Enright: Finally, does it bother you that *The Mad Man* and *Hogg* always get discussed together? To me, aside from an omnivorous attitude toward sex (though John Marr in *The Mad Man* obviously has some taboos that *Hogg*'s narrator doesn't) and some particular fetishes, the books couldn't be more different. If I flip to any page in *Hogg*, I'll probably see some scene that'll haunt me for the next few days. If I crack open *The Mad Man* at random, I'll encounter a character or a situation that'll make me smile and maybe even laugh. John is such a great character to take us through the sexual underbelly—he's likable and, aside from his brilliance, a pretty regular guy. But maybe you see the commonality that I don't?

Delany: I think the affect of the two books is very different, though certainly both focus on the sexual. They were written thirty years apart—and in two hugely different eras, pre-Stonewall and post-Stonewall. Does the discussion bother me? Well, once a book is finished and out in the world, I aspire to keep them in that part of my mind where bother is, as it were, not a bother—if you can follow what I mean.

Enright: Anyway, I appreciate your taking the time to read and respond to my questions—and for writing such great books. You said you were busy; as a reader, I'll say I hope that at least part of that business is writing a new book for me to devour.

Questions on the Comic Art Form: Erin Cusack Interviews Samuel R. Delany

Erin Cusack/2005

Previously unpublished interview. Printed with permission of Erin Cusack.

Erin Cusack: Comics artist Will Eisner uses the term sequential art when describing comics. Scott McCloud, author of *Understanding Comics, The Invisible Art* (1993) provides the definition: "juxtaposed pictorial and other images in deliberate sequence." What is your perspective on these definitions, and is there any specification (or non-specification) you would like to contribute from your understanding of the comics art form?

Samuel R. Delany: I've written at length about the intellectually crippling part the mania for definitions (and the equally crippling mania for origins) plays in the criticism of the paraliterary genres. (The paraliterary genres are the genres that your ordinary man-on-the-street, if you asked him and he answered quickly without thinking, would likely say are not really literature—are not aesthetically first rate: comic books, westerns, science fiction, mysteries, pornography . . .) But whether literary or paraliterary, no artistic genre can be defined. Genres are far too complex. Nor does any have a single origin. They are *always* the result of multiple forces and many events in the world. Because we might be talking of a single aspect, we might want to highlight one historical moment in its development rather than another, but that's the best we can do. To assume we're doing anything more authoritative than that—to assume that we've found *the* defining moment—for the entire modern phenomenon is just critical arrogance and/or selling short the complexity of the phenomenon under discussion. Good critics respect history, but precisely because they respect and realize it *is* a complex interplay of events and forces, they don't try to simplify it into these highly conservative and distorting (and finally rather authoritarian) models. Because each genre of artistic production exists primarily as a set of interpretive codes that *most* readers share, even while some of those codes of necessity are going to be somewhat different for *each and every* reader—and because a whole set of those codes has to do with how important *originality* and *new developments* are in the specific examples of the genre we hold up as particularly valuable—artistic genres belong to a category of social human objects that resists definition.

I mean, how can you give a rigorous and boundary limiting definition of some category of object, the most important example of which—when, sometime tomorrow, it arrives within our ken—we will recognize precisely *because* it is different from all the others that *do* fit the definition we came up with yesterday? No one has been able to define poetry, or define the novel, or define drama, or even define the essay . . . not to mention art, sculpture, music, or dance.

Part of the complexity of each of these has to do with how readers interact with the given object. A good part of modern poetry is because we agree to read it *as* poetry. A good deal of modern art is because we agree to look at it, there on the museum wall, *as* art. Sitting in the concert hall, we agree to listen to a particular concatenation of sounds *as* music.

No dance critic, for instance, would begin an analysis of any single dance or even a set of dances or even some historical subsection of dance like ballet or ballroom dancing with an attempt (totally impossible) to define all dance:

Many dances are a case of movement that is supposed to give pleasure to whoever watches.

Many dances do. But there are whole sets of religious dances throughout the world where the pleasure of the viewer is quite secondary or simply irrelevant to their purpose.

One of the most delightful modern dances I ever saw, given during an evening's performance along with a number of other modern dance works, involved a bare stage, where, after a few seconds, once the lights came up, a voice sounded out, describing how a dancer comes out to the center ("A single dancer walks to center stage, and, as the music begins, rises up on point . . ."), begins to dance, then is joined by many more, then still more, till ("suddenly the back wall of the stage pulls apart, revealing three quarters of a mile of football field, where hundred of dancers leap about, who now all rush forward, onto the stage . . .") finally hundreds are on stage, and the voice goes on to describe them doing perfectly impossible things ("Three dancers run up the stage's left wall and begin to pirouette across the theater's ceiling, upside down, above the orchestra . . ."), finally to leave a single dancer on the stage once more, who (the voice explains) comes forward to the stage apron and takes a low bow.

At that point, the stage lights went off again.

But other than what occurred in the audience's mind (which, given the laughter and applause throughout the whole "performance," was considerable), this dance involved neither actual movement, actual human beings, nor music!

But for that evening, the rather sophisticated dance audience in the Joyce Theater on New York's Eighth Avenue was willing—even delighted (the piece got a
rousing ovation)—to look at something that, under other circumstances, might
have been considered a poem, a dance scenario, or even an essay or a play, as a
dance.

Actually it was very witty—and sometimes touching—as it was intended to be.

Only the paraliterary genres—which are often viewed as socially second-rate
genres—are assumed (incorrectly, I feel) to be subject to definition. One (though
it is by no means the only) reason they are assumed to be such is because they are
seen as simpler, less protean, and, yes, finally less humanly and socially important
than other genres.

The fact that paraliterary critics like McCloud constantly appeal to definitions
and origins makes this a vicious circle (paraliterary critics tend, these days, to be
the *only* critics who do), which I would like to see paraliterary criticism break
out of.

Well, part of what makes modern comics—and this is especially true of a
relatively unusual graphic novel (both as to its story and its art) such as *Bread &*
Wine—is that we agree to read a given text as a comic. The best readers will read
such texts with the full, rich, wide-ranging interpretive techniques comics have
built up since the government started using them to instruct soldiers (many of
whom could not read or write worth a damn) back in World War One. I think, by
the way, that's a far more important weigh-station in modern comics history than
Egyptian picture writing or any of the other—dare I call it—nonsense (not because it isn't historically interesting, but because it displaces so much that would
be so much *more* telling) that McCloud cites in *Understanding Comics* (and that
all but swamps *Reinventing Comics* [McCloud: 2000]). One of the problems
with "definition" and its handmaid "origin" is that, in pursuit of them, we get
so caught in legitimating our despised genre that we forget the material history
of our actual object of consideration. McCloud *knows* about those instructional
comics—he's seen them and paged through them. (The fact that he includes "in-
struction" in his definition is his unacknowledged nod to them.) But, in his own
history, he's overlooked discussing them directly, because he's more interested in
associating comics with more respectable arts, historical events, and objects.

This is very risky.

When McCloud writes about how we read modern comics (the gutters,
closure, the various ways we respond to various aspects of them, the way they
deal with time . . .), he is, I think, unfailingly brilliant. McCloud on the "history"
and "origins" of comics is, I think equally, off in some legitimating Cloud Coo-
Coo Land. Comics *are* interesting and rich. McCloud's book is proof positive of

that. But you don't have to borrow that interest and value from other arts and other epochs. Better to dig it out of the objects themselves—and out of your own relationship to the object—an aesthetic project that goes directly back to the great nineteenth-century critic and fiction writer Walter Pater, by the bye. (It doesn't originate with Pater. It passes through him. But he's one of the people who brought it to a boil, when it did.)

I think we have to start off giving the paraliterary genres—comics, mysteries, advertising, westerns, science fiction, and, yes, even pornography—the same intellectual respect that we give the literary genres. (To anticipate one of your later questions, that's part of what a text is. Indeed, the concept of text was revitalized toward the middle of the last century to accomplish precisely that: movies [and also popular music] were once considered secondary and silly, "by definition." When popular critics such as Sontag, Kael, Sarris, and others decided that film was perhaps the most influential art of the first half of the century—they had to invent the modern notion of text to allow in films. Sontag called it "the great democracy of texts"—which presumably has to allow in comics too, to be consistent with itself.) What we can do, however, is describe the aspects of a particular genre that interest us.

That's what good criticism is.

In even so brilliant a work as *Understanding Comics*, McCloud makes the same self-crippling gesture by getting caught up in definitions, rather than spending those pages on what strike me as the *most* brilliant parts of his exegesis, such as when, say, he describes the way the gestural and most cartoonish parts of the drawing are perceived as subjective by the viewer—as a "self"—and the most "realistic" representations are perceived as objective—as McCloud says, as an "other."

What the comics medium can do is move the viewer in and out, back and forth, between those states, even as the eye moves over a single page, even within a single panel.

You'll see that happening in Wolff's drawings in our graphic novel *Bread & Wine*:

Consider the series of drawings on page 22, giving the account of Dennis's father's death: In the second row of panels, first is the silhouetted figure of the long-haired workman getting drunk at the bar—Dennis himself: his figure is dark, mysterious, even menacing.

Then, in the wider panel beside it, you see the figure of Dennis's father—also drunk—weaving through the street at night, looking for his grown son. But his form is merely sketched in a swirl of lines, with which art students have been taught for many years, now, to draw quickly in order to get down basic shapes and suggest their movement.

But it's also subject to McCloud's considerations: *vis-à-vis* the silhouette, because it's a form of simplified, stylized cartoon, that figure is "you"—you are, for a panel, Dennis's inebriated, physically unbalanced dad, in the street at night, the lights and darknesses falling every which way about him, illuminating nothing for him. In the same way your body pushes away from the dark mass of "Dennis," in the first cramped panel on that row, in the second, roomier panel, your body tries to find its place in that open swirl. The non-realistic and sketchy visual rhetoric with which Dennis's father is rendered invites you into it.

In the next, larger and lower panel, the van swerves around the garbage truck: All lines here are heavy, thick, like woodcuts. (This serves to slow the feel of the action—to render it in a kind of comics slow motion.) The "same" figure—so airy and unbalanced, in the panel above—is here in silhouette! Now he looks far closer to the way Dennis himself was drawn, just above it, at the bar. The figure who, a panel ago, was your "self" is now the most opaque and menaced/ menacing of "others": The immediate reading of the panel is that you, the viewer, are behind the figure, who is facing the oncoming van. Once the figure is struck, though, the van will move on toward you! A second look, however, suggests the figure might as easily be fleeing the van *toward* you, the viewer. (The reflected light on the back of the figure's lower leg keeps resolving—then failing to resolve—the ambiguity of the direction of the figure's motion.) In a moment, Dennis's father will fall into your arms, and you must somehow protect him from his death. (But the words, "struck him, killed him . . ." toward the panel's bottom let us know you failed.) Because of the way these three panels are drawn, your own relation as viewer to the figure is thrown into question by the rendering, by the visual rhetoric, by the information it provides as well as the information it withholds. You are first pulled into, then wrenched from, that *en passant* position of subjectivity and thrown into a moment of objectivity by the headlights bearing down—an objectivity that turns out to be even more ambiguous than the drunken cartoonish subjectivity. (Which way *is* the figure running, toward you or away?) If you let yourself experience it, the effect is that Dennis—recounting the story, above—for a moment isn't really sure who was struck, his father or himself. He wants to save his father, to protect him; but he is equally menaced by that death . . .

Now, none of this is in Dennis's words—which are not even given, only synopsized by Chip—the pudgy naked guy who listens, his eyes half closed, next to Dennis on the motel room bed. Dennis's eyes are completely shut as he talks, suggesting the semi-dream state, or at any rate the imaginative reconstruction, of the incident below them.

We can understand—and, if we let ourselves, feel all this bodily, with a little nudging from McCloud, between the sketchy, cartoonish second panel and the heavy dark woodcut-like panels before and after it—the complex nature of the effect of his father's death on Dennis himself.

Words alone can't do it. And certainly they can't do it in the same way.

For me it's an interesting visual moment in the story—one that experienced comics viewers (or, perhaps, comics viewers who are familiar and attuned to McCloud's most insightful critical moments) will have an easier time apprehending than those who aren't.

Cusack: I think, as McCloud also points out, that without the word "pictorial," juxtaposed static images in deliberate sequences could well be the definition for letters or even the entity of words. What do you think about the relationship between comic panels and prosaic text? Are they both legitimate forms of reading through abstraction?

Delany: Definitions function largely to exclude. Descriptions—because, by definition, they are not exhaustive—are welcoming and often function inclusively, along with other descriptions. Often criticism in the 1930s felt it was competing with science, where definitions and exclusions were really necessary. But science and art are not the same. And definition is largely a thirties lit. critical notion. It hasn't been a major part of literary criticism since the sixties.

The difference between definition and (the term I prefer) functional description might seem small. But finally it's very important, not only for what it does to the logic of your argument, as you get farther and farther away from it, but also for the attitude (exclusive or inclusive) that each term carries with it, attitudes that control how you'll continue and what you'll end with.

I have no problems with a sentence such as, "The overwhelming majority of what most of us recognize as comics juxtapose pictures or other images in a deliberate sequence, intended to convey information and/or to produce an aesthetic response." What McCloud actually writes, however, is:

> **Comics** (ko'mics) **n.** plural form, used with a singular verb. 1. Juxtaposed pictorial and other images in deliberate sequence, intended to convey information and/or to produce an aesthetic response in the viewer.

I wouldn't argue with McCloud's "definition," because in western critical discourse, immediately that suggests that his definition might be corrected. I don't think it can. What I would rather do, is suggest that you look closely at the visual and verbal rhetoric *around* McCloud's definition, as it occurs in McCloud's own book: First, there's the argument that it ends, where visually it apes a definitional entry on a dictionary page. It more or less concludes a movement in a presentation in which cartoon-Scott speaks with a largely invisible (or silhouetted) audience, during which a sequence of previous definitions are tried and found wanting. At the same time, film and animation are discussed in marginal relations to the rest of the central discussion.

Among all that, however, I feel two panels are particularly important for reading McCloud's discussion productively. The two are among the smallest panels in the sequence. One comes at the very beginning of the discussion—the last panel on page 5—and one comes in the middle of the whole thing—the second panel on the top row of page 9. Both are rich with irony. Both are put there to make the ordinary comics reader smile—and even laugh.

I point them out, however, because, in their tone and their feeling, they seem *most* closely related to comics and *least* related to what we usually think of as academic criticism. They are doing something far more likely to be done in comics, and while it *can* be done by formal critics, it has to be done very differently. But I also think that—critically and crucially—they are doing much more.

Let's start with that last panel on page 5: "But to define comics," cartoon-Scott is saying, "we must first do a little aesthetic surgery and separate form from content." The picture, however, does not show a doctor with a scalpel. It shows, rather, Scott with an ax, getting ready to swing!

Then, we turn over the page: Form and content are presented as a glass pitcher (labeled "comics"), and content would seem to be the dark liquid the pitcher contains.

The ax with which Scott was ready to separate them has been left behind on the previous page. It was just a joke, an exaggeration, a moment of hyperbolic irony . . . Here, on page 6, we see (in panels 2 and 3) that separating them is only a matter of lifting the full pitcher and pouring its contents (initially labeled "Writers, Artists, Trends, Genres, Styles, Subject Matter, Themes") out into a glass—from one form into another, presumably to show what remains constant, when we *vary* its form.

Cartoon-Scott drinks the glass of "content"—suddenly to cough and spit out what he's imbibed. Recovering, he tells us: "The trick is NEVER to mistake the message for . . . the messenger." (The last word occurs over a panel that shows the glittering, empty vessel sitting in the light.) But the coughing and a number of other things—particularly in the two small panels I'm concentrating on—suggests that perhaps some confusion has already occurred. Clearly cartoon-Scott did not drink what he thought he was drinking down—simple tasty content removed from its form and put in a harmless new form, the glass.

In some way, *did* he mistake messenger for message? Or did he mistake content for form?

Before we get to the second of my two privileged panels, let's stop and look at the largest panel on page 6—the one in the lower corner. Here cartoon-Scott describes the happier fate of other artistic genres: as he does so, six glass pitchers, each the same shape as "comics," hang against the starry night, in two matched rows of three each. The six glass pitchers are labeled:

Written Word   Music   Video
Theater   Visual Arts   Film

Beside them, cartoon-Scott explains: "At one time or another, virtually all the great media have received critical examination, in and of themselves." And in the last panel on the page, he goes on: "But for comics, this attention has been rare . . ."

If we look at the six pitchers of the other "great media," and compare them to "comics," we can note something: Save the gleam from the stars that illuminate their surfaces, the glass pitchers are *completely* black. The "comics" pitcher was filled just to the neck with dark content, but empty and transparent above that, allowing us to make a visual distinction between form and content before any separation—the pouring out—occurred. But because we are looking at these pitchers against the night, we as viewers can't tell: Are the pitchers of the other media completely empty and transparent—that is, composed of nothing *but* form? Or are they *so* filled with content that the two, in their cases—form and content—are perfectly coextensive and thus really one? Is each pitcher perhaps its own content? Or is what it contains actually the form? That's certainly what would explain cartoon-Scott's coughing, when he (and we) thought he was drinking simple content. From the way they are drawn in this particular panel, whatever we decide to do with the rest, it's arguable that such a distinction is undecidable.

Recall that ax—hold it in your mind there—as we go on and look at the second of these two little ironic panels I mentioned.

The second panel I want to highlight is, as I've said, in the middle of the top row of three panels on page 9. In the previous two pages (and thirteen panels), Scott has been talking from a lecture stage to an implied audience, who every other panel or so adds another term to his placard on which his "definition" of comics grows. It started out with Eisner's definition "Sequential Art." But by page 9 it's grown to "Juxtaposed Pictorial and Other Images in Deliberate Sequence."

At this point, in *our* panel, making a somewhat surprised cartoon-Scott look off to the left, someone in the audience calls out (possibly from a box seat: the caret on the dialogue balloon suggests that the origin of the voice is above some of the audience): "What about BATMAN?! Shouldn't it have Batman in it?"

Responding, another voice calls up from the front of the auditorium, from someone we presume is more serious than our (certainly young) heckler, who possibly even gives voice to Scott's thoughts—or who, more likely, voices an aspect of our own thought (cartoon-Scott is silent in this panel): "Who let him in?"

After this interruption, Scott continues with his argument, which climaxes just below the little ironic panel: the right hand gutter of the ironic panel and the right hand gutter of the panel with the dictionary definition are totally aligned, the only two gutters among the first six (and two rows of) panels that do line up.

I would suggest that both bits of irony (even to their alignment)—both the picture of Scott with the ax, ready to separate form from content, and the ironic Batman heckler—perform one job, a job that reinforces the ambiguity in the large panel of the classical pitchers against the night sky in the lower corner of page 6 and Scott's confusion over what he was actually drinking—form or content—once he pours out the liquid from the "comics" pitcher in the row of panels above it: Both are ways of suggesting it might be harder to separate form from content than it first seems, or even to tell which one is which. They continue, both before and after it, what the coughing suggests and what is portrayed for the traditional genres: What you think content may, indeed, be form.

If that ax persisted over the page break, and we used it on the beaker full of comics content, it would shatter the vessel of "form" and the "content" would run out all over the floor and be forever irretrievable.

As well, however naïve the heckler's question seems, it still raises the question: To what extent is "Batman," to which we initially respond as if it were pure content *par excellence*, actually a defining form? Maybe it's a genre—another kind of content, at least as McCloud initially labels it (Look: "Genre" is there on the liquid in the "comics" beaker.) But aren't all genres finally a *kind* of form? Isn't style—another thing McCloud lists under "content"—a matter of form? Throughout the history of criticism, "style" and "content" have been set up in opposition as frequently as "form" and "content." Many people would say that style should be part of the vessel, rather than what the vessel contains.

Are the "artists" and "writers" of comics part of its content or part of its form . . . ?

Indeed, in the initial picture on page 6 of the transparent pitcher of form, because the word "comics" is in thick letters that are part of the glass (part of the vessel, part of the form) *above* the liquid content's surface, we assumed that the writing in white, *below* the surface of the liquid, labels the liquid itself—the vessel's content:

"Writers, Artists, Trends, Genres, Styles, Subject Matter, Themes"

But perhaps all of these *are* actually formal, and label only the vessel . . .
(How does one write on *liquid* anyway?)

Are perhaps (as the panel on the lower left of page 6 suggests) all genres *nothing* but complex forms?

Certainly that's what all the ironies and ambiguities of these panels lead us to consider.

In short, McCloud's ironies and ambiguities, now drawn large, now drawn small, remind us that the idea of the beaker or vessel of form and the malleable liquid of content is something of a fiction, an oversimplification, a formalization in itself, which perhaps makes things initially easier to understand, but which finally covers over as many (or even more) problems as (or than) it solves. Without such oversimplifications, definitions of such complex social objects as kinds of art are impossible. Indeed, a definition functions largely as a sign that such an oversimplication has always-already taken place.

Up till now, I've been sidestepping your questions a bit—but, after my discussion of your first two as a grounding, I'm ready to take them on more directly.

"What are your perspectives on these definitions"—Eisner's and McCloud's?

My indirect answer is that even McCloud constantly includes little ironies to problematize his own oversimplifications, though to find them you have to read particularly carefully, even inventively.

My direct answer to it is that I don't think *either* Eisner *or* McCloud is at his most interesting when he's *defining* comics. (Largely, that's because both are trying to do an impossible job, which—in my opinion—both should skip over, to get on with the fun part.) I find the ironies and ambiguities that they themselves include that problematize their definitions far more interesting than the definitions themselves. I think both are more interesting still, when each describes how comics work, either in whole or in part. I'll even say I don't think *I'm* that interesting either, when I'm explaining why their defining attempts are futile and dull.

I believe all three of us are more interesting when we are *reading* comics—or reading parts or aspects of comics—carefully and closely, with our own readers. That's what the job is. You pick a comic up. You read it. If you like it, you read it a few more times—then, if it seems worth it, you write about what was really interesting in it. What got to you? And how? And why? And what do you think the formal mechanics of its getting to you entailed? (This last is the question *Understanding Comics* answers again and again with so much insight.)

I believe criticism has to assume that anyone who decides to read some of it (criticism, that is)—about comics, about novels, about modem art—knows enough to recognize a comic or a novel or a painting when she or he sees one. Sure, a critic might point out some things about some of them you never noticed before—even something in common with a lot of them.

That's exciting.

That's what McCloud does.

That's what Dorfman and Mattelart do.

Some of the things Dorfman and Mattelart point out, if you haven't thought about them before, might make you stop and think again—wondering if, indeed, comics don't have a negative side as well as all stuff that's worth celebrating, which McCloud and the rest of us are concerned with; things which we, busy praising, might overlook. That's part of criticism too.

But don't expect *anyone* to say all that needs to be said about all of them.

And the most interesting things are not going to be some (impossible) definition—or some necessarily privileged origin: Though history is often revealing and fascinating about how things got to the state we currently find them in.

Now (finally!) to the core of your second question: "What do you think about the relationship between comic panels and prosaic text? Are they both legitimate forms of reading through abstraction?"

Many years ago I wrote (rather authoritarianly) that I distrusted people who "read" comics. Comics were to be "looked at." People who "read" comics were simply approaching them in the wrong way—like people who went to "see" an opera. No matter how exciting and colorful the production, basically you go to *hear* an opera. People who do go to see operas, are almost always disappointed with what they see: The soprano will be too fat, the tenor too old. The special effects that operas have been demanding since Offenbach and Wagner could only really be accomplished in films with computer graphics today. The sets and costumes are there to *prompt* your imagination—not to *do* all the imaginative work.

Likewise, I felt, first and foremost comics were to be appreciated visually. I even went so far as to compare the words in comics to the librettos of operas—some of the world's greatest operas have perfectly mindless librettos. ("Lucia de Lamamour," "Fidelio") Without the music, they'd be laughable.

(Beaumarchais wrote it in the eighteenth century and George Bernard Shaw [in *Man and Superman*] quoted it at the beginning of the twentieth, "Anything too silly to be said can always be sung.")

While I still feel that comics are basically a visual medium, in the last twenty-five years we have had some writers enter the comics field who have had as much influence—if not more—than any artists in its history: notably Alan Moore and Neil Gaiman, following on the "relevant comics" of writer Dennis O'Neil and artist Neal Adams in the 1960s and '70s. If I was ever to write another comic book, certainly I would approach the words very differently from the way I did in my first two graphic novels, *Empire* and *Bread & Wine*—and that difference would have to do almost entirely with having seen what Moore and Gaiman were able to do in the field *as* writers.

Cusack: Written word, theater, music video, film, and other media have all received critical attention and examination. Why do you think comics or graphic novels have consistently been the exception to this sort of standard critical review?

Delany: I *don't* think that grows out of any anxiety over the combination of words and images—the explanation that McCloud offers. (If it did, why would so many critics, from Susan Sontag on, declare that film *was* the great art of the last century?) I think it has to do with parts of comics history that McCloud leaves out.

I think it has far more to do with the fact that comics as you and I would first recognize them, rather than starting as hieroglyphics, grew out of newspaper comic strips and cartoons into those training manuals for illiterate soldiers I mentioned, back around World War One. When those comic book manuals began to make the transition into their peace-time form, telling stories and such, they were very much assumed to be working class art—and art for the least intelligent, the most non-intellectual segment of the working class.

Initially they were very cheap: five and ten cents. They didn't go up to a quarter until the middle sixties. The pictures were assumed not to be doing things that the words couldn't do. Rather, they were assumed to be there because the audience for them was too undereducated to *deal* with the words at all! The concept that comics were for children and/or illiterates—which persisted up through the forties and fifties, and even endures today—is mostly what has held back serious criticism of comics, with exceptions such as Will Eisner's *Comics and Sequential Art*, Dorfman and Mattelart's *How to Read Donald Duck* (1971; Ariel Dorfman was an elementary schoolmate of mine), Martin Barker's *Comics, Ideology, Power, and the Critics* (1989), Water and Bissett's *Comicbook Rebels*, Witek's *Comic Books as History: The Narrative Art of Jack Jackson, Art Spiegelman, and Harvey Pekar*, Umberto Eco's "The Myth of Superman" (1960), McCloud—or, indeed, some of my own work (*Silent Interviews: On Language, Race, Science Fiction, and Some Comics* [1993], *Shorter Views: Queer Thoughts and the Politics of the Paraliterary* [2000]).

Another very strong current is easy to overlook today, because it is simply not as strong as it was in this country before the Second World War: anti-Semitism. In the United Sates, mainstream literary publishing was dominated by Protestants, while secondary publishing—paperbacks, pulp adventure magazines, science fiction, mystery, westerns, comics (in short, writings for the working class)— was often owned, occasionally edited (though many of the publishers made a point of hiring Christian editors, to make themselves appear more like literary publishing), and frequently written by Jews. Often, the most conservative politics in the country was pandered to, especially in the early years of this secondary paraliterary publishing. But more and more, throughout the thirties and the forties, the general worldview put forward in these narratives, not only in comics but in science fiction and the urban mysteries that it produced, was what has become known as "the liberal Jewish worldview," in which women were granted a larger more active part than in the traditional "genteel literary tradition" (as it was known) and there was a far more cosmopolitan approach to matters of ethnicity and race. More conservative forces—which were pulling together over those same years and getting ready to climax with the House Un-American Committee investigations and the subsequent McCarthy period in the early fifties— were quick to see all this as communist inspired. Thus all of it tended to be dismissed (if not damned) by the mainstream of American culture as working-class/ non-intellectual/politically dangerous, Jewish garbage.

Cusack: When abstracting an image through cartooning, we achieve amplification through simplification. Do you think this is true? Because cartoons are less specific, do they embody a greater world of meaning?

Delany: Well, I certainly think they're subject to the old Marshall McLuhan adage, "Low resolution equals high involvement." And if, either in its range or its intensity, meaning has to do with the *amount* of involvement, well—there you go. A really fine mind, reading a really fine comic—something written by Alan Moore or Len Wein, Greg Rukka or Brian Azarillo, something drawn by Eduardo Russo, Kyle Baker, Kevin O'Neill, Eddie Campbell, Frank Miller, Peter Kuper, Grant Morrison, Jason Lutes, or E. J. Su—can usually have a pretty interesting time, if he or she knows comics and how to read them richly.

Cusack: You have written both traditional novels and unconventional graphic novels. What is your opinion of the graphic novel, and how do you personally differentiate what conceptual material is better suited for the graphic novel genre as opposed to the literary novel genre?

Delany: I like them. Otherwise I never would have written them. Some graphic novels I've read I've found powerful and complex.

The most obvious difference between graphic novels and serially published comics is that the graphic novels tend to be longer. The graphic novel gives both writer and artist more room in which to set up richer and more complex aesthetic forms. Because of the length, sometimes a graphic novel can develop a sense of density that may be harder to achieve in a twenty-two or twenty-three page comic book.

Once I taught a graduate seminar on Alan Moore and Eddie Campbell's *From Hell* (1992–98), before its sixteen parts and eleven volumes were collected into a single book—several years before the film appeared (2001). Moore conceived the project as a totality; and Campbell carried it out brilliantly. The different kinds of comics rhetoric the original eleven volumes employed make the whole a veritable encyclopedia of comics styles:

Here we get historical and architectural information presented as directly as any of those World War One military manuals on how to care for your gun. There we get a dozen-page fantasia of a psychotic madman riding about London, in a style close to the hyperbolic reality of a dream. At another, we watch a secret induction ceremony into the Masons. Another place, we move through the cellar crypts of Bedlam, or the lightless underground canals of Limehouse.

One understands why the film was the palest shadow of the comic; for one thing it started by taking two characters, the intellectual tension between whom fueled the entire 470-page series, and collapsed them into one, so that the whole thing pretty much lost all its intellectual drive.

To take on *this* question more directly: I don't believe any content *a priori* makes better (or worse) graphic novel material. Your job as writer, as artist is to discover the form that will make it work most effectively. Certain formal devices are useful for achieving certain effects. But you start by deciding what effect you want to achieve. I mean, can you think of material—and styles—more different than Jason Lutes's *Jar of Fools* and Frank Miller's *Sin City*? Or Moore and O'Neill's *League of Extraordinary Gentlemen* and Moore and Campbell's *From Hell*? All four are quite extraordinary—and as different in feel and style as four such projects can be.

Sometimes the form-content separation is a useful fiction. Other times, an equally useful—and equally provisional—creative fiction is the one that articulates: "Just go on and tell your story." But to gain control of your effects, you have to be aware of the emotional fall-out created by going from one *kind* of picture to another, big to little, little to big, light to dark, dark to light—or from one page to another. You have to be aware of the amount of time between pictures—and even the way the captions relate to the picture: Do the words extend the picture's action (in which case they should usually go toward the picture bottom)? Or do they intensify its atmosphere (in which case they should usually come near the top)? The standard traditional comics rule is no more than thirty-five words per panel—and no more than six panels to a page, with four the ideal number. But there are many reasons to violate that—in both directions. (Moore delights in nine panel pages—and makes the resultant claustrophobic feel a part of the story.) The best thing is to read widely in many comics and graphic novels, paying attention to the many formal techniques they use for various effects. Then use them yourself—and/or invent new ones.

Cusack: Do you think the study of Intellectual Heritage should abandon the motto "All text all the time?" Are other forms of media, such as comics or graphic novels, necessary in understanding our Intellectual Heritage (given that comics have been employed as storytellers for a large part of human history) or even better equipped to bridge the gap between seemingly disparaging world philosophies?

Delany: As I've already suggested, if your definition of "text" is restricted to written texts in verbal form and excludes everything else, it's an old-fashioned definition, one which hasn't been current for thirty-five years. More than twenty-five years ago, critic and social philosopher Gayatri Chakravorty Spivak described "text" as anything that presents itself as a play of presences and absences—anything that was light and dark, anything that had this idea but not that one as part of it. In short, a text was anything that could be read—and critics have been reading art works—paintings and sculptures—since Ruskin, since Winkelmann and Lessing in the eighteenth century and before. Nobody becomes a sophisticated intellectual limiting himself or herself only to canonical written texts. I believe one has to experience all the arts, widely.

Yes, you must read widely in the approved canonical texts. You also have to read widely in a lot of texts various people disapprove of. Life gets interesting at the point where you realize that you rather like—and approve of—some texts that others don't; and you neither like nor approve of some texts that many do.

Now that's a really dangerous thing to say—because, as every teacher knows, there are a lot of highly seductive texts—what one might called "sophomoric" texts—that can be greatly enjoyable and seem extremely fresh and new to not particularly widely educated readers. The problem is that they tend not to lead readers on to other works, especially once they become broadly popular. Rather, they stop and catch readers and make them think, often, that they have now encountered the best there is, so the readers just stall out and never progress. *The Lord of the Rings, A Hitchhiker's Guide to the Galaxy*, even *Harry Potter* often function in this way. On another level, the works of Charles Bukowski can easily strike young male readers like this. Occasionally visual artists' work functions in the same way: Salvidor Dali and Pavel Tchellechev—so that many people, in reaction, find themselves disliking such works disproportionately, mostly for their seductive qualities, which so often forestall artistic growth in the viewers who discover them and become enthusiastic over them. There are even comic book artists like that—Jon Muth and, to some extent, Art Spiegelman, and Frank Frezetta.

Cusack: What is an important moment in *Bread & Wine* that could only be communicated graphically?
Delany: I think Wolff found a purely graphic and highly comics-like way to communicate Dennis's joy in being with me—through the classical use of a page-break, between pages 37 and 38. It probably doesn't work for every reader—but it works for a lot of them.

However, other than to say look at this page, or look at those pages, look at these panels, then tell me if they move you in an emotional or psychological or bodily—or even intellectual—way that's basically nonverbal, I don't know how to do more than point, or indicate sketchily, those nonverbal responses. The only alternative is reading them closely with you—the job, as far as I see, of all criticism. Indeed, if I *could* tell you that—in words that do other than describe how the pictures make an educated viewer feel—then I *could* communicate it other than graphically!

I've always valued the freedom in the interrelation of reader and text in all the silent genres—books, comics, painting, sculpture. As soon as we introduce sound into the art work, from music, to spoken dialogue in plays, to TV, we become time-bound (yes, it starts even with silent films) in a way that the silent genres are not. I've always felt for that reason that the silent artistic genres were privileged. And, yes, they include comics.

The Wiggle Room of Theory:
An Interview with Samuel R. Delany

Josh Lukin/2006

From *the minnesota review*, 65–66 (Spring 2006). Reprinted with permission of *the minnesota review*.

To many, Samuel Delany is the radical gay black New York critic who has written on the roles of race, sexual orientation, New York City, and semiotics in his life and in American society. He has appeared in documentaries about the city. In 1993 he won the William Whitehead Memorial Award for a Lifetime's Contribution to Lesbian and Gay Writing and this year won the Lambda Literary Foundation's Pioneer Award. His 1987 book *The Motion of Light in Water* is a classic of African-American autobiography, and his bestselling volume of sexual memoir and urban sociology, *Time Square Red, Times Square Blue* (1999), is a staple of queer theory courses. But Delany is probably best known for his novels. Styling himself a Marxist, but deeply influenced by Foucault and deconstruction, his class-conscious and poststructuralist sensibilities are reflected in his science fiction and fantasy works, such as *Dhalgren* (1975) and the four-volume *Return to Nevèrÿon* series (1979–87).

Born in 1942 and educated at the Bronx High School of Science, with a single year (unfinished) at CUNY constituting his experience as a university student, Delany published his first novel at the age of twenty and lived for over twenty-five years as a professional writer before becoming a professor of comparative literature at the University of Massachusetts in 1988. He has taught at Wesleyan, SUNY-Buffalo, SUNY-Albany, the University of Kansas, the University of Wisconsin, the University of Michigan, the University of Minnesota, and Cornell. His many science fiction novels include *Nova* (1970), *Trouble on Triton* (1976), and *Stars in My Pocket Like Grains of Sand* (1984). His volumes of memoir are *Heavenly Breakfast* (1979) and the graphic novella *Bread & Wine* (1999). He has also published three pornographic novels—*Equinox* (1973), *The Mad Man* (1994), and *Hogg* (1995)—as well as a volume of literary fiction, *Atlantis: Three Tales* (1995). His most recent publication is the short novel *Phallos* (2004). In addition to sexuality, literary theory, and canonicity, Delany's critical essays cover topics as wide-ranging as the fiction of Stephen Crane and A. S. Byatt, the poetry of Hart Crane and Ron Silliman, and the theater of Shakespeare, Wagner, and Artaud. Now the author and editor of forty or more books, Professor Delany teaches in the English and creative writing programs at Temple University.

This interview was conducted in writing between September 19 and October 4, 2005, by Josh Lukin, a lecturer in English at Temple University.

Lukin: Your first teaching gig occurred in 1959, when you taught remedial reading to young Puerto Rican men at your local community center in New York City; you taught your first creative writing class in 1967 at the Clarion Writers' Workshop; your first university visiting professorship was at SUNY-Buffalo in 1975; you started your first permanent teaching position, a full professorship at the University of Massachusetts, in 1988. You have only spent one year in college, and, if I'm not mistaken, never had to apply for a teaching job. How does that happen to a person?

Delany: The process is simple—and probably self-evident. Someone in a university, a dean or a significant portion of the faculty of one department or another, who is in a position to hire, must think highly enough of your intellectual accomplishments to want to retain you despite your lack of formal education. In 1975 Leslie Fiedler recommended me for a term as the visiting Butler Chair Professor at SUNY-Buffalo. There I met Marc Shell and Murray Schwartz, then both junior faculty. After my term at Buffalo was up, I saw neither for a baker's dozen years; but during that time both followed at least some of my work. When, in 1987, Schwartz became dean of the College of Arts and Sciences at the University of Massachusetts and Marc was hired as head of the university's Comparative Literature Department, they were looking for someone with scholarly interest in some branch of popular culture, such as science fiction, as well as a familiarity with developments in literary theory. Books of mine such as *The Jewel-Hinged Jaw* (1977), *The American Shore* (1978), and *Starboard Wine* (1984), which had recently gotten me the Pilgrim Award for Excellence in SF Scholarship, probably played a large part in their decision to recruit me. So, for the next eleven years, I was a professor of comparative literature at the University of Massachusetts at Amherst.

I've been lucky enough that this has happened to me three times. Six years ago this process brought me to Temple University.

Lukin: You were first "known" in the science fiction field, then as an "academic," then as a notable voice in the gay world, and perhaps only recently as a writer that a young African-Americanist can study without risking stigma. In each of these milieux there have been occasions when you or your work has been dissed for your/its association with the other ones. Is there less of that now than there used to be?

Delany: All writers with any sort of public get dissed from time to time. I never paid too much attention to it. Nor did I ever think there was a great deal of it—when it came along, I tended to ignore it. I'd even go so far as to say that people who like my work, in an effort to show how interestingly controversial I am, make more of the dissing than I do—to the point where, occasionally, I think they actually exaggerate the amount of dissing there: a clause about my rampant sexism in a David Foster Wallace article on something else entirely, a sentence in a John Podhoretz op-ed piece praising the Giuliani administration's handling of the Times Square boondoggle at the end of the nineties and just after, an absurdly erroneous statement in a book on SF about my beliefs about AIDS transmission. And usually within weeks, someone writes, "What are these people on about? Have they actually *read* the piece in question?" Readers, black and white, who are put off by, say, the particular gay topics I have been handling for thirty years now, are likely to ignore Delany entirely. The same applies to those who don't take science fiction seriously. For them, the fact that I write it pretty much pollutes everything else I might do. They're not even going to *bother* to diss me.

Because, since 1975, my work has more and more dealt with gay material, another factor enters the equation. The conservative view of matters gay is still rife with the idea of contagion, so that I suspect they are afraid that if they objected, they would too quickly find themselves tarred with the same brush: You know—why are you even *talking* about stuff like that?

A cousin of mine recounted to me an incident of that sort within my own extended black family. Some years ago, her mother, my marvelous and wonderful Aunt Laura, decided to read my 1988 autobiography *The Motion of Light in Water: Sex and Science Fiction in the East Village.* Fifty pages into it, she phoned my equally wonderful Aunt Bessie, to declare, "Bessie—do you know what that boy is writing about . . . ?" and proceeded to tell her. Five hours later, and another 150 pages on, Aunt Laura phoned Bessie again: "Good Lord—Bessie! This is just terrible . . ." and three hours after that, she phoned a third time: "Bessie! I don't believe what I'm *reading . . . !*" To which my feisty eldest aunt finally announced back: "Well, if it's all that terrible, why have you had your nose buried in it for the last eight hours?"

So Aunt Laura phoned her eldest sister no more. But that's the way the black community in general has taken my work. Those that read it seem to like it; the rest avoid it, because even to decry *Equinox, Hogg, The Mad Man, Times Square Red, Times Square Blue,* or *Phallos*—not to mention *Dhalgren* and the *Return to Nevèrÿon* series—would open them to Bessie's authoritative censure.

Lukin: A theme of *About Writing* that has appeared in your earlier nonfiction but is rarely addressed in creative-writing guides is "the writer's reputation," in part as it relates to the structure of publishing. In the past five years, we've seen a renewed Delany presence in bookstores thanks to the Vintage Books reissues of your early fiction; but notwithstanding your own work's renaissance, you advised writers at Clarion West a couple of years ago to consider self-publishing.

Delany: In 1979, basically some eighty-odd independently owned publishing companies operated out of New York City. By 1989, only five remained. Yes, there were many more than five names, but the overwhelming majority had been bought up by international monopolies—Bertelsmann, HarperCollins, Beatrice, global monopolies of that sort (Doubleday, Bantam, and Dell, and two or three others, for example, are now one company owned by Bertelsmann operating out of a single office at 666 Fifth Ave)—so that in terms of corporate ownership, there are only five. The spectacular collapse—or, better, displacement of ownership—of U.S. publishing during the 1980s is an event whose results have been repeatedly narrated. It upset the economic careers of many "mid-list" writers, such as myself. It's one of the major reasons why, at age forty-seven, when I was offered a professorship, I accepted. Shortly before the offer, while I was a Fellow at Cornell's Society for the Humanities, at the Andrew D. White House, in 1986, I had watched most of my books go out of print, one every two weeks, as my major mass market paperback publisher, Bantam Books, radically revised its policy toward just the sort of writer I was.

It's not that before this collapse I advised students against self-publication and afterwards I advised them to try it. Rather, it's a case of what self-publishing came to mean in both situations. When there was a greater variety of commercial publishers and more economic competition between them, self-publishing was a way to avoid competition. It announced that you couldn't take the heat. That's why I advised against it, back then. At that point, nobody really took self-published writers seriously. Self-publishing was for books such as *Thoughts of God, by John Francis, Forty Years a Backwoods Doctor,* or (the title is Auden's) *A Poultry Lover's Jottings.*

Today, the collapse not only means that there's no real economic competition, but the kinds of things that publishers are looking for have changed. Commercial publishers today are far more distrustful of good writing than they have ever been before, and usually won't consider it unless it comes with some sort of ready-made reputation or gimmick. In the last half dozen years, writers have shown me rejection letters from publishers such as Harcourt Brace that actually say, under the letterhead, "We're sorry. This book is too well written for us." This means that competition is of an entirely different order than it was, say, thirty years ago, when such a letter simply would not have been written.

Because of computers, because of the Internet, you can self-publish at a level far higher than you once could. The product can look extremely professional. And if that's the kind of brick wall you've been bloodying your head against, small publishers and self-publication are, today, reasonable things to consider.

Lukin: In *Silent Interviews, Shorter Views,* and "Midcentury," you write at length of the discovery of theory and the role it played in your thought, leaving me with the impression that it saved your thinking by giving you a place to stand outside some constraints of the hegemonic discourse. What do you see as the place of the "theory canon" at the present time?

Delany: To begin with, your impression is wrong. From Braudel's contention that "Without theory there is no history" to Derrida's assertion that "We are never outside metaphysics," one of the most important insights of the most recent leg of the collection of theoretical dialogues that go by the general name of poststructuralism is that a "place to stand outside hegemonic discourse" is an illusion. Yes, you say "outside *some* of its constraints." But as I know you know, and I suspect, given your current work on abjection, disgust, and exclusion, you concur with, I don't believe the inside/outside metaphor can provide a way to overcome them. The fact that, even accidentally, you are drawn however *en passant* to use it—just as again and again am I—is a sign of how strongly the discourse of inside/outside, us/them, our position/the opposition is in place in the hegemonic discourse we would both like to revise.

Though I am black and gay, I am as much a racist, a sexist, an anti-Semite, and a homophobe as any right-wing Christian bigot: I *must* be; it's desperately *important* that I be; if I am ever to be able to talk to such people and effect some change in their beliefs and behavior, I *have* to be. To be what I would hastily call a civilized man with a civilized sense of democratic fairness is something you do on *top* of that. It's a refinement of that, if you like. It only gets to seem, with the blindness to basic processes that comes from practice, something you do in *place* of it. But the other is always there. I've always talked with such people whenever

I've had a chance. Even more so I listen to them—long and carefully, about their feelings and experiences, as well as many other topics—whenever I've found myself next to them in bars and on Greyhound busses or I have one as a seatmate on some air-bus to Detroit or Denver or San José, or when they're taking out their kids in the park. But I will never be able to effect any meaningful change other than one or another form of terrorism by fooling myself into thinking I can do anything by "standing outside" some hegemony.

This is neither a matter of New Age mysticism nor some earlier form of personal acknowledgment of historical guilt. (I'm wholly with Joanna Russ in this matter, who, back in 1975 wrote that, in terms of men looking at their own sexism, "Personal guilt about such things is a complete waste of time.") Really, this is straight Nietzsche, as when he says in *The Genealogy of Morals*, which I quoted as an epigraph to the first part of *Times Square Red, Times Square Blue*, "The great epochs of our life are where we win the courage to rechristen our evil as what is best in us."

My beliefs are based on firm convictions about hegemonic discourse in general and even more on some theoretical precepts about what discourse actually *is:* It's an associational linguistic structure that we all inhabit—specifically the one that constitutes the world. If we didn't inhabit the same discourse, we couldn't understand racist jokes when we heard them nor could we find others' use of them offensive when the contradiction with our own situation is too painful to allow us to laugh. While the part of us that we consider our "self" may each be positioned differently within it, none of us is outside it. That is *particularly* true for those of us who are black, or disabled, or overweight, or Asian, or women, or gay, or part of whatever group we have been socially assigned to, because if we didn't know that discourse down in our bones, we'd be dead.

People have noted for years how fast racism or sexism or classism reasserts itself as soon as a certain vigilance is allowed to relax. That's because they don't come in from outside. They are a *necessary* underlying factor within the egalitarian behavioral structure itself. Such a behavioral structure is not about ignoring differences. It's about noticing them, valuing them, realizing that there are certain situations, cultural and defined, when these differences are important—and realizing that they are crashingly irrelevant in others. (That's what valuing means.) If the structure of when and where they are relevant and irrelevant gets loose or generalized, you have racism, classism, and sexism all over again. If you're lucky, you can enlist habit on your side, especially with the young. But (to put it in Lacanian terms) you're still fighting the Imaginary—and history is always settling the Symbolic into the Imaginary, even as theory is always un-tangling the Imaginary into the Symbolic. Until the properly stabilizing Symbolic discourse is in place, you're particularly vulnerable.

Lukin: I meant, in my last question, of course, precisely the tendency of so many people to reject the new or the marginal, to "be still, be quiet, obey the king," as you yourself once wrote, to appeal for validity to the Official Story, to affirm the dreams of full presence, the reassuring foundation, the origin and the end of the game. How should I have characterized the, um, *opposition* to that?

Delany: I believe at this point we're discussing a topic that I first wrote about in "Shadows" (particularly pp. 20–50), a near-book-length essay I put together be-fore my novel *Dhalgren* (1975) was published: It dealt with how verbal forms, to-tally consecrated by use, can be referentially empty (or transcendent: often it's the same thing) and thus highly mystificational, like the "it" in "it is raining" in En-glish (I once had a student who argued that the "it" in "it is raining" referred to "you know, the sky, the weather, the whole *thing*"; if that's not transcendent—and in a particularly American mode—I don't know what is), or possessives when they refer up the power scale—when a worker says "my boss," a subject says "my king," or a slave says "my master." One reason *why* the inside/outside metaphoric system is finally so powerless is because it is an extension of a whole set of metaphors that come from armed encounters, the military "*citre et trans*" metaphors ("this territory and—over there—that territory"), the metaphors of military opposition, which are particularly useless when what is perceived to be in opposition is actu-ally two discourses. The only thing that can affect the "conflict" of discourses is some form of education. It may, indeed, be a form of education that we have not yet discovered.

People who retain some fondness for my early science fiction occasionally point to a parable from my mock Bildungsroman, *Empire Star* (1966), in which the naïve hero, Comet Joe, learns the difference between what I called, back then, "simplex," "complex," and "multiplex." Most recently an extremely perceptive young woman, Ariel Haméon, reviewing Professor Jefferey Tucker's book from last year about my work, *A Sense of Wonder: Delany, Race, Identity, and Difference,* put it perhaps even more crisply than I did in the initial novella, forty years ago:

> There's Comet Joe's simplex recognition that there are lights beneath that extra-planetary Brooklyn Bridge; the more complex view he got as he walked and saw the lights shift and change; and the multiplex understanding he gained when he ran fast enough to suss the pattern in both the bridge's struts and the lights behind them (*New York Review of Science Fiction,* 17 [2004]).

In the course of running, Joe falls and skins his knees—there's a price for gaining the multiplex view. But, I'd also like to point out, my (written in) 1965 vision of simplex, complex, and multiplex, is very much a pre-theoretical view of its complex (I use the term on purpose) topic.

Before he fell, if Joe had taken one more conceptual jump, he would have landed in the foothills of modern critical theory. If, in the transition between the three states of comprehension, he had been able to generalize along the following lines, he would have arrived at what today we might recognize as a fundamental theoretical insight:

> When I first stood here, motionless, looking at the underside of the bridge, with its plates and struts and lights, hundreds of feet above my head, I saw just a random pattern of lights and darknesses. I assumed—wrongly, I now know—that what I saw was all that was there, and that such a random pattern represented the fixed and immutable truth of the bridge. That was my simplex view. Once I began to walk along, however, and saw the same stricture from a succession of points of view—while, now, as I moved, a strut moved from in front of a light I hadn't seen before and another light vanished behind one of the struts that, from my new position, occluded it—I realized that the pattern of lights and struts was complex and would appear differently from different places. That was my complex view. When I ran, however, the patterns changed even faster, and suddenly I was able to see an even more complicated *overall* pattern that, because I was moving at a greater velocity, I could make out and retain—the multiplex view . . .

Here is where, of course, Joe tripped, bringing his insight to an end. Had he not tripped, however, he might have gone on a step:

> Yes, I have seen a more comprehensive pattern, and I feel I am that much closer to apprehending the truth of the bridge's structure. But because I have gone through the process I have already, I'm now aware that were I to run even faster, or perhaps were I to run in a different direction or take any number of other trajectories along the ground here, or climb up higher, or observe the bridge from closer, or even from above it, or on it, or were I able to take some of it apart, the possibility always remains that I might suddenly see still *another* pattern in its organization, equally multiplex, yet totally other. Yes, I have seen a larger and more comprehensive pattern, but from what I had to do in order to see it—moving from simplex to complex to multiplex—I now induce that the greater pattern I have seen, despite whatever explanatory use I might

successfully put it to, is *not* privileged—any more than the first simplex view I had, or indeed the complex view. Though I can put what I have learned to any provisional use that happens to yield to it, I must not confuse that provisional use with theoretical absolute truth—or I will be, at least theoretically, just where I was when I started.

That would have been the specifically theoretical insight. But that was the one which, in 1965, twenty-three-year-old Delany was not quite up to. Still, I hope you can see how turning loose the privileged status of the new multiplex pattern— even though one may still find that pattern highly useful—leads to a certain philosophical humility. For these who take it seriously, it means we start listening to those who come to us with different points of view in a new and far more appreciative way. The point is, this is *not* just muddle-headed relativism—the assumption that *all* points of view are equally correct or of equal interest, to you, me, or anyone else. You're still free to critique what you see and hear. But it means that you don't dismiss them out of hand just *because* they're new or different. The fact is, there's no way to exclude all possibility for the future's bringing into your or someone else's ken new contextual information with some bearing on the topic to hand.

This is the insight that works its way through the argument in Derrida's critique of John Searle and his reading of John Austin in *Limited, Inc.* (1988); by extension, Derrida's argument goes on to suggest that all the strategies we use to foreclose on an otherwise endless discussion . . .

—Hey, I really and absolutely understand what you/the text is saying.

—You/the author/the text has completely and totally communicated his/her/its/your intentions to me.

—My understanding of you/the text is now identical to what this or that authority has to say on the topic, so that clearly my interpretation now cleaves to the truth.

—Indeed, *any* argument in the form, I don't expect/want/need further contextual information that might adjust my understanding.

. . . are just that: attempts to foreclose argument that have nothing to do with—at least theoretically—the presence (or absence) of truth.

Lukin: That view, which I'll call perspectival pluralism, connects to a point you once made about the location of meaning, vis-à-vis recent arguments over Michaels and Knapp's "Against Theory." Do you remember?

Delany: Yes. You had called my attention to an online discussion of the claims in "Against Theory," led by the analytic philosopher John Holbo. But in explaining his refutation of Knapp and Michaels, Holbo tacitly assumed the "communication" model of language, i.e, the model that says: I have a meaning—an (capital I) Intention, an "aboutness"—which I place into a word or a set of words, which I then toss out into the air. These words strike your ear and release their Intention into your brain—an Intention that wasn't there before and that, upon completion of the act of hearing or reading, *is* there, now: it has been communicated.

But this is far too "Imaginary" to serve as a model for language. Also, it's just wrong. Its inaccuracies spawn endless arguments of the sort that Holbo and his interlocutors were engaged in. Indeed, it has been spawning them since Cratylus argued with Socrates.

A better one is: From my learning experiences in my culture, I have many words and associated meanings in my brain. You have many words and associated meanings in your brain. Because we have lived and experienced similar discourses, many of those meanings are the same or highly similar. Because we have lived in many different discourses, and because we have experienced the discourses we have from different positions within them, many of these meanings, at all levels, are different.

Now, suddenly—because of the language that bombards me, moving around meanings in my brain, some of which I can identify as yours and some of which I feel are mine—I get a desire to produce a meaning, an "aboutness," an intention (small "i," i.e., an urge that my utterance produce a particular effect, agreement, perhaps; perhaps dominance or awe. Possibly laughter. But, first, the desire to produce a meaning is *not* the intention. And, second, "meaning," "aboutness," and "intention" are different things, even if they appear to lie in the same direction). Responding to the desire, the discourses that I inhabit and my particular position in and among them, choose some words for me, and (after a more or less critical review of them prompted by other discourses, if I'm that sort of guy) I fling them out into the air.

The words strike your ear, where, within your brain, the discourses that *you* inhabit guide them to the meanings *you* have associated with them. These meanings are thus called up in *your* brain. But my meanings never go directly into your brain and yours never go directly into mine. Communication, on *that* level, is simply an illusion, fostered by cultural and discursive similarities and congruences. Within the discourses you inhabit, the meanings have already struck up a desire to produce another meaning. Thus dialogue continues.

Once we have a sense of the process, we have to note that slippages and mistakes can occur at any point. We can misspeak, mishear, misperceive, misthink. There are misinterpretations. And, sometimes (once we enter the world of texts, of art . . .), we find slips in the shape of the signifier—such as natural signs that are so close to words (the rock whose ridges and erosions happen to spell "Help!") that a language-like response is called up in our brains. Since language is the entire discursive, reflective (not communicative) process, the question "Are the rock's ridges really language or not?" is a non-problem. The answer to that question is technically "no," not because the rock is devoid of Intention or the desire to produce a meaning (i.e., a semantic paraphrase), an intention or an "aboutness," but because a word is not language; a meaning or an Intention or an aboutness is not language. A mistake is not language. A desire for meaning is not language. Only the whole complex process together is language (including mistakes). Articulations without discourses (which are in your brain, not in the world) are not language. And discourses without utterances are not language. All of these things are analogous to wheels and gears and gas tanks and sparkplugs and batteries and camshafts and oil baths and cooling pipes and hubcaps and carburetors and seat-belt buckles in a car.

Indeed, the kind of argumentative problems that arise between Knapp/Michaels and Holbo are analogous to the sort of problems garage mechanics might have if, back when Adam was cutting up the experience of the world with names for things, he had named the trips between New York and Philadelphia, or Camden and Trenton "cars," and people only learned by trial and error what the machinery that facilitated those trips had to do with getting them there on time. The question about the word on the rock is rather like asking, "If the north wind comes along and suddenly blows me from the streets of New York to Elizabethtown—"the way, say, Phaedrus recounts to Socrates that Boreas, the North Wind, once carried off Oreithyia from the bank of the Ilissus—"is that *really* a car?"

Lukin: Does theory have a contribution to make to creative writing pedagogy?
Delany: Well, a small, but important one has to do with what the writing process is—the nature of the process that produces the sentence, in the sense of how the mind produces language and the relation of the production of such language *to* (here they are again) intention, reason, and logic.

The most dramatic version of this argument I've encountered recently was between the poet Hart Crane and the critic-poet Yvor Winters. They debated it in letters during the twenties. The debate is particularly involving because only Crane's side still exists: Winters's letters have been lost. Nevertheless, it's fairly easy to reconstruct his side, or at least what Crane assumed Winters's side to be.

Basically Winters felt that, starting with Whitman and Emerson, American poetry and poetics had put too much stress on the unconscious, by critically privileging the rhapsodic, the dithyrambic, the delirious currents in language. The purpose of literature (Winters felt) was to train and recomplicate our thinking, our reasoning, our intelligence. Reason, logic, and intention should be the *source* of poetry in particular and art in general. Crane had run across this argument before—in of all places, O. P. Ouspensky's mystical treatise *Tertium Organum.* (It's a paradox that, generally speaking, mystics want their religion to be mystical and their art to be inchoately logical—rather than the other way around.) At first Winters was taken by the high intelligence with which Crane explicated and defended his poetic practice. But eventually, after the publication of Crane's *The Bridge,* Winters came to the conclusion that Crane—like Pound and Eliot—was only using his intelligence as a smoke screen to allow himself to indulge these undisciplined forces from the unconscious, a kind of automatic writing, a childish and immature verbal playfulness, which hid great aggressions and hostilities, and which had not made peace with a model of the mature and complete man—responsible, heterosexual, and socially accountable—and which, because it eschewed these qualities, could lead to no good end. When, a few years later, the tale of Crane's homosexuality and his alcoholic suicide came back to him, Winters felt that his disavowal of Crane—and all other "overly-romantic" poets from Rimbaud and Whitman to Mallarmé and Crane himself—was justified. What had first struck him as beautiful and grand, now he was ready to dismiss as immature, mannered, and self-indulgent.

I believe Winters was wrong, theoretically (whether he was wrong in his assessment of Crane's poems or not is, finally, a personal matter). I think Winters was wrong in his basic assumption that intention, reason, and logic are the compelling source of language. I think the corollary that goes along with it is also wrong: That language "communicates" these in some direct manner. My theory, if you will, is a version of a theory that has been put forward by Dante Alighieri, William Butler Yeats, and Jack Spicer—to name three poets whose work you might be familiar with. This is the idea of the poem as dictated—and, by extension, the idea that the source of language resides in some faculty of mind (man's, or in Dante's case, God's) we cannot directly know. Consciousness (with its handmaids reason, intention, and logic) sits in total ignorance of its inner workings and can only request it to offer up language. Sometimes it obeys. Sometimes it disobeys. Sometimes it offers up the kind of language "we"/consciousness ask/s for. Sometimes it offers up very different language from what "we"/consciousness ask/s of it. As that language is offered up, consciousness—with reason, intention, and logic—can oversee that language and accept this or that part of it, reject this or that part it. Revision is always possible. We ask for rhapsody—and sometimes we get rhapsody. We ask for reasoned argument, and—if we're lucky—what we get is what consciousness recognizes as reasoned argument.

This mysterious faculty of mind seems to be, to some extent, trainable. But we must never become too arrogant in our demands on it or too slipshod in our critique of what it offers. We have to listen carefully and make our revisionary requests humbly. Otherwise, it turns off—or produces only vacant shells of chatter and gossip.

I think this is what Crane—along with Spicer, Yeats, and Dante—understood. This is the model I try to impart to my writing students. They must not be afraid to use their critical faculties on their own work—but they must use them with care and—yes—a certain craft. But the craft has very little to do with what the commercial distributors of public narrative and public language call "a mastery of the medium." Indeed, as I try to point out, in reality such "mastery" is almost entirely a matter of submission—submission to existing grammatical models of language, of narrative, and of dramatic effect.

Lukin: It seems to me that, in the past eight years or so, you've registered more and more on the radar screens of major literary scholars. What do you think of the reception of your work by Hazel Carby, Ross Posnock, or Walter Benn Michaels?

Delany: I enjoy them when they enjoy my work and seem to understand it. I try not to get too flustered when they don't like it or seem not to get it. Writers like Steven Shaviro, Madhu Dubey, and Carl Freedman seem to like some of what I do—and I hope that's not the only reason why I like them. Hazel Carby has been generous in her statements about my work, especially in *Race Men* (1998). She's never really chosen to write about any of it at length—but certainly no onus falls on her to do so. While I have a few questions about some of Ross Posnock's exposition of his position, in *Color and Culture* (1998), which may even account for Jeffrey Tucker's misunderstanding of it, I can only be grateful for what Posnock has said about my novella "Atlantis: Model 1924" in the last chapter of his book. When critics have proffered practical criticism, mostly in reviews, I've occasionally felt I profited by their negative responses.

To the extent I understand the arguments in Michaels's recent *The Shape of the Signifier* (2004), there's a lot to be drawn to. The basic argument seems to be that the overvaluation of history (*my* history *makes* me a Jew, a black, determines my culture and thus my beliefs) as the ultimate cause of everything, i.e., a "historicist" view, leads dialectically (he never uses the word, of course) to a subsequent undervaluation of history (it's all in the past; you can't change it anyway; the material support for ideological differences fell with the fall of the wall and the subsequent dissolution of the Union of Soviet Socialist Republics; come on, as folks who live together in the present, we're all far more alike than we are different), i.e., a "posthistoricist" view, and this axis and any position along it he calls "historicism." (This is different from the historicism Popper cited in *The Poverty of Historicism* [1957]—the assumption that history can become a quantitative, predictive science—though it's interestingly related to it.) Symptoms of this historicism are everything from New Historicist Greenblatt's desire to talk with the dead, in which Greenblatt eventually realizes much of their talk is his own voice come back to him, to various embodied metaphors such as Morrison's bodily returned ghost in *Beloved* or Leslie Marmon Silko's privileging of tribe over class in *Almanac of the Dead* (where the classic Marxist is executed by the Native Americans he comes to help because he keeps insisting they are a class, not a tribe, and, what's more, in their failure to realize they're a class, they are a dupe of capitalism).

Somehow Bret Easton Ellis and I (in Michaels's seven-page reading of a small section of my novella, "The Game of Time and Pain") are his "antihistoricist" novelists—clearly, within his system, we are something of his heroes. But, in the end, he remarks, ruefully, of my tale (which is about a slave who, because of some incidents in his youth, is inspired to lead a slave revolt that is ultimately successful in overturning the institution), "As a strategy for making fun of the identitarianism of writers like Morrison and Spiegelman, this is pretty effective; as a politics—or, at least, as a left politics—it isn't: the absolute commitment to freedom of contract [which is how Michaels reads S/M practices—with-a-safe-word] can hardly function as a basis for a critique of economic inequality." Since I do come off, in this schema, as a *small* good-guy (in a Coda, he turns tail and pulls out the Big Guns on Ellis's *Glamorama* and DeLillo's *Mao II*; historicism here would seem to be what allows the media, governments, and religion to take the "standpoint, people who *believe* differently" must be treated as "people who are different"), perhaps I should be grateful and not look a gift horse in the mouth. As a writer of light fictions of ideas, apparently I escape the major critique he levels at serious satiric realism, in the works he finds wanting here.

But some things bother me about Michaels's argument. His earlier praise of Ellis's *American Psycho* hinges on statements like, "the group that constitutes Bateman's [the American psycho's] preferred target, pretty 'girls,' doesn't constitute a people: women are not a culture." Yet, one of my major revelations when, as a young gay man, I got married in 1961, was that they damned well did and were. In his discussion of my tale, Michaels draws the conclusion, "So Delany's masochists are ... not a people (on the model of Jews or African-Americans)." But the whole later half of the Nevèrÿon series grows largely in direct dialogue with the work that the gay community, particularly those interested in S & M, were doing at that time. Ironically, I was in correspondence with a couple of the SAMOIS writers, whom Michaels cites in the accompanying discussion, when those stories were being written. Before 1969, the gay community of the U.S. tended not to think of itself *as* a community. Afterward, it did. The eleven stories and novels making up *Return to Nevèrÿon* are, historically, so very much post-Stonewall stories, that I wonder how comfortably I can wear Michaels's "antihistoricist" mantel. If Michaels's point is merely that a people/community/political group need not be hereditary, to me this seems self-evident. (But what's the force of his denying "peoplehood" to pretty girls or to women and to masochists? Suppose they *want* peoplehood? Would he deny it to them then? That's precisely the point of conflict that demands tolerance, so that people can learn from their histories what in their lives they want stabilized and what they want to let go of. The overvaluation Michaels decries is the—yes—historical fallout from decades of *intolerance*—not from too much wishy-washy liberal tolerance.) But why look for a politics in the section of a tale that deals with what inspires an individual, who feels himself outside a group (the young slave was not born into slavery; his masochism dates from *before* his enslavement at age fifteen), to move forward to join one? So much of the story is about subsequent group and communal action, why not look for it there?

It seems, at any rate, that someone as comfortable with theory as Michaels would suspect that the last place to look for a politics is at the point that the narrative constructs as the *origin* of identity, however briefly or however (as it turns out in this tale) falsely.

Also in his analysis, Michaels makes a couple of statements that I find wildly over the mark: "his [Delany's] point is that it [sadomasochism] can be a 'turn on' *only* if you do it by agreement, that the agreement is the turn on." No, that's not my point. It's not even true. If it were, you wouldn't have the fundamental need for the S/M community to establish itself as such—and in the gay community, the sub-community of S/M practitioners, female and male, did, a decade post-Stonewall, the most work the fastest—in the first place. Michaels also writes, "It's not just that masochism is legitimated by freedom of contract ... masochism is itself the love of that freedom." Well, as an ex-lover of mine once told me, when I was drawn to indulge similar hyperbole more than twenty years ago, "Sit down, Maudine—and eat your pie:" No, masochism is not a love of freedom; masochism is taking sexual pleasure in pain, bondage, degradation, or subservience.

For Michaels, both the overvaluation of country and the overvaluation of the family are symptoms of historicism. Michaels wants beliefs to come back into questions of value. He wants us to be able to say, I suspect, America was founded on some really extraordinary ideas—political beliefs—about freedom and truth and the pursuit of happiness and the right of all people to them and to the situations that make them possible. He wants us to be able to say, my family has some social ideas about things that I think are dead wrong, and I don't share them and I don't want my kids to grow up sharing those notions either. He wants to maintain clear distinctions *between* loving and valuing; *between* feeling and believing; *between* subjectivity and subject position. But one would became downright drunk on intellectual clarity, if one could actually live in such a world as he envisions—that is, a world where more than a dozen people could agree on the definitions of those distinctions and agree further on what those distinctions *actually* entailed. (Because we don't live in such a world, that's why the notion of tolerance *is* such a great American *political* belief.)

But there's another set of overvaluations and undervaluations at work here. When we undervalue the things we have been given and did not choose for ourselves (and history tells us often they are aspects of our socioeconomic privileges and the social education that those privileges netted us, which, though we have it and rely on it daily, we remain blind to), we tend to overvalue our elective communitarian discoveries—and someone has to remind Maudine that, no, sadomasochism is just an appetite, and, like the standard missionary position, it too can get out of hand. It needs to exist—and always-already has—in a *social* world, a world sometimes more conducive to its intelligent carrying out and sometimes not. It can get banal. It can get too wild. Consent is *not* built into it, any more than it is built into vanilla carryings on—which is *why* consent has to be added socially. And if it isn't, directly or indirectly, you're likely to have problems.

Though one can come to love the freedom to practice it with multiple partners, and deeply resent it when that freedom is taken away, masochism itself is no more a love of that freedom than it is a love of capitalism or socialism—or is a belief that dictatorship is the best means of government or a belief in participatory democracy. There are highly neurotic masochists—and eminently levelheaded ones. (And—like standard missionary folk—some are psycho.) Some are

Republicans. Some are Libertarians. Some are rich. Some are poor. And, guess what? The same goes for sadists. The uncritical assumption that correspondences between sex and some such characteristic are necessary rather than contingent (that they are identities in the logical sense rather than contingent metonymic associations that other situations and other discourses can reassign) is what produces the intellectual debacle of, say, James Miller's appalling biography *The Passion of Michel Foucault* (1993)—as it produces the somewhat *extreme* sentences Michaels writes above.

Lukin: In your second interview with *Callaloo*, back in 2000, you downplayed the significance of identity markers and even ideological allegiances as signs of critical acuity. Yet I, at least, sometimes find myself discussing elements of your work in terms of the trope of marginal or subaltern status. Is there any usefulness or peril to that way of talking about work that addresses such issues as yours does?

Delany: What you call "downplaying identity markers" I would call simply the fall-out from my theoretical position that identity is a contingent collection of attributes—a constructed category, i.e., held together by discourse.

I have no problem with your—or anyone else's—discussing my fiction about subalterns in terms of subalterns. Here, at least, I think Rorty's notion of different language games can be useful. But my preferring one language game over another can always be because I haven't seen the abuse that particular language game lends itself to—as I have with, say, the kind of hyperbolic enthusiasm that Michaels exhibits in the sentences I pointed out. I do understand—and have experienced firsthand—the desire to use that sort of language. That's why I'd rather ironize and joke Michaels out of his use of such hyperbole ("Sit down, Maudine . . ."), even though I think that kind of language can stabilize some truly *pernicious* results. But I also know that, quite apart from this, no matter how ironic your critic, when you realize someone finds inaccurate and misleading your account of something meaningful to you, it's hard not to feel: Hey, you're attacking my transcendent yearning directly.

All I can pose to that is an old dictum from the creative writing workshop: No, your basic feeling is not being attacked. Try to communicate your yearning (yes, I drop the transcendent) through accuracy and specificity. Use your own language. Start by realizing you are *not* unique, and look for the differences between your experience and the way that experience is usually spoken of.

"My mistress' eyes are nothing like the sun . . ." and, well, neither is sadomasochism. I suspect that Michaels would find this argument "posthistoricist" because, even in its celebration of difference, it also might be seen to be saying, "Hey, we're all brothers and sisters under the skin. There really *are* no differences." To which I can only reply, "Boy, are there differences! Lots of people really *don't* want to play together. And people really do believe different things." As I wrote many years ago, Lévi-Strauss's declaring "all men engage in the same amount of intellection" is fine when he's talking about the similarity between a tribal shaman in South America and a nuclear physicist in Berkeley, California. But what happens when *one* of his men is a thirty-seven-year-old Polish construction worker, reeking of beer, and wondering if he's going to be let go because his immigration papers are not in order, and the *other* man is a twenty-two-year-old woman secretary, just graduated from Bryn Mawr, working in an advertising company located on Lexington, wondering if this is what she wants to be doing with her life and what advancement is possible for a woman in such a job, both of whom are pressed bodily up against one another, with a tool bag between them, hurting both their knees, in a subway car at rush hour—both of whom just then are thinking about each other, and both thinking things the other, just then, wouldn't find very pleasant.

In such a situation, the "amount" of intellection is more or less irrelevant. To get home without an incident, both need a little tolerance (i.e., a political belief), a little repression (if Freud is right and civilization always hinges on castration and repression, i.e., a little socialization), the two of them—politics and socialization—put together with whatever bit of mental *bricolage* (i.e., theory) is appropriate to the situation. But this is precisely where you *need* the wiggle room that theory gives you—just as classical Marxism tries to initiate the notion that our two rush-hour riders actually *do* have shared socioeconomic interests that might at least produce a political alliance, were both educated to appreciate their socioeconomic specificities. Is my position here an oscillation between undervaluation and overvaluation, both of which obliterate subjects? Or is it, as I would hope, a non-privileged multiplex view? And is the distinction a matter of language games—or *is* it more substantive?

Right now, I'm not sure. Why? Because I would need to know more about each of the individuals as people—*and* their class. As well, either one or both might be queer; either one or both might be black—as, since World War II, there are black and Eurasian Germans and black and Eurasian Swiss, there are black and Eurasian Poles. And depending on what each feels about it, as well as what each believes, it might be relevant.

As people have become more mobile in the world and are willing to talk more and more about their subjectivity, identity markers have become more and more loosely joined, more and more mobile in themselves. That's why we have to turn away from Hegel's notion of getting rid of all the inessentials and letting oneself deal only with the essential, to a theory like Derrida's that reminds us of the power of the context to add more unusual or surprising factors—because greater context is even more likely today to bring in surprising information than it was in Hegel's and Hölderlin's day. On a purely theoretical level (one of Zizek's more recent points), Derrida wasn't saying anything Hegel didn't know.

Lukin: I think "demystification" is a helpful way for a reader to frame the intellectual imperative that drives your writing. How would *you* characterize your intellectual project?

Delany: Needless to say, I'm highly complimented. But I would frame my own project far more modestly. For thirty-odd years, since I published "Shadows," I have been trying to promulgate—and develop—a more and more sophisticated notion of discourse. Would it be overstating things to say that the world needs one desperately? I don't think so. Every time we back-slide from the Freudian notion of the "unconscious," citing its mentalistic or biologistic clumsiness, every time we lose sight of the class war because we've once again become entranced with the relativity of superstructure and infrastructure and the impossibility of establishing an absolute boundary between them that holds up theoretically, or every time we find some other notion of the Symbolic too baroque to pursue with any seriousness, we also brutalize the concept of discourse—understanding—itself. In essays such as "Wagner / Artaud" or "The Rhetoric of Sex / The Discourse of Desire" or "Shadow and Ash"—or even now and again throughout *Phallos*—I have tried to limn some parameters of one aspect or the other of discourse directly. But more often, as in, say, *Times Square Red, Times Square Blue*, what I see as my primary goal in my own intellectual overview becomes a tertiary thematic in the specific work.

I resist, as they say, the notion of "demystification" because it suggests something apocalyptic, in the sense of pulling away the *kalyptra*, the veil, of revealing the truth—that is to say, it suggests someone "who knows." And I don't know or claim to know. What I tend to find myself doing more and more is insisting on what we *don't* know—and that we would do ourselves a favor by ceasing to carry on as if we did. As a novelist, I move here and there and explore, looking largely for the fascinating pattern—for something that I might call form, or beauty, or sometimes even creation. As a nonfiction writer, I try to write about what I see and have seen *here* against what I see and have seen *there*—and what people have said about what is there, what is here, and to compare that to what I saw when *I* looked. Any demystification that, from time to time, readers can find—and that's entirely dependent on the readers' position within the greater discourse—is a happy accident.

Some Questions from Steven G. Fullwood for Samuel Delany

Steven G. Fullwood/2007

Previously unpublished. Printed with permission of Steven G. Fullwood.

Fullwood: Tell us about *Dark Reflections*?

Delany: *Dark Reflections* is a novel—a highly structured novel . . . which is to say, in the sea of informally structured works pouring out around us, it's a highly experimental work. In three cross sections, it gives the story of a fictional African American poet, Arnold Hawley, who grew up in Western Massachusetts, and who, after school in New England, comes to New York's Lower East Side and lives there for the rest of his life. He's a gay man, who grew up largely before Stonewall.

He's somewhat older than I am. Given that we are both committed to our work, he's lived a life about as different from mine as it would be possible to imagine. He's never been partnered. (Since I was teenager, I've almost always had a life partner.) He's a poet who, over the forty years the book depicts, has written eight collections of poetry. (I've never written poetry, though I've written some twenty-five novels.) Although the sixth of his books won a prize and was moderately successful, he's not a well-known writer—which is to say, his life is much like that of many writers—serious, hard working, deeply committed writers—working in the United States today.

Much of the book comes out of my last eight years, during which I've been a professor of creative writing at Temple University. I wanted to write a novel that young people seriously interested in writing might read, which would sketch something of the life awaiting them. Within that, I also wanted to make an aesthetic object that, in itself, would attempt to reflect some of the beauty one commits oneself to by going into the literary arts.

Fullwood: At this point in your long and varied career, share a moment when you knew that you could call yourself accomplished?

Delany: There *are* no such moments. And any time you think you've found one, all you have discovered is a moment where you have been blinded, fooled, or duped.

Sadly, the worst thing that can happen to a writer is that she or he gets to a point where she or he believes—or he or she believes someone who tells him or her—that he or she now knows how to write; that one has found one's voice; that one is now "accomplished." Perhaps it's something of an exaggeration, but it's far closer to the truth to say that we must learn to write all over again with every sentence we begin—and that what teaches us anew is the structure, the content, and the form of what we are writing about. Paying minute attention to that alone is what can sometimes produce good writing.

Fullwood: What's life like on a daily basis for Chip Delany?

Delany: It's a concatenation of moments I can pay attention to that give me pleasure, and many more that slip by while I am looking at something else—dust on the floorboards, a book in my hands, the light on the edge of my glasses while they sit beside me on the desk . . . It's a familiar view of trucks and cabs and motorcycles out my fifth-floor apartment window. It's familiar book jackets as I pad past my shelves, barefoot, in the morning on my first trip to the john. It's an unfamiliar black woman in a sweatshirt and a scarf I might see at the diner in Philly where often I stop for breakfast, or an interesting point an Asian student makes in a question to a visiting lecturer in the afternoon.

Fullwood: You have over three dozen titles to your name. Tell me which ones I should read (if I haven't already) and, in one sentence, why.

Delany: No. That's entirely *your* choice. You are free to choose—or not to choose—and any suggestions I make, however pleasant or well-intentioned those suggestions sound, are still a form of bullying. Advertisements and general cultural hype bully us every day, and I don't want to join that. If you find a book of mine—or of anyone else's, for that matter—pick it up, read the first page, or a page in the middle. Then decide if you want to go on with it or not.

That's what it's about.

It's not about making sure you've read everything the Joneses or the Jarmushes, the professors or the pundits have read. That's just bullying yourself.

It's about reading freely, widely, and adventurously.

As to why?

That's something you can only know after you've read it.

Fullwood: What are you working on right now?

Delany: Another novel, another novel . . . *always* another novel.

Fullwood: Your epitaph?

Delany: Good Lord! That's something I think should be left to other people, don't you? I've got far too many things I want to write about while I'm living than to waste time trying to direct anyone as to what they should say after I'm gone. Really, that seems rather misguided and trivial.

On *Dark Reflections* and Other Matters: A Conversation with Samuel Delany

Carl Freedman/2007

The following interview, previously unpublished, took place, entirely in writing and by e-mail, during the summer of 2007.

Freedman: I'd like to begin with a major concern of your work as a whole, which is also an area in which you've been especially innovative: the representation of sexuality, and specifically homosexuality. Gay themes are hinted at in your early novels *Babel-17* and (arguably) *The Einstein Intersection*, then treated more overtly in *Dhalgren* and *Trouble on Triton*; still later, in *Stars in My Pocket Like Grains of Sand*, *Flight from Nevèrÿon*, and *The Mad Man*, homosexuality is a central concern—and sometimes is represented quite graphically. Your latest novel, *Dark Reflections*, is already one of my personal favorites among your books. The protagonist—an African-American poet, Arnold Hawley—is homosexual, but at the same time he is also relatively asexual. In one aspect, the book is about his *failure* to become an actively sexual gay man. Though sexuality is certainly a concern of the book, it's by no means the only concern and not necessarily the most important. While surely a gay novel, *Dark Reflections* is not so *emphatically* gay as *The Mad Man* or *Stars in My Pocket*. I've just finished my third reading, and increasingly I suspect *Dark Reflections* marks something relatively new in the literary representation of sexuality. Christopher Isherwood once said that the reason he completely excluded homosexuality from the stories in *Goodbye to Berlin*—even though it was certainly part of the personal experience on which that autobiographical cycle of stories was based—was that, in the 1930s, it would have been impossible to portray homosexual experience at all without distracting all attention from everything *else* he wanted the book to be about. Are we within—or within sight of—a literary situation radically different from that which Isherwood found so stifling eight decades ago, a situation, now, where overtly gay themes can coexist more easily with other concerns? Is the heterosexual reading public more prepared to accept that homosexuality can be one part of a character's make-up without necessarily being all-defining? Certainly, as a gay writer who has been publishing books for close to half a century, you've witnessed some extraordinary changes in the social and literary situation of gay writing.

Delany: Certainly the great novel of (dare I call it) modern gay life is Isherwood's own *A Single Man* (1964). Like Joyce's *Ulysses* and Lowry's *Under the Volcano*, it's also one of the great twenty- four-hour novels. A late-middle-aged literature professor living in Los Angeles, whom we only know as George, has just lost his lover to death. But because this is pre-Stonewall, he must make the transition between being a person with a life partner and a domestic sexual outlet to the situation essentially of a "widower," without any of the social or institutional supports that would be commonplaces in the life of a married heterosexual male: no one offers him a few days off from school to take care of the funeral arrangements. No one at school offers him condolences, and he goes to his lectures and is expected to deliver them as if nothing has happened. A few people who know try to give him a bit of sympathy, but since there is no officially and socially condoned way to do it, they are largely at a loss. He's excluded from the ordinary civilities of human compassion, because of social custom—or, more accurately, its lack. The irony of the title becomes heart-breaking.

Now George and Arnold are both older gay men. But the differences between them are great: Full professor versus adjunct; white versus black; European versus American; scholar versus creator; west coast versus east; and finally partnered versus unpartnered . . .

We mustn't allow any of this, however, to make us forget that gay men have been a staple of the novel from its inception. Petronius Arbiter's *Satyricon* and Lucius Apuleius's *The Golden Ass* (in Robert Graves's lucid translation) from the second century CE were novels I looked through as a fourteen- or fifteen-year-old, specifically *because* they were rumored to contain accounts of homosexuality. When I asked my Aunt Virginia for the Scott Montcrief two-volume translation of *À la recherche du temps perdu* as an eighteenth birthday present, when I took it into my bedroom to read, the first section I turned to was *Cities of the Plains*. Along with those, I devoured Vidal's *The City and the Pillar*, Calder Willingham's *End as a Man*, Donald Webster Cory's *The Homosexual in America*, André Tellier's *Twilight Men*, and Cocteau's *The White Paper*.

This meant, two years later in 1960, when Leslie Fiedler rose to fame pointing out the homoerotic subtext of the American classics, from *The Last of the Mohicans* to *Huckleberry Finn* and *Moby-Dick* (not to mention *On the Road* and *One Flew Over the Cuckoo's Nest*), I was already familiar with these literary and paraliterary attempts at presenting the real thing.

Classical literature is rife with studies of gay men, even when they are not named as such: the tale of Gilgamesh and Enkidu, the oldest Sumerian epic; *The Iliad*, whose subject is laid out in the first lines, "I sing, Goddess, of the wrath of Achilles"—Achilles, who was a cross-dresser, by nature a pacifist, and the lover of his young ward Patrochlus—none of which, apparently, gets in the way of his bravery.

Ordinarily I don't find these originary genealogies of much interest, because they rarely represent anyone's actual reading. In my case, however, they did. Along with a fair amount of classical French, English, and Russian literature—Jane Austen, the Brontës, George Eliot, Dickens, and Hardy; Dumas, Flaubert, Gide, and Camus; Tolstoy and Dostoevsky—this, along with Steinbeck, Faulkner, and James T. Farrell, was my adolescent reading, with every spare moment among them devoted to science fiction, Edmund Wilson, and James Baldwin.

One reason, before I began my first published book, I picked up Fiedler's *Love and Death in the American Novel*—a few weeks after my marriage in August of 1961—aside from its general fame, indeed, its notoriety, was because Fiedler was the father of a high school classmate (not that I knew Jay Kurt Fiedler that well) and because its most notorious chapter ("Come Back to the Raft Ag'in, Huck Honey"), somewhat abridged, had run as a feature article in the Sunday *New York Times Book Review*, where I'd first read it. In that chapter, Fiedler's thesis is that American literature tended to privilege relationships between men over hetero-sexual relations. Often, as in the case of Twain, these relationships are between white and black men—or in the case of Melville and Cooper, white men and Maori, Amerindians, or Pacific Islanders.

I had already noticed that, in the staple American novel, the women characters—whether Fitzgerald's changeable Daisy Buchanan, Twain's timid Becky Thatcher, or Hemingway's dying-in-childbirth Catherine Barkley—were so socially and imaginatively stymied as to function mostly as emotional place holders, all but devoid of agency or even general liveliness. Because of the so-cial fields that the Daisy Millers or the Myra Henshaws inhabit (and Cather's *My Mortal Enemy*, her study of the Henshaws, is surely the most impressive portrait among the lot), their rebellions finally amount to nothing in terms of their own personal happiness—they accomplish little of any value for themselves, for all their early winning charms as rebellious heroines.

When I read Fiedler's whole book, a few months later, I found that he went on to say that the appropriate material for a work of literature that aspired to greatness—surely an idea lifted from Leavis's appreciation of D. H. Lawrence, if not buttressed by a vulgar notion of Freud's view of sexual development—was mature heterosexual relations, presumably between equally well-realized male and female persons/characters. As Fielder suggests in the unnumbered pages of his book's introduction, "The failure of the American fictionist to deal with adult heterosexual love and his consequent obsession with death, incest, and innocent homosexuality" leaves American literature a long way to go.

On first reading this, I reached two almost simultaneous conclusions. One)—If Fiedler was correct, neither *The Iliad* nor *The Odyssey* could qualify as mature works of literature, because basically the first is about the anger of a gay warrior over his unfair treatment, who does not believe that the war he has been bamboozled into fighting is a just cause. And he's right. And *The Odyssey* is entirely about what Odysseus and Penelope do when they're apart, rather than how they relate together. Two)—And this was something I was beginning to learn through conversations with my brilliant poet wife—as long as the social expectations, the social opportunities, and the social education of women were what they were, those utopian "mature heterosexual relations" that Fiedler wrote of as the proper subject for great literature were a contradiction in terms.

This was the impossible and contradictory burden I lugged into the field of writing, and with which I attempted to negotiate my first seven novels, *The Jewels of Aptor* through *The Fall of the Towers* trilogy as well as *The Ballad of Beta-2*, *Babel-17*, and *Empire Star.*

Then Marilyn and I broke up—that is to say, we no longer lived together for a goodly while. My next three novels—*The Einstein Intersection, Equinox*, and *Nova*—were books in which, while I did not forget any of what I had learned up until then, I ceased trying to take on (in what were frankly foredoomed experiments) these problems front and center. Rather, I wrote the tales I wanted to tell, but when they brushed up against elements that redounded on these larger problems, I still tried to write as honestly as I could.

It was not till *Dhalgren*—when Marilyn and I got back together, briefly, for a couple of years, first in San Francisco, then, after another separation, in London—that I decided I was going to take on the problems that did impinge on my own life directly—and maintain that honesty in my presentation of what social forces fed into them. At that point, I certainly knew there was no dividing the social problems of gay men from that of women (lesbian or straight), blacks, and the various European and Asian minorities, chief among them Jews.

Though we skip over another dozen books—*Trouble on Triton* and the whole Return to Nevèrÿon series, as well as my work of the last fifteen years—*Dark Reflections* is very much a continuation of that same strategy. I wanted to tell Arnold Hawley's story: a reason I wanted to tell it was because it is so different from the story, say, of John Marr in *The Mad Man*, a character far closer in type, temperament, and experience to someone like myself than is Hawley.

You've been wonderfully generous in your praise of *Reflections*. Even though the book has not been out a year, I am aware that a number of readers have already declared they can identify with Hawley far more readily than they can, say, with Marr.

Perhaps it's not particularly politic to point it out. It might even smack of ingratitude. But the readers who find Hawley easier to identify with than with Marr tend to be heterosexual.

The sexual freedoms John Marr indulges on a spring walk along Broadway or through Riverside Park, night or day, are freedoms that gay men have constructed socially for themselves over decades but to which straight men—and women—just do not have access to the same degree—at least not yet. Thus it's hard for many of them to put themselves in Marr's position when reading the novel—though I have my share of letters from gay men claiming *The Mad Man* is a favorite work, because it writes of what those freedoms feel like in a way they can recognize.

Through geographical and sociological accident, Arnold Hawley has missed out on both the pre-Stonewall gay sexual freedom of the 'forties, 'fifties, and 'sixties, and the post-Stonewall gay sexual freedom of the 'seventies. Thus, Hawley's attitudes to gay sex are much closer to those of many straight folks to straight sex, even fairly liberated ones, than they are to Marr's.

For a decade now I've felt that Michael Cunningham's *The Hours* is the most important American novel, straight or gay, since Fitzgerald's *Gatsby*. One thing that makes *The Hours* so important is that it *does* paint a mature relation between a woman and a man, which is, even with the tragic ravages of AIDS, largely exemplary. Both the woman and the man are gay, however—and the woman is currently partnered with someone else. By turning this rich, rich friendship into a repressed love affair that subverts the validity of Clarissa's sexual and domestic relation with her lover, the *film* totally and brutally mismanaged the book's fundamental situation. But the fact is, this beautifully written novel—thirty-odd years after Fiedler made his call—is the only one which *has* answered it, in about the only way possible, until the society undergoes a great deal of change.

Cunningham once quipped, "They had to wait until I wrote a novel in which nobody gives anyone a blow job in order to award me the Pulitzer Prize." Although Arnold does give a blow job, he gives *only* one—and is very uncomfortable with the results. I wonder if there isn't a hint of Cunningham's point in the "accessibility" and "identification" that some straight readers say they feel for *Dark Reflections*.

Freedman: Probably so. A heterosexual reader myself, I find Arnold Hawley much easier to identify with than John Marr. Also I find Arnold's *world* more recognizable than John's. But I think generic as well as personal issues are at stake here. *Dark Reflections* seems to me perhaps the most consistently realistic piece of fiction you've written, whereas *The Mad Man*, as you yourself write in the "Disclaimer" that introduces it, is "a pornotopic fantasy: a set of people, incidents, places, and relations among them that have never happened and could never happen for any number of surely self-evident reasons." Perhaps, though, this is a question to be discussed a bit further: I mean the historical relation(s) between genre and gender, and between genre and sexuality. Certainly quite a few formal and historical matters are raised by your interesting genealogy of writings about homosexuality. Achilles and Patrochlus, like Gilgamesh and Enkidu, are same-sex lovers. But can we apply a modern term like "gay" to them? Wouldn't Foucault raise some pertinent objections here? How can we understand the differences between same-sex eros in Petronius and Apuleius, on the one hand, and, on the other hand, in your own brilliantly pseudo-classical novel *Phallos*?

Delany: A good question, certainly. But we have to remind ourselves precisely what Foucault is talking about when he discusses the forces through which discourse creates—or fails to create, as the case may be—social objects such as "homosexuality." The very fact that we all—you, I, and doubtless Michael Cunningham—associate "blow jobs" with homosexuality is part of the discursive web that is *what* homosexuality is. Foucault's point, of course, is that, at different times in history the web of associations was so differently structured that to speak of "homosexuality" as we understand it—in terms of all the various associations, strong and weak, that make it up—is a major distortion of what was there.

Specifically: the Greeks and the Romans after them were completely unconcerned with "blow jobs." For them, same-sex sexual relations between men were all-but-entirely about penetration, and specifically about who was on the top and who was on the bottom, at what age, and for how long. The literal meaning of "blow job"—sucking penises—would almost certainly be understood, unless there was a lot more elaboration around it, as something that nurses or eunuchs did to quiet down obstreperous male infants who were crying too much. And, apparently, often it worked. If you translated Cunningham's quip literally into the Greek of Plato and then translated it back—literally—into contemporary English, you'd probably have something like "They had to wait until I wrote a book in which nobody gave someone else an infant pacifier until they could award it a Pulitzer Prize." Homosexuality has dropped out of the equation and the message has become nonsense—because homosexuality as *we* understand it wasn't part of ancient Greek discourse: and the literal meaning of "blow job," the sucking of penises, would have been associated far more strongly with another practice: i.e., the quieting of infant males, though most Americans today would probably associate *that* with child abuse!

Now some people will find this concept difficult to absorb, or to absorb completely. Though they can understand these individual differences, they believe nevertheless there must be some core concept of "homosexuality" that remains constant in spite of all these *social* changes, which they perceive as happening around that core without ever transgressing it, cutting through it, restructuring its basic ontology. What they mean, of course, is that they feel there is some core concept that is not going to change *for them*—and, probably, as far as they go, they're right: It's not, at least any time soon.

But regularly I've written about certain concepts I thought would be unchanging for me that have, indeed, changed. In *Dhalgren*, for example, Kid and Lanya discuss their memories of the moon landing in July of '69 (not a full month after Stonewall). As people of a certain age may recall, that event was a three-day long televised affair—like a royal wedding or the funeral of a president; and if you were in another country (I was in Toronto, Canada) strangers came up to you on the street and congratulated you just for being an American.

Freedman: Yes, the same thing happened to me in Durham, England.

Delany: It monopolized a week of world headlines. When, seventeen years later in 1986, photographs of individual atoms in salt crystals taken with a new high-powered electron microscope were first published in the *New York Times*, it was nowhere near as big an event—though it changed the structure of lived and perceived reality, for the people who looked at them, bringing an entire realm of theory into the directly perceptual, quite as much as the reality of the moon changed for those who watched humans first visit it.

Like nine/eleven, the moon-landing was an event all but impossible, certainly, for an American to ignore. And, as Kid remarks in *Dhalgren*, while, before, the moon had been a place people had been looking at in the sky for millions of years, for the last five hundred of which had rhymed with June, no one had actually *been* there. But afterwards, it was totally changed: It was a place where people had walked, had run, had jumped, danced, taken pictures and spoken from. And this was enough to make it feel—the next time Kid looked up in the sky and saw it—that it was now a different object.

And it was.

When I wrote that, of course, I was describing a feeling I'd had myself—as did many others to whom I spoke. Among the first of these "world" altering experiences I underwent personally was my first plane flight, when, at age twenty-three, in three hours I flew across lands and roads it had taken me four days to hitchhike over a month before—which I wrote about in *The Motion of Light in Water*. (Much closer to the beginnings of commercial air travel, it was a time when passengers applauded the pilot for a perfect three-point landing—which, save in a few international air flights today, is no longer done; and now, when it does happen, gets laughs.) In my short piece, "Eric, Gwen, and D. H. Lawrence's Aesthetic of Unrectified Feeling" and, more briefly, in the extended essay, "Midcentury," I've written about the "televisionizing" of the country, which took place when I was between eight and ten.

(My personal sense is that the computerizing of the nation hasn't made anywhere near as big a change in the conceptual lives of people as some of these others, other than to devalue information by flooding the "market" with it, even though far more has been written about it than about all of the others put together: Currently major military operations are going on in Bangladesh, where people are being thrown in jail, confined to their houses, and no gasoline is being sold to prevent people from leaving their cities. I mentioned this in a class and only two students were aware of it, this past Friday—one an Indian young woman, who explained she had to call her parents every night to find out if they were still alive, or had eaten that day. No food deliveries are being made at stores. A perfectly non-political uncle of hers had already been thrown in jail. Now this should be first-page international news, but it is as unknown to Americans today as the Rwanda genocides during the time they were happening.)

In "The Tale of Plagues and Carnivals," I described my experiences in the Albert Hotel—the experience I also talk about in the Fred Barney Taylor documentary *Polymath* (2007)—of my exposure to the transsexuals who lived there, and how, over time, responses I had assumed were unchanging and inchoate to my being, began to change—as a result of the reality of day-to-day encounters.

This sort of thing is at the core of much of the discussion today of "cosmopolitanism" in matters of gender and race. Because, at certain social levels, people of highly different social and socioeconomic cultures are pushed—at least in cities—much closer to one another, "cosmopolitans" are likely to have experiences of how much people *can* change more frequently than people who live in a community at a more rural saturation.

But with that as background, we can go on to a more direct encounter with your question about *Phallos*.

Phallos is a novel of historical irony. Fundamentally a comedy, it's far closer in feel—I suspect; or I hope—to Cocteau's play *La Machine infernale*, or Giraudoux's *La Guerre de Troie n'aura pas lieu* (or, even more, Giraudoux's ironic novella *Elpinor*—his story about the first named soldier to die in the Trojan War, who falls not in battle but slips, rather, from a wall while climbing a ladder and—accidentally—breaks his head), or Sartre's dramatic retelling of Aeschylus's *Oresteia*, *Les Mouches*, than any authentic ancient tragedy—*or* comedy, for that matter. *Phallos* uses the unstated differences between homosexuality then and now as a kind of allegorical stand-in for the differences between homosexuality pre- and post-Stonewall: those "extraordinary changes" you wrote of toward the end of your first question.

Freedman: In other places you've said that *Phallos* and *The Mad Man* were written with a gay male audience primarily in mind—although you don't object to anyone else reading them. How would you describe the intended audience for *Dark Reflections*?

Delany: Well, I very much hoped it would be a novel for adults. Many of my books in the past—certainly *Phallos* and even *Dhalgren*—envision a bright sixteen- or seventeen-year-old, not unlike I once was, lurking among whatever readers the book manages to attract, curious to see what it's actually about.

But not this one.

Dark Reflections grows almost entirely out of my last eight years' teaching in the Graduate Creative Writing Program at Temple University in Philadelphia. It's written specifically for my most talented, most intelligent, most dedicated graduate students, who tend to be age twenty-four to fifty-five.

It's for those people who, indeed, would have given up (in 1987) a thirty-two-thousand dollar a year job for a twenty-nine-thousand dollar a year job, in order to have an extra day each week to write, whether poetry or prose.

It's a book that says: Let's assume you have enough talent so that people in actual publishing venues will, from time to time, recognize it and support you through a volume or two. This is the life and the kinds of publishing experiences that await you: First of all, whatever you're doing is eventually going to be superseded. And unless something really extraordinary happens, you are *not* going to be picked up by Knopf, or by Penguin-Viking, or by Farrar, Straus & Giroux—not in the current contracting publishing economy; not with the number of dedicated and talented people who are out there today, all competing with one another. It's a book that tries to show that all sorts of young people actually *are* working in commercial publishing today who really *want* to see their companies support good literature, but they simply don't have the freedom or the support to do any more than gesture in that direction. Even when they manage to make those gestures, the pressure of their own survival means they can't put their first energies to it—or, like Vikki LaSalle, they will get fired for it if they are actually successful. Or, like James Farthwell, they will quit in disgust (and go on to compromise, anyway). Or they will drink themselves to death—like Sam.

Personally I've seen *all* those editorial endings—and each of them more than once.

Back in '75, when Marilyn's first book placed with Viking Press—she was twenty-eight—they offered her a thousand dollar advance. A year and a half later, for her second, Viking offered only $750. When, two years after being accepted and a year after being published, her *first* book finally won the National Book Award for Poetry—the highest award for poetry in the country—Viking generously upped her *second* advance back to the *same* thousand dollars it had given her for her *first* book. Now, that's how, in this country, *successful* poets are treated!

Dark Reflections is also for my best fiction writing students in another way: Most are desperate to write a series of stories that can pass for a novel; they have no idea how hard that actually is. I wanted to show them how it might be done. It's not just a matter of writing three or five stories about the same person. It means using a lot of intelligence to weave the tales together on at least three different levels—thematic, dramatic, and formal.

I don't know how much I've succeeded in fulfilling any of those tasks. A number of messages from disparate readers, who seem to have "gotten it," make me think that some of it, at any rate, I've pulled off. But I have no way of knowing for certain. And, yes, they tend to be readers who have been with me a long time, like yourself.

Of course, *Dark Reflections* is also a book about the great Wagnerian wager of the Ring: How much of your personal life must you give up in order to seize the Rhinegold, i.e., to pursue effectively Power or Art?

Freedman: Let's move on to a slightly different, but closely related, topic. It seems clear that, in the modern era, most important writing has been written from one or more marginal viewpoints. (A nice pedagogic device is to demonstrate how

difficult it is to name a major modern author who was a middle-class heterosexual Englishman: Forster was gay; Lawrence was proletarian; Dylan Thomas
was Welsh; Virginia Woolf was a woman; and so forth.) This is emphatically true
of you: not only are you a gay writer and a black writer, but you're a writer much
of whose work has been in such marginalized genres as science fiction, sword-
and-sorcery, and pornography. One implication of *Dark Reflections* and your
comments about it (and also of your latest nonfiction book, *About Writing*) seems
to be that, increasingly, simply to be a *writer* is to be marginalized. I suppose this
phenomenon can be traced back to the Romantic Movement, perhaps further; but
it seems to be deepening rapidly. As late as the 1960s, Norman Mailer, James Baldwin, and, to a lesser degree, James Dickey, were popular celebrities in a way that's
nearly impossible for any serious novelist or poet today. Are there any gains here,
among the losses? What promises (or threats) do you, as the man who invented
the World Wide Web (I'm thinking of your "General Information" system in *Stars
in My Pocket Like Grains of Sand* [1984]), see in the newer electronic media? Since
you mentioned the Taylor documentary *Polymath*, I might say, in passing, that,
though I enjoyed watching it, there is not a single Delany text that I would will-
ingly trade for it.

Delany: To which I would respond, equally in passing, that's a trade no one—
especially Fred Taylor, the filmmaker—would ever ask of you. He's a maker of experimental documentaries. That is to say, he's fundamentally an artist. Thus, he's
doing what filmic artists basically do: He is looking around for images, vocal and
visual, which interest him, and juxtaposing them in ways he finds suggestive. But
he is not trying to replace either the topic of his film—me, or any of my work—
with his.

Even though it's a documentary, even though there is a lot of information
in the film that seems as though its informative content might be the sole purpose for recording it on a strip of celluloid, basically he's creating a work of art—
and his own work of art, at that. Discussions of the world in matters of art tend
to flatten out the suggestiveness of the art object and leave it dominated only by
its functionality, its usefulness, its truth value. Science fiction—as the "literature
of ideas"—has suffered as much from this as any genre in the West—unless you
want to talk about the way "realistic" fiction in general has suffered from the same
thing: that somehow the value of fiction itself lies not in its imaginative suggestiveness, but in its "truth."

Recently, out in Colorado, at Naropa University, I heard an interesting afternoon lecture in the great, gray Performing Arts Center, by Donald Preziosi, in
which Preziosi revisited the famous "Book Ten" of Plato's *Republic*, where the

poets are so famously excluded from Plato's ideal republic. Preziosi points out that, for Plato, all representation was itself subversive, because even the most conservative representation opens the possibility that what is represented one way can always be represented another. This is built into Plato's very "Theory of Ideas," so to speak, and into the absolute existence of things-as-Ideas in that scarily anti-Foucauldian, anti-Heraclitian "Platonic Realm," to be imitated by human craftsmen with whatever variations in the fallible, fallen world. Plato's doctrine is one, you remember, in which permanence and steadfastness are equated with the good and beautiful. For Plato change is basically a process of perishing and decline, a symptom of weakness and decay.

Now my own critique of Preziosi would be that, in terms of his view of art, he has let "representation" become too strong. Art for me is a system which allows freedom of juxtapositions, suggestions, and interpretations: thus representation is only one of the things that juxtapositions, suggestions, and interpretations working together in a particularly limited—and operationalized—way can bring about.

At least thirty years ago—I no longer remember in which piece it was—I wrote that the pyramidal model of society no longer obtains. (It's one of the things I learned when I was trying to force a pan-social picture of a scientific society into that artificial pyramid, which I used in the three books of *The Fall of the Towers*.) When, in '56, the white-collar class of the United States outstripped the size of the blue-collar agricultural/industrial class, the traditional model of a small upper class, a broader middle class, and a huge and sprawling working class was no longer adequate to picture our country. Today society is made up of endlessly intersecting margins—some of which are more powerful than others; and many of which are less powerful and knotted into relatively unchanging social positions. An awareness of this is what modernism constantly swerves away from—I wonder sometimes if the insistent blindness to this isn't what *post*modernism *is*.

Auden talks about this with insight and intelligence in *The Dyer's Hand*: At the height of romanticism, the artist—Hugo, Sand, Wagner—was the most honored of the state's civil servants. (Look at their funerals! In all three cases, they were grander affairs than that of the assassinated President Kennedy.) Once the Edwardian era was done, with World War I marking the cut-off date, this becomes less and less the case as the twentieth century progresses, and—as you point out—the artist is perceived as more and more marginal: Eventually, his or her importance is precisely *that* he or she is marginal.

The romantic hero—Byron's Manfred or Childe Harold, say—is born at the center of the nodes of power, but for reasons half psychological and half socio-logical *chooses* to live a marginal life, outside the workings of that power, and brings upon himself his own destruction as a result. The shift of this story away from men to women—in, as I said, Cather's great novella *My Mortal Enemy* [1927], where she shows that the cost of such a defection may be much higher than one thinks during the headiness of adolescence, when one first makes the choice, es-pecially for women—marks Cather's novella as one of the great short meditations on the American cultural experience; as Cather's *Song of the Lark* [1915] is one of the great full-length meditations on the topic.

I mention them because both are novels which certainly taught me a great deal about what the novel was and could do—and, therefore, are books that *Dark Re-flections* hold its small dialogue with . . . should anyone be interested in following it out.

Freedman: Getting back to the matter of representation, I think I tend to agree with Preziosi, though I wasn't able to hear the lecture you mention. Though it's certainly possible to overemphasize the representational (or the paraphrasable) content of art, I think that, after about six decades of grim academic formal-ism in America (i.e., ever since the New Criticism became dominant), the op-posite error is more prevalent. One index of the power of artistic representation is that representation is nearly always what the real enemies of art have in their sights. Has any writer ever been clapped into prison because of suggestiveness of style, or imagery, or symbolism? When writers get in trouble, it's usually be-cause they're trying to represent something that the men with guns don't want represented: whether, say, it's Flaubert representing adultery, or Lawrence repre-senting heterosexual genital intercourse, or Solzhenitsyn representing Stalin's la-bor camps. And then there are the philosophical reactionaries, from Plato, as you point out, to the *Tel Quel* group, who object not so much to the representation of this or that in particular as to any representation whatever. Of course, we mustn't think that representation is limited to realistic prose fiction. Aren't several of your own works, like *Hogg* and *The Mad Man*, especially relevant in this context?

Delany: I'm tempted to answer the first part of your question—about Flaubert, Lawrence, and Solzhenitsyn, say—with a flat and definite "Yes." Though I think one could append an important and truthful elaboration to that "Yes," which, first, is the only argument I know that allows us to get beyond the Platonic di-lemma and, second, that certainly problematizes—if it doesn't explain outright—what Sollers, Kristeva, Barthes, et al. at *Tel Quel* were on about.

Traditionally criticism tends to speak of juxtapositions, suggestions, and interpretations as if they followed *after* representation; as if they were something that
grew out of representation. But that is not the case.

Actually juxtapositions, suggestions, and interpretations are *always* aesthetically *anterior* to representation. The artist creates the effect *of* representation—
and specifically the different ways in which a given situation might be represented
in art—through an analysis (i.e., through one or several interpretations, if you
will) of what elements need to be juxtaposed so that they will tender their inter-
critique of suggestions.

The little squiggle that the artist puts down with her pencil toward the top of
the page, by itself, doesn't look like much of anything. But when five or seven or
twenty are arranged together, they begins to *suggest* the edges of leaves. The artist goes on to arrange many clumps of these squiggles in an overall cloud form,
which *suggests*, indeed, tree-leaves on branches. Now, below that, she draws
two descending lines, which flare toward the bottom, *suggesting* a tree trunk—
though either line without the other or the squiggles above would suggest little.
A few more wavy verticals between those lines (the edges of the tree trunk)—
not horizontals—*suggest* the grain of tree bark. Now no single line, taken by itself, represents anything. But when all these *suggestions* are juxtaposed, something interesting happens. We realize that the artist has been particularly clever:
By only suggesting *one* edge of the leaves, we get a sense, looking at her tree, that
it is standing in the sun (more of those verticals are on the right side rather, suggesting the un-represented sun is shining from the left), which only lets us see
the outside edge of each leaf because the inner edges are in shadow. Indeed, her
drawing has far more sense of presence, seems far more realistic, immediate,
and vivid than a drawing where the artist has carefully inscribed both edges
of every leaf on every branch. Indeed, such a picture—one by Audubon, say, or
the Douanier Rousseau—appears by comparison labored, childish, and primitive. That's because the artist has been too intent on *representing* what we know is
there, rather than *suggesting* what we actually see. But that is how all realistic "representation" works.

The things alone that differentiate the work of various artists in their representations of this or that object *is* the analysis of those anterior juxtapositions
and suggestions that allows representation—the effect of multiple suggestions
that we recognize as representation—to manifest.

Indeed, this is so much the case that the artist who tries to go straight for representation without the anterior analysis of the suggestions and juxtapositions
of the pre-representational condition—the initial elements of the artwork itself

(as Theophrastus quotes Heraclitus, "The universe's beauty begins as the sweeping together of an array of random things." [Robinson, Fragment 124.] Again Heraclitus saves us in our argument with Plato)—often we perceive as a hack, unless, like Rousseau, he can convince us that his vision has validity on another level.

By the same token, once we perceive that such analysis *has* taken place, it's all but impossible to deny the appellation of artist to the creator—at least other than in the very short run. That's why calling works like *Hogg* or *The Mad Man* or *Phallos* "pornography" has never bothered me. Or, for that matter, calling them science fiction—not to mention literature.

The structure of discourse *about* art is largely protective *of* art. Much of that protection is distractionary. Recently some writer in *Slate* magazine made one of those absurd comments that the uneducated are forever making about SF to make their own ignorance seem like knowledge. Doubtless you've seen it dozens of times in your career as a science fiction scholar, as have I. Equally doubtless, you have, I'm sure, as little respect for it as I do: Literary writer X (often someone with a relatively recent Pulitzer, the prize Gass excoriated as "the People's Prize"—in this case, I believe it was Michael Chabon) "has waded into the muck and morass of the hopelessly infantile and played-out genre, science fiction, and, with a new and intelligent work, given it a much needed lease on life." Now, certainly it isn't Chabon's fault that idiots think to praise him by insulting you and me. This sort of stupidity, which probably half the readership at this point recognizes as such, is entirely to protect the concept of the artist from the pollution perceived to pullulate dangerously around the notion of genre. But it's lost its power to offer such protection anywhere outside the Oprah Club, or possibly in what remains of the Book of the Month Club—that is to say, nodes of literary power that are entirely economic and totally without critical weight.

One of the things the Internet has done is make these forays in genre boundary reinforcement all but impossible to carry off with a straight face. As soon as this one was made, Ursula Le Guin wrote a devastating parody of the whole business, which zipped around the Internet, probably to be read by more people than who'd read the original copywriter's (whatever you say, he was not a critic) dumb, dumb pronouncement. I hope he appreciates the favor I do him by withholding his name.

Intelligence really is more interesting than stupidity. So whether it is ceding Sergio Leone his deserved place among moviemakers—despite the marketing, the titles, and credits imposed on the beginning or the surround of his films, or his early death and limited output—or Guy Davenport his position, with his sixty-odd stories, or Grace Paley with her forty-six, among the finest American writers, it happens by a fairly natural process through which intelligent people seek out the intelligent analysis of the anterior situation behind all art (no matter the part representation itself plays or does not play in the final product), that allows art itself to come forward.

(With Baudelaire's *Fleurs du mal,* Joyce's *Ulysses,* or Ginsberg's *Howl*—three literary or poetical works brought to trial in different centuries—I think you'd be hard pressed to pin down *what* was being "represented" that was being objected to, *other* than the clouds of uncomfortable suggestions and connotations that actually constitute the work: Lesbians sitting on the beach or walking in the woods . . .? A woman sitting on the strand or a man taking a bath . . . ? Crazy guys on drugs . . .? That's why, in all three cases, eventually the trials failed or their verdicts were reversed.)

As long as the artist remembers that juxtapositions, suggestions, and interpretations *precede* representation—and are what, finally, create it (and not the other way around)—it doesn't matter if the rest of us now and again forget; though certainly the artist has an easier time and can communicate about a wider range of material and subject matter if more people understand the actual inchoate process. Not only do those elements allow representation to be, they also allow the experimental in art to exist. (What makes academic formalism boring is only that it so rigorously represses suggestion and interpretation, among the three, and tries to limit all discussion to the most sedimented juxtapositions: the ones that mediate the particularly sedimented suggestions we call [yawn] plot.) But that's another topic, even as it's absorbed by this one here.

Freedman: Clearly, this conversation could continue, but that seems like as good a point at which to stop as any. Thank you very much, Chip, for your time and for sharing so many interesting thoughts with us.

Index